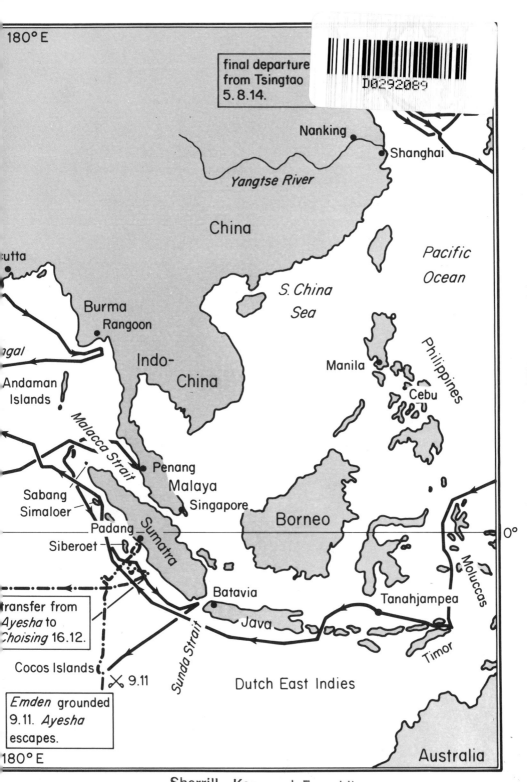

180° E

Nanking
Shanghai

Yangtse River

China

Pacific
Ocean

S. China
Sea

:utta

Burma
Rangoon

Philippines

Indo-
China

Manila

Cebu

gal

Andaman
Islands

Malacca Strait

Penang
Malaya

Singapore

Borneo

Sabang
Simaloer

Padang
Siberoet

Sumatra

0°

transfer from
Ayesha to
Choising 16.12.

Batavia

Tanahjampea

Moluccas

Java

Cocos Islands

9.11

Sunda Strait

Timor

Emden grounded
9.11. Ayesha
escapes.

Dutch East Indies

Australia

180° E

GENTLEMEN
OF WAR

GENTLEMEN
OF WAR

The amazing story of Captain Karl von Müller and the S.M.S. Emden

Dan van der Vat

WILLIAM MORROW AND COMPANY, INC.

New York 1984

Library of Congress Catalog Card Number: 83-63293

ISBN: 0-688-03115-3

Printed in the United States of America

First U.S. Edition

1 2 3 4 5 6 7 8 9 10

For my mother

CONTENTS

ILLUSTRATIONS

SMS *Emden*[1]
Captain Karl von Müller[1]
Hellmuth von Mücke[1]
Devastation at Madras[2]
SS *Clan Grant*[3]
HMAS *Sydney*[2]
The *Emden* destroyed[4]
The wrecked transmitter mast at Direction Island[1]
The station office[1]
The severed cable[1]
Captain Glossop's letter[1]
Official praise for the cable station staff[5]
The landing-party embarks[1]
The Germans leave the island[1]
The *Ayesha*[1]
Australian landing party arrives[1]
Welcome at Constantinople[1]

ACKNOWLEDGMENTS
1 The Imperial War Museum
2 The Robert Hunt Picture Library
3 The National Maritime Museum
4 Australian War Memorial
5 Cable and Wireless Group

ACKNOWLEDGMENTS

The literary sources which I consulted are fully described at the end of the book. The main sources of what follows were the files of the German Military Archive (*Bundesarchiv-Militärarchiv*) in Freiburg, and I should like to express once again my most grateful thanks to the staff of that institution for their help. No less helpful were the staff of the Public Record Office at Kew, Surrey, whose material was of equal value. My thanks also for various items of information to the Royal Geographical Society, the office of the Naval Attaché at the West German Embassy in London, the Imperial War Museum in London, the Deutscher Marinebund in Wilhelmshaven, the public libraries of the Borough of Richmond-upon-Thames, and to Peter Preston, the Editor of the *Guardian*, for allowing me to disappear to finish the writing. I would also like to acknowledge with much gratitude the support and enthusiasm of Ion Trewin and his colleagues at Hodder and Stoughton, and of Dinah Wiener and Felicity Bryan, my agents at Curtis Brown. Finally, colleagues, friends and family are to be admired for tolerating the consequences of one man's latter-day obsession with things naval, Anglo-German and of 1914–1918 vintage.

Nothing in what follows is either fiction or 'faction'. The professional historian and the purist will miss footnotes and page-by-page attribution to source, which I have omitted in the, for me, overriding interest of narrative flow, as I did in the case of my previous book *The Grand Scuttle*. But I did my homework as best I could, and every statement is derived from the sources named either here or at the end of the book. Where quotation marks are used, they enclose remarks or statements recorded as having been made by those to whom they are attributed in the text. I have invented nothing; I may of course have drawn the wrong conclusion from stated facts, but I try to say clearly, whenever I extrapolate, what is mine and what is not. I have sometimes been obliged to choose between one version and another when they conflicted, and I have tried to be logical in doing so. Any error that may have slipped in is mine alone.

Ein ruheloser Marsch war unser Leben
Und wie des Windes Sausen, heimatlos,
Durchstürmten wir die kriegbewegte Erde.

Our life was like a march without a rest,
And, homeless like the soughing of the wind,
We stormed across a world disturbed by war.

Friedrich von Schiller, *Wallenstein's Death*

GENTLEMEN
OF WAR

PROLOGUE

DIRECTION ISLAND, 9 NOVEMBER 1914

A Chinese 'coolie' employed at the cable station on Direction Island in a remote part of the Indian Ocean was the first to notice the motionless grey silhouette of a warship about a mile offshore. It was dawn, 6 a.m., on 9 November 1914, and the menacing shape lay silently off the mouth of the lagoon serving the island as a natural harbour. The coolie excitedly pointed out the ship to a British night-duty operator just coming off shift, and he set about rousing the rest of the station's personnel. As the light rapidly improved in the manner of tropical dawns, Dr. Ollerhead, the station's medical officer, noticed that the foremost funnel was a two-dimensional dummy. The ship flew no flag. Soon her steam-launch could be seen, towing two large rowing-boats full of men. The station manager, Mr. D. A. G. de H. Farrant, joined the watchers on the roof of a bungalow and agreed with the general conclusion that the installation, which included a wireless transmitter, was about to be raided. Mr. Farrant, as stout-hearted as he was stout, issued a stream of orders. A wireless operator rushed to his Morse key and began to transmit an alarm call; another donned earphones and heard a loud alien transmission, obviously from the intruder; he tapped out a challenge on the same wavelength and heard the warship jamming in response.

By this time the staff knew that the ship now threatening them was His Imperial German Majesty's Ship *Emden*, the light cruiser which had led His Britannic Majesty's navy a merry dance all over the eastern Indian Ocean for the past two months and become a legend. In the transmitting room of the cable station, other operators were sending the news calmly and efficiently along the three cables which joined at Direction Island, linking it with Australia, the Dutch East Indies and Africa and ultimately with the entire network of cables connecting the various far-flung parts of the British Empire. The alert went to the naval headquarters in Singapore and Cape Town, Melbourne and London. Mr. Farrant had already planned what to do in

11

such a raid after receiving a warning of a possible German attack from the Royal Navy: a damaging raid on a similar installation in the Pacific had cut the link between Canada and Australia for seven weeks. The wireless operators carried on transmitting for several minutes, despite the jamming, in the hope of reaching a British heavy cruiser with which they had been in contact the day before. They knew it must be the *Emden* because they had been following the progress of the war, taking advantage of the station's almost unique access to information in the area; they were aware that there was no other German ship in the Indian Ocean. So they tapped out 'SOS – *Emden* here . . . SOS – *Emden* here . . .' until a German officer in a tropical uniform and solar topi burst in with pistol levelled, followed by several sailors armed with rifles.

The personnel were ordered away from their equipment and out of the building and the Germans, armed with axes and hammers, set about smashing everything in sight. Others placed explosive charges at the bottom of the transmitter's aerial mast, and within minutes the structure collapsed. The staff's request that the mast should be blown up in such a way that their treasured tennis court, which they had laid out themselves, would not be damaged, was met by the raiders, who apologised for what they were doing and conducted themselves correctly throughout. While some of the sailors attacked the cable station itself, others dragged up cables from the seabed and hacked away at them until they were severed; then they dragged the ragged ends as far apart from one another as possible. Meanwhile all the thirty-four staff, European and Asiatic, were gathered in the sun outside the station and told that they were for the time being under German martial law. The Imperial naval ensign was run up the flagpole and a lookout posted on the same bungalow roof from which the station staff had viewed the ship.

The raiders and their victims were soon on excellent terms. Mr. Farrant congratulated the officer in charge on his Iron Cross, to the latter's amazement: the operators had picked up a Reuter message announcing that all the officers on the renowned raider *Emden* had been awarded the decoration by the Kaiser. One of the British present politely invited a German officer to play a game of tennis with him to while away the time. The offer was declined with some asperity and a larger measure of incomprehension. What might have become a difficult clash between two manifestly different varieties of sense of humour was forestalled by the clear sound of urgent alarm bells ringing out from the ship. At the same time her siren sounded repeated short blasts and the lookout called urgently from the bungalow roof.

The three officers shouted a stream of orders and the landing party, fifty men in all, rushed back to the wooden jetty and their boats with all their equipment. The three small craft set out in pursuit of the cruiser, which was already under way. But they could not catch up with the ship, which was pulling away from them, abandoning them. The Britons still on the bungalow roof could see another cloud of smoke to the north-east. By 9.30 a.m., the raiders were back. Once again the staff were herded together under guard, while other men positioned four Maxim machine-guns on the beach, facing out to sea. The commanding officer meanwhile climbed onto the bungalow roof and studied the area to the north intently through binoculars. Soon the crash of distant gunfire could be heard, salvo after salvo, and then the different sound of shells exploding. Half an hour later the officer came down again and issued another stream of orders. It was clear that the *Emden* had engaged an enemy warship, and it sounded to the expert ear that the guns of the foe were ominously large. She might not come back.

In the lagoon there lay a white-painted schooner of some 97 tons called the *Ayesha*. The Germans had noticed her on their first landing and had intended to place explosive charges aboard with the intention of sinking her. This plan was now cancelled, and the sailors asked Mr. Farrant how much food he had on the island. On learning that he had a four-month reserve, they told him that they would, with regret, require him to hand over half. The British tried to dissuade the Germans from their now apparent intention of setting off in the small sailing ship; they said it was in poor condition and had not been in use since a steamer had taken over the job of supplying the island every three months and taking away the copra which was its only product. The Germans took no notice, and when their determination to try to make a run for it became clear to the genuinely admiring station staff, these set about helping with a will. Out at sea, nothing could be seen or heard at all now. Unless both ships in the action had crippled each other out there, one or other would be back, and given the odds against their solitary ship, the Germans had to accept that it was highly likely to be the enemy that came back because he had heavier guns.

The German sailors worked all afternoon loading supplies and making ready. As dusk was about to fall, the German commander, a clean-cut man in his prime with heavily accented English and two stripes on his sleeves, apologised once more to Mr. Farrant. Then, using their steam-launch as a tug, they set off, the *Ayesha* in turn towing the two rowing-boats. They soon vanished in the darkness. There was still no sign of a warship.

13

As soon as all the Germans were aboard the schooner, which was named after the favourite wife of the prophet Mohammed, the station staff inspected the damage they had done. It looked a lot worse than it actually was. The cable upon which most time had been spent was a spare length, kept on the seabed in case of emergency. Of the three links joined at the island, only one, the line to Perth, had actually been severed, while one of the other two was slightly damaged. Part of Mr. Farrant's preparations had been the burial in various places on the island of vital spare parts. These were soon unearthed, and within minutes of the Germans' embarkation the station was able to send a brief cable reporting that it had been visited by the *Emden*, which had then been engaged by a warship presumed to be British.

It was only the next morning that His Majesty's Australian Ship *Sydney* arrived to 'borrow' Dr. Ollerhead. The staff then learned that the *Emden* had gone aground on North Keeling Island a few miles to the north over the horizon, and that there were many dead and wounded. The Australian cruiser looked remarkably unscathed. Her own landing party of armed sailors were astonished to find out that the German detachment landed by the *Emden* had vanished into thin air. The *Emden*'s spectacular career, during which she had spread alarm and despondency all over the Far East and tied down huge forces, was over, but the *Ayesha* had got away. It was an end and a beginning . . .

PART I

THE WAR CRUISE OF
SMS *EMDEN*

Old and young, we are all on our last cruise.
Robert Louis Stevenson, *Virginibus Puerisque*

1

THE SWAN OF THE EAST

The ship whose name was to reverberate around the world and which would become the most renowned fighting vessel of the First World War was, like a child, born without a name. Her lease of life was granted by the German Emperor, Kaiser Wilhelm II, on Saturday, 23 December 1905. The absolute monarch signed one document after another as he tried to clear his desk at Potsdam in time for Christmas. Among them was an order for the replacement of two superannuated small cruisers due to be paid off. One of the two ships thus called into existence was for the time being referred to only as *Ersatz Pfeil* – replacement for SMS *Pfeil* (arrow). On 6 April 1906, the first day of the new financial year, the Imperial Naval Office in Berlin placed the order with the Imperial Yard at Danzig (now Gdansk in Poland). The keel was laid on 1 November 1906. Delays, caused by the stresses and strains of Germany's huge shipbuilding programme at the peak period of the misconceived naval arms-race with Great Britain, held up the launching for nearly ten months. But at noon on Tuesday, 26 May 1908, Herr Fürbringer, Chief Burgomaster of the Reich's north-westernmost city, proudly announced at a ceremony at the naval yard that he had been ordered by His Imperial and Royal Majesty 'to give this new ship the name of his loyal city of Emden' of which he had the honour to be leading citizen. He duly swung the ritual bottle of *Sekt* against the forward-raked bow and called for the obligatory three cheers for the Kaiser. And so the last piston-engined cruiser to be constructed in Germany took to the water (the other light cruiser sanctioned by the Emperor at Christmas 1905, SMS *Dresden*, had turbines). She was to cost a total of 6.38 million gold marks (£319,000). Like nearly all other ships of her general type in the Imperial Navy, she had been given the name of a medium-sized city as part of the policy of fostering enthusiasm for the new, costly and enormously expanded fleet. Each city so honoured was expected to take a keen interest in the progress of its floating godchild and Emden took great pride in its namesake from the outset. Like all family relationships, the connection was to bring grief as well as joy. Wishing the ship *bon voyage* in the name of the city of Emden, the mayor said: 'Justify the trust that is placed in you, be a strong shield for your crew, maintain the fame of the German flag at home and abroad, in peace and, if necessary, in bloody conflict for German rights and German honour.' Grandiose sentiments of this kind were commonplace at the launchings of warships in those jingoistic times (and are not entirely unknown today). But if ever there was a ship that lived up to such high-flown official admonitions, her name was *Emden*. In fact it is no exaggeration to say that she handsomely exceeded the instructions she received at her launching, more so than any other warship built by Germany before or since.

The *Emden* started her trials under her first captain, Commander Engels, on 10 July 1909, and her crew was brought up to full strength on 21 August. Eight days later the Kaiser, as was his wont, chose his newest cruiser as escort for the royal yacht *Hohenzollern* for the annual 'Emperor's Manoeuvres' in the Baltic. After successfully completing her sea-trials and testing her guns, torpedo tubes and minelaying equipment, the *Emden* was assigned to the Fleet Reserve at Kiel, the principal Baltic naval base, on 30 September. Six months later, on 1 April 1910, she was put into active service with the seagoing fleet, inheriting the crew of the paid-off, old light cruiser *Arcona* led by Lieutenant-Commander Waldemar Vollerthun. The *Emden's* first sailing orders were signed by the Kaiser on 26 March, entailing the repainting of the ship in white for service in the tropics (her original colour had been the warship grey introduced by the Germans in 1902 and eventually imitated by every other navy). She was to replace the superannuated light cruiser *Niobe* in the Cruiser Squadron commanded by Rear-Admiral Gühler and based in the Far East. But before that she had some calls to make, to show the flag. Her first mission was to attend the celebration of the centenary of the Republic of Argentina in Buenos Aires on 25 May 1910. So on the morning of Tuesday, 12 April 1910, she left Kiel and entered the Kaiser Wilhelm II Canal linking the Baltic with the North Sea across Schleswig-Holstein. After pausing off Cuxhaven to send a sick man ashore, the *Emden* entered the open sea that evening. She was never to see German home waters again.

Ten days later she dropped anchor in the Brazilian port of Porto Grande, her first landfall after crossing the Atlantic at an average speed slightly in excess of her economical cruising speed of 12 knots and without noteworthy mechanical problems. On the 26th she left for Montevideo to link up with the light cruiser *Bremen*, under the orders of whose captain, Commander Goette, she temporarily came from now on, until the two ships left Buenos Aires on 31 May and parted company. From there she sailed round to Punta Arenas in southern Chile, thence to Valparaiso and then southward again to the port of Talcahuano, near Coronel, about halfway down the long Chilean coastline. Here she carried out an experiment which the crew found distinctly less than enjoyable. The ship was crammed with every ounce of coal that she could be made to carry. The normal capacity of her bunkers was 790 tons, but when she left Talcahuano on 24 June, she was carrying 1,080 tons. The extra fuel cluttered the decks and every available nook and cranny aboard, including much of the less than generous space provided for the crew of more than 350 men. The *Emden*'s next task was to pay a call at Papeete, the capital of the French island colony of Tahiti, where she arrived on 12 July 1910, just in time for Bastille Day on the 14th. She arrived with 190 tons of coal left, after a voyage of 4,400 miles via Easter and Pitcairn Islands. This was a remarkable demonstration of consistency and fuel economy which won praise and a scattering of decorations from the Kaiser when he read the report in October. The *Emden* left Tahiti on 17 July and reached Apia in the German island colony of Western Samoa five days later, where she joined SMS *Scharnhorst*, the heavy armoured cruiser which was Admiral Gühler's flagship, and came under command of the Cruiser Squadron, Germany's sole 'blue water' or overseas naval formation independent of home ports. For the next eight weeks she was with the Squadron as it worked its way across the Pacific. On 17 September 1910 the *Emden* docked at the Squadron's base at Tsingtao, port of the German enclave of Kiao Chow in north-east China, for the first time. From there she engaged in the normal activities of the Cruiser Squadron, visiting northern Chinese ports and patrolling the Yangtse River in the heyday of western domination and exploitation of China; showing the flag in Japanese waters; and calling at the chains of islands in the eastern Pacific owned by Germany at that time. By the end of the year the new cruiser had shaken down well and her crew had completed the process of working up their sailing and fighting efficiency, which was just as well: she was ordered to abandon her annual overhaul at Tsingtao to go to Ponape, an island in the Caroline group due east of the Philippines and some 400 miles north of the Equator, to suppress a revolt which had begun in October.

The *Emden* set off for her first action on 28 December, linking up with her sister-ship, SMS *Nürnberg*, which had just left Hong Kong, two days out from Ponape and arriving there on 10 January 1911. Under the command of the newly promoted Commander Vollerthun of the *Emden* as senior officer present, the two ships shelled a 1,000 ft.

hill fortified by the rebels, who had murdered the German district commissioner, on the small neighbouring island of Jokaj. Then a landing party of sailors and native troops stormed the position after a six-hour struggle through daunting terrain. But the rebellion continued on Ponape itself, and more bombardments and landings against bitter and stubborn resistance were necessary over a period of six weeks before the last rebels surrendered. Fifteen men were tried, convicted and executed by firing squad for the murder of the district commissioner, two other white officials and a larger number of indigenes during the uprising, which had arisen over a road-building project; 426 others were banished to the German possession of Yap, some 1,200 miles to the west. The two cruisers and their two accompanying gunboats lost one officer, two sailors and two native soldiers killed, and one officer, five ratings and nine soldiers wounded. The *Emden* left the 'pacified' colony on 1 March and was back in Tsingtao on the 14th. It was at this time that Admiral Gühler died suddenly of typhus during a visit to Hong Kong. He was replaced by Rear-Admiral von Krosigk. The ship completed her overhaul and resumed squadron duties. The rest of 1911 was seldom eventful, apart from a typhoon at the end of July which damaged the ship in Yokohama during an official visit to Japan, making a week's repairs back in Tsingtao necessary, and the replacement as captain of Commander Vollerthun by Lieutenant-Commander von Restorff on 23 November, six months after half the crew had been relieved by the usual annual fresh draft from the North Sea Naval Station at Wilhelmshaven. The other half was relieved in the same way in May 1912; the last such draft was to arrive in May 1914. Junior officers were rotated no less frequently. Meanwhile the pattern of exercises, colonial patrols, courtesy visits and keeping watch on the unrest in China continued; in March 1913 Admiral Krosigk was relieved by Rear-Admiral Maximilian Graf von Spee in the command of the Cruiser Squadron. Two months later, Lieutenant-Commander Karl von Müller relieved the newly promoted Captain Restorff, formally assuming command on 29 May 1913.

In the middle of the following month, news of serious unrest in northern China reached the Squadron at Rabaul in Kaiser Wilhelmsland (now New Britain), a German island north-east of Papua-New Guinea, during a cruise in the South Pacific which was promptly abandoned. The warships headed for the Yangtse via Yap; the *Emden* called briefly at Tsingtao for coal and minor repairs, entering the Yangtse River on 10 August and reaching Nanking two days later, where she met HMS *Hampshire*, a British heavy cruiser, and comparable ships from Japan and the United States. The colonial powers were determined to protect their interests and enclaves in the turbulent new republic of China against various groups of rebels, who were firing on western steamers and even gunboats with rifles and cannon from the banks. On 27 August, the *Emden*, upstream and south-west of Wuhu, came under fire from artillery positioned at a fort near Tongling, at a range of 1,300 yards. Already cleared for action, the cruiser fired five salvoes from her port broadside of five 4-inch guns, her main armament. The twenty-five shells from the Squadron shooting champion silenced the fort. The ship, continuing upstream towards Hankow as ordered, came under rifle fire which she returned with machine-gun volleys. SMS *Emden*, already known as 'the Swan of the East' for her white livery and her especially graceful lines among mariners in the China seas, was now saluted as the boldest and most dashing of the colonial powers' warships for the manner in which she ran the gauntlet on the Yangtse, and her captain was subsequently decorated. The cruiser returned to Tsingtao after two months on the turbulent river, but for the ensuing eight months she spent more time in Chinese waters than anywhere else, in case of a renewal of unrest. On 12 March 1914 the ship's navigation officer, *Kapitänleutnant* Hellmuth von Mücke, was appointed First Officer (his rank, literally 'lieutenant-captain' as in 'lieutenant-colonel', lies between lieutenant RN and lieutenant-commander). On the same day the captain was promoted full commander; as luck would have it, he damaged the destroyer *S90* a fortnight later by starting to leave harbour at speed without first untying her from the *Emden*'s side, for which he received a written reprimand. Neither his decoration nor his promotion was affected.

In mid-June, after completing the last major exchange of crew, the men of the *Emden* and the rest of the Squadron's ships in port at Tsingtao entertained HMS *Minotaur*, the heavy cruiser which was the flagship of Vice-Admiral Sir T. H. M. Jerram, the British Commander-in-Chief, China. The officers and ratings of the Imperial Navy, the formidable new seapower second only to the Royal Navy itself, set out to overwhelm their British guests with lavish hospitality and genuine friendliness at their only major overseas naval base. The inevitable football match between the two navies was a 2:2 draw at full time, but the British shot home three more goals during extra time. The German sailors were adjudged outright winners of the gymnastic competition and honour was satisfied. Relations between the hosts and the visitors at all levels during the four-day visit attained extraordinary heights. Fully aware of the growing tension at home in faraway Europe, but at least partly suppressing its implications for themselves, the men of the two navies played together as if there were no tomorrow and parted with protestations of undying friendship and promises never to fight one another. These undertakings were kept, though no doubt not in the manner intended by those who gave them: the *Minotaur* never fired a shot at any member of Graf Spee's Squadron, which is not to say that she would have refrained from doing so had they met after war broke out.

On 20 June Spee took the *Scharnhorst*, the *Gneisenau* and most of the rest of his Squadron out of Tsingtao for a cruise in the South Pacific. Of the cruisers, only the *Emden* was left in port, with a handful of auxiliary craft. Commander Müller was thus for the time being Senior Naval Officer of the East Asia Station. The rest of the Squadron was never to return. Five days earlier the *Emden* had received a very substantial reinforcement in the eighteen-stone shape of Captain Julius Lauterbach, master of the Hamburg-America Line cargo-liner *Staatssekretär Kraetke* and a lieutenant of the naval reserve. Reservists of his category had to serve two months per year with the navy but could choose when; Lauterbach had asked Spee for attachment to the *Emden*, and he joined the ship at a time when several officers and men were sick aboard and even in hospital ashore with dysentery. The departure of the main body of the Squadron to Samoa on the 20th meant that the *Emden* had to delay her scheduled trip to Shanghai at the mouth of the Yangtse, a fact which caused the crew no grief because of the insufferable humidity of the area at this time of year. Instead they looked forward to a promised voyage to Mexico in the autumn, which was a much more attractive prospect.

Meanwhile, in Tsingtao at the end of June 1914 it was the hottest summer old hands could remember for at least ten years when, on the 29th, the news came by wireless that the heir to the throne of Austria-Hungary, the Archduke Franz Ferdinand, and his wife had been assassinated at Sarajevo the day before. As officer of the watch, Lauterbach took the news to the captain, who like everybody else there at the time attached no special significance to it beyond seeing it as another ingredient added to a menacing brew of tensions in Europe. Although the Kaiser had broken off the Kiel Navy Week as a result, it was learned in Tsingtao a week after the event at Sarajevo that he had allowed the annual Emperor's Manoeuvres to go ahead, with the royal yacht *Hohenzollern* once again accompanying the High Seas Fleet at sea. War remained very possible, but did not seem imminent. From the South Pacific, Spee ordered the *Emden* to sit tight in Tsingtao, finally cancelling the visit to Shanghai. The next day, 9 July, the Admiralty in Berlin warned that hostilities were likely between Serbia and Germany's ally, Austria-Hungary, and that they were also likely to spread. Heightened watch was henceforward maintained in the wireless office for transmissions from foreign ships. Otherwise it was quiet, apart from a typhoon on the night of 22 July, until the 24th, when the Austrian cruiser *Kaiserin Elisabeth* entered harbour. The elderly vessel, slow and of little more fighting value than a large gunboat, had sought a friendly landfall because she would have stood no chance against any modern cruiser of the Triple Entente powers, Britain, France and Russia. She was thus a harbinger of war and was recognised as such by the men of the *Emden*, who nonetheless made her welcome. The Austrians proceeded to mobilise in style and at their leisure, with frequent pauses for parties and visits ashore, for the best part of a week. Aboard the *Emden*, the only modern warship at the disposal of the Central Powers in East Asian waters, the wireless telegraphists were busier than ever logging the dread messages relayed nearly halfway round the world by Germany's chain of powerful wireless stations from the Admiralty in Berlin. On the 25th it was the Austrian ultimatum to Serbia that reached the China Station; two days later they learned from the Admiralty that diplomatic relations between the two Balkan powers had been broken off; the day after that, that Austria had declared war on Serbia. On the 29th came the order: 'Seek contact with Cruiser Squadron.' Spee was still somewhere in the South Pacific. The *Emden* began to prepare for war.

Commander Müller was not only captain of a warship but also, in the absence of the Squadron, senior naval officer responsible for naval preparations at Tsingtao, for all German naval vessels along the China coast, and, in the event of war, for all shipping under the German flag within reach, with full powers to requisition and commandeer. He also had orders from the Admiralty and from his own Admiral on what to do in the event of war with various combinations of powers, but these left him with considerable discretion and therefore a heavy burden of responsibility.

Karl Friedrich Max von Müller, soon to become the most famous ship's captain in the history of Germany, was as a boy destined for the army. This befitted the son of a colonel in that Prussian army which had upset the balance of power in Europe by its smashing defeat of France in 1870. Müller was born at Hanover on 16 June 1873. After grammar school (*Gymnasium*) there, and later at the main Baltic naval-base city of Kiel to which his father had been posted, Müller went to a military academy at Plön in Schleswig-Holstein and from there to the army officer-cadet corps. But at Easter 1891, having won his father over just before he turned 18, Müller made the unusual transfer to the navy and became a midshipman, or naval ensign, within two years. In October 1894 he was a signals sub-lieutenant on a battleship; two and a half years later he was promoted lieutenant. In 1898 he began a two-year stint as an officer of the watch on a gunboat based on German East Africa (now mainland Tanzania) with several voyages to German South-West Africa (Namibia): it was during this assignment that he contracted malaria, the disease he suffered from for the rest of his life and which was the cause of his untimely death.

Despite consistently good, sometimes exceptionally good, reports from his superiors, and the breakneck expansion of the navy from the turn of the century to the outbreak of war, promotion was slow for Müller. In 1903, less than three months before his thirtieth birthday, he was gazetted *Kapitänleutnant*, by which time he was a gunnery officer aboard a battleship. He took a number of staff courses between brief tours of duty in various capacities on battleships. In autumn 1907 he joined the staff of Prince Heinrich of Prussia, the Kaiser's younger brother who commanded the Baltic Fleet, aboard his flagship, SMS *Deutschland*. After nearly six years, Müller was promoted lieutenant-commander at the end of 1908. From 1909 to 1912 he served in the Imperial Navy Office in Berlin as a staff officer, where he made a distinctly favourable impression on Admiral Alfred von Tirpitz, architect of the massive expansion of the German navy and now its political chief. Despite Prince Heinrich's commendations and the now regular glowing reports from other superiors, verging on the lyrical in praising his expertise in gunnery ('First-class, completely reliable officer. Warmly recommended to future superiors. Signed: v. Tirpitz' 1912), Müller passed his 39th birthday without attaining the naval officer's *raison d'être* as a seaman – command of a ship, however small. At this age David Beatty, Britain's most famous naval officer of the First World War, was already a rear-admiral. But at the end of 1912, Müller was ordered to take command of the *Emden* in the following spring.

It was his boldness and resolution in dealing with the rebels along the Yangtse that finally produced the long-overdue career breakthrough. He became a hero in the newspapers of all the imperialist powers as well as the German press, and the rapidly expanded navy with virtually no history could hardly fail to acknowledge this rare demonstration of dash and gallantry. He was given a medal (the Order of the Royal Crown, third class, with swords) and a very approving report by Graf Spee at the end of 1913, carrying a recommendation for promotion. He became a full commander in March 1914.

Why the sterling qualities of an officer like Müller were not recognised sooner is impossible now to establish. But it has to be said

24

that in a service which was for a long time the favourite plaything of an absolute monarch with strong autocratic and capricious tendencies it was not enough to be of exceptional quality and to have no enemies. The Imperial Navy was dominated by three rival centres of power – the Navy Office (political), the Admiralty Staff (military) and by no means least the Kaiser's Navy Cabinet (at court). Quite clearly Müller was not the kind of man to push himself forward, even when he had daily access to no less a man than Tirpitz, at that time the most important of the three naval chiefs. There are hardly any intimate insights into his character to be found anywhere. Unlike so many others with connections with the *Emden*, however tenuous, he wrote nothing for public consumption and his long report to the Admiralty after his ship's last battle is a model of detachment which gives hardly a clue to the character of its author. We are left with a shadowy picture, made up of asides by others more concerned with their own affairs or versions of events and of official assessments. From these emerges a man of immense reserve, no less highly regarded by his inferiors than his superiors; however we do not even know whether he had a sense of humour. But we can at least judge him by his deeds, which we are about to consider.

The ship's second-in-command, by contrast, was a natural extrovert who was to become as famous as Müller for one of the most remarkable escapes in the history of warfare. The Odyssey of Kurt Hellmuth von Mücke, erstwhile First Officer (executive officer and first lieutenant) of the *Emden* and commander of the ship's landing party, is a worthy sequel to the maritime Iliad of the cruiser's campaign in the Indian Ocean.

Eight years and nine days younger than his skipper, Hellmuth von Mücke was also born into the minor military nobility, the son of a captain who later joined the Imperial civil service. He was born in Zwickau, Saxony, and became a naval officer-cadet in April 1900, a midshipman after a year, sub-lieutenant in September 1903 and full lieutenant only one year later. He served in a battleship, a light cruiser and destroyers until he became Flag Lieutenant to the Admiral commanding reconnaissance forces (cruisers) in 1907. In April 1910 he was promoted *Kapitänleutnant* and got his first command as captain of the destroyer *S149*, simultaneously serving as Flag Lieutenant to no. I Torpedo-boat Flotilla, of which *S149* was leader. In 1911 he added the role of adviser to the torpedo inspectorate to these responsibilities until he was posted in autumn 1912 to the staff of the junior rear-admiral of the reconnaissance forces. He had, however, been asking for an overseas posting, which was given to him one year later – navigation officer of the *Emden*. As we have seen, he became

First Officer six months later. As such, he was responsible for the day-to-day running of the ship and was principal disciplinarian. Endowed, among other qualities, with natural leadership abilities, charm, physical presence and good looks, he proved to be a man of almost infinite resource at sea and on shore. Modesty was not one of his failings. His extrovert nature was an excellent foil for the watchful but withdrawn captain who occasionally found it necessary to rein in his formidable 'Number One', as he would have been called in the Royal Navy.

Of the 400 men who took SMS *Emden* to war in 1914, one other deserves introduction at this point. He is Reserve Lieutenant Julius Lauterbach, whose own escape back to Germany and the fantastic adventures he had on the way out-Conrad Joseph Conrad. He was an officer of the watch and for a while navigation officer, but his real value to the cruiser was as prize officer in an area of ocean he knew intimately as a merchant captain.

Lauterbach too was the son of an army officer who was originally destined to follow in his father's footsteps. He thus spent six years in a military academy. Born at Rostock on the Baltic in 1877, he went to sea before the mast at the age of 17 without the approval of his family and became an officer-cadet. He loved the sea, sailed all over the world in sailing ships and steamers, became expert in navigating the China coast and was appointed master of a Hamburg-America Line ship at the age of 29. Only four years younger than the *Emden*'s commander, he had known him slightly at the officer-cadet school they both attended before going their different ways to sea. Even as a very young man, his photographs show Lauterbach to have been of giant frame. In early middle age he ran to fat, but a great deal of his 255 lb. bulk was muscle. He soon acquired the voice, the boisterous nature, the jollity and the beer-storage capacity appropriate to his size and was apparently given to singing a ditty which began: '*Zu Lauterbach hab' ich mein' Strumpf verloren*' (literally, 'I lost my socks in Lauterbach' – there are at least four places called Lauterbach in Germany; the name means 'clear stream') which has overtones of losing one's shirt and is sung to the tune of 'Where, oh where, has my little dog gone'. One cannot escape the conclusion that this larger-than-life, back-slapping mariner pickled in beer would have been overwhelming to tedious at close quarters or on prolonged acquaintance; but his adventures are part of the story of the *Emden* and his undoubted qualities are another example of the exceptional human material the cruiser carried to war from Tsingtao in summer 1914, as we shall see below.

26

The port which was the *Emden*'s base for the four years leading up to the war was an instant Germany city implanted on the coast of China. Seized with the surrounding area by three German cruisers in 1897 after two Lutheran missionaries had been murdered in the district, it became a bustling harbour, naval base and commercial centre in less than two decades. What was originally a poverty-stricken fishing village surrounded by barren land rapidly acquired its Friedrichstrasse, its yellow-stuccoed Post Office, the Café Metropol for the consumption of coffee and cakes on sweltering sub-tropical afternoons, the more apposite Fürstenhof beerhall, the banks in the Wilhelmstrasse, the carefully manicured arboretum, the barracks, the Central Hotel and the theatrical and concert hall. There were hundreds of towns like it between Emden on the Dutch border and Königsberg in East Prussia; none of them however was built on the site of a hot and humid Chinese coastal settlement by a splendid natural harbour, made habitable for Europeans by sea breezes. There were also resort facilities, a Catholic and a Lutheran church, a railway station on the new Shantung Railway, coal and ore mines, hospitals and schools of the highest quality. Over all flew the black, white and red tricolour of the German Empire. It looked as permanent as Hong Kong and considerably more orderly. The showpiece of the German Empire overseas was to fall to Japanese and British naval and military forces in the opening months of the coming war. Building on the excellent German infrastructure, the Chinese have developed Tsingtao into a major industrial city with a population well in excess of a million.

From 20 June 1914 the naval protection of this imperial jewel was the responsibility of the one modern warship moored in its harbour, the light cruiser *Emden*, whose captain was senior naval officer, answerable to the Governor in the absence of Admiral Spee.

Displacing some 3,600 tons, the ship was 387 feet long and just under 44 feet wide, with a draught of about 17½ feet. Two-thirds the length of a typical capital ship but less than half the width and lying rather lower in the water, ships of this category always gave a distinct impression of elegance, even delicacy. The delicate impression, despite her armament, was not altogether false. Her conning tower was protected by four inches of armour-plate; for the rest, she had an armoured deck two inches thick amidships. Her main armament consisted of ten 4.1-inch (10.5 cm.) guns, two forward, two aft and three set into each side, giving two broadsides of five guns each. She was powered by two standing triple-expansion engines of three cylinders each, with a total of twelve boilers that could withstand a maximum pressure of 227 lb. per square inch, yielding a top speed of

24 knots. Her forward-sloping bow was a survival of the days when ramming was an important part of theoretical naval tactics; and she burned coal. Her tragedy was that she was out of date before she was launched, compared with her British contemporaries, which outclassed her in guns, armour, speed and range.

The centrepiece of the Imperial German Navy was the High Seas Fleet, the bulk of its fighting strength and destructive power until the Germans grasped the significance of the submarine in a war against Britain. The High Seas Fleet was conceived by Tirpitz and enthusiastically fostered by the Kaiser as a challenge to the world maritime supremacy of the Royal Navy; as such it was a principal cause of the First World War. Germany, the world's leading military power, could live very well without a navy; Britain, whose power and Empire depended on dominant seapower, could not, and she reorganised her naval strength to form the overwhelming Grand Fleet, to contain the High Seas Fleet in the North Sea in case of war. The pride of each battle fleet was the capital ship, the battleship or battlecruiser (which had a battleship's guns but greater speed, gained at the expense of some armour protection); the mine, the torpedo and the submarine were soon identified as such great threats to these that enormous numbers of smaller ships were built to protect the largest ones. The capital ships were screened by destroyers whose main weapon was the torpedo and main advantage high speed; to counter the destroyers and to act as scouts, the battle fleets deployed cruisers with guns powerful enough to blast destroyers out of the water. The big ships swallowed rafts of money and were often politically controversial in both countries. This led the British to economise on destroyers and light cruisers and the Germans to sacrifice heavy and medium cruisers from their expansion plans and to keep their light cruisers as light as possible. The High Seas Fleet and its supporting ships were built in the first instance for service in the North Sea and the Baltic, the Grand Fleet for service anywhere in the world. The Royal Navy's ships were of long range in coal or oil capacity and in comfort for their crews; the German vessels carried less fuel and their crews spent much of their time in barracks ashore between short forays at sea, which made their ships stronger but their accommodation spartan. Further, the British outgunned the Germans in nearly all classes of ship: where a German battleship had 11-inch guns, a British one would have 12-inch; when the Germans installed 12-inch guns, the British were going for 15. As if to compensate, German barrels lasted longer and their armour was better, as were their rangefinders.

Thus German cruisers like the *Emden* were built with the needs of the North Sea-oriented High Seas Fleet in mind, while British ones were built for greater independence and flexibility, to police an Empire as well as protecting battleships. Germany's solitary overseas formation, as we have seen, was Graf Spee's Pacific or Far East command, names given to it by the British: for the Germans it was simply *the* Cruiser Squadron, the only one they had. In 1914, Germany had eight major cruisers (Britain had thirty-four). Of these, five were battlecruisers and one a disastrous hybrid, a heavy cruiser trying to pass as a battlecruiser – all but one of these were attached to the High Seas Fleet – and the other two were the *Scharnhorst*, Count Spee's flagship, and her sister-ship, the *Gneisenau*, also with the Cruiser Squadron. The last two named were the only two heavy cruisers (the largest category of non-capital ship) in German service. They were supported by five light cruisers broadly comparable with the *Emden*, though two or more were commonly on detached duty. The other four were *Leipzig*, *Nürnberg*, *Karlsruhe* and *Königsberg*. Apart from a handful of destroyers and a scattering of slow, lightly armed gunboats in the vicinity of Germany's sprinkling of overseas imperial possessions, these cruisers and the detached light cruiser *Dresden* were the only German surface warships on the open sea when war broke out on 1 August 1914. (One battlecruiser and one light cruiser were in the Mediterranean.) All of them were to distinguish themselves in one way or another in the opening months of the war before they were inevitably cornered by superior British forces. Not only did the Royal Navy outnumber the German Navy by a ratio of at least six to four overall; not only did the Cruiser Squadron also have the modern Japanese Navy and detachments of the Russian and French navies to contend with; but each German cruiser also had the extra handicap of being outgunned and outrun by the main enemy's ships in each category: British light cruisers were bigger, more strongly protected and faster, and they had 6-inch guns to the German 4-inch; and their heavy cruisers were heavier still, also faster and more protected, with 9.2-inch guns against 8.2-inch. German construction quality, hull strength and gunnery control equipment, however, tended to be superior. All this meant that any warship sent in pursuit of the *Emden* after she was detached from the Squadron would be superior, and that any modern warship from the Royal Navy larger than a destroyer which she might meet by accident would also be superior. Luck and her captain's wits might save her; her guns, her engines and her armour would not.

But she did at least possess the Great Equaliser, the torpedo, fired from two underwater tubes placed transversely to fire broadside-on on either side. She normally carried five 17.7-inch torpedoes with a range of some 11,000 feet. One of her torpedo officers was Sub-

I ieutenant Franz Joseph Prinz von Hohenzollern-Sigmaringen, a nephew of the Kaiser.

The range of her guns, which could each fire sixteen shots per minute out of a normal stock of 150 rounds per gun, was about 13,500 yards. She had a steaming range of about 3,790 nautical miles at her economical cruising speed of twelve knots with a normal supply of coal of 790 tons; 4,460 at eight knots; and only 1,850 at twenty knots (1,226 at her maximum speed of 24 knots, in theory). By using every square inch of spare space, she could carry a total of 960 tons of coal without losing fighting efficiency and with corresponding gains in range. But the problem of coal supply in enemy-dominated seas was her greatest weakness in her role as a commerce-raider. At the same time it was as a commerce-raider that the *Emden* reached the full potential of her class in a war against Britain – despite having been designed for fleet support rather than for independent action.

2

'FAIR TO SEE AND YET BOUND TO DIE'

The ever-conscientious Commander Müller regarded with the utmost seriousness his temporary responsibility for the naval protection of the German colony of Kiao Chow, which extended inland by a radius of thirty miles from its splendid harbour of Tsingtao. Warned by his Admiral that the rest of the Squadron would probably be away for three months and that he might not be relieved before then, Müller was given written and oral orders on what to do in the event of war, but was left with considerable leeway on how to carry them out. In the event of 'war-scenario C' his instructions were to organise and support the despatch of all coal-steamers out of Tsingtao to predetermined rendezvous points as reserves for the Squadron, and to ensure that his own and any other usable warship were not trapped in the harbour in the event of a siege or blockade. 'War-scenario C' envisaged war between Germany and her allies and the Triple Entente of France, Russia and Britain. Thinking aloud, Müller had already told Lieutenant-Commander von Bötticher, a staff officer with Spee, that he felt the best way of executing his orders was to threaten enemy commerce on the open sea in order to draw hostile forces away from Tsingtao, which would help German vessels to escape. Assisted by his young adjutant, Sub-Lieutenant Albert von Guérard, Müller spent much of his time going over contingency plans. In particular he prepared for all officers a war-game for which 'I took as basis a war with England and the Dual Alliance [France and Russia] and the start of tension as on 1 August'. Since this was precisely what happened, his arrangements worked extremely smoothly when war came.

Preparations began in earnest at the end of June. The captains of three small river gunboats in various parts of China were ordered to disable their ships and get the crews back to Tsingtao. A warning was sent to the Austrian *Kaiserin Elisabeth*, which decided to come to Tsingtao. An old cruiser or large gunboat, the *Cormoran*, was in dock under prolonged repair. Two ocean-going gunboats were already in port and two more were called home from various places in the region, as was the elderly but far from outdated destroyer *S90* (400 tons, completed in 1900 and capable of up to 26½ knots). German consulates in the Far East were asked to watch for potential enemy ships and report their movements; merchant ship captains were warned to be ready for requisitioning or for entering neutral ports to collect supplies and sail to the predetermined meeting points to be available for the Squadron. Other ships were to take refuge in neutral harbours to avoid falling into enemy hands. Particular attention was naturally paid to the deployment of coal-ships, all of which were to be commandeered for the Squadron and sent to strategic places in Far Eastern waters. Like everybody else involved at the time, the Germans in the Far East believed that it would be a short war to be decided by the fighting on land in Europe. Their formidable disadvantages locally could be offset only by evasion – and good organisation.

Shortly before the outbreak of war, Müller suggested to Spee that in the event of 'war-scenario B' (conflict with France and Russia), the *Emden* should run south-west and lay mines off Saigon and other Indo-Chinese ports to upset trade and morale in French colonial territory. The Squadron would have been a very powerful asset to Germany in such case; but 'scenario C' was infinitely less favourable, because of the pattern of alliances built up in the immediately preceding period. If Germany and her allies became involved in conflict with either France or Russia, the other Power would join in. As it was, Austria-Hungary declared war on Serbia, Russia took Serbia's side, Germany took Austria's and then invaded France, via Belgium and directly, to knock out the French before tackling 'the real enemy', Russia. Britain was not bound by treaty to intervene on the side of France and/or Russia but there was an 'understanding' to this effect; the violation of Belgian neutrality, of which Germany had been a guarantor no less than Britain, left the British with no choice but to declare war on Germany. For a few days the Germans, especially their navy and above all the Cruiser Squadron, hoped against hope that the British would not be drawn in. Germany was at war with Russia as from 1 August and with France from the 3rd; the British came in at midnight on the night of 4 August, and scenario C was complete.

The implications for the Squadron were momentous in the extreme. Under 'B' it would have had to contend with elements of a Russian navy still not recovered from its smashing defeat by the Japanese at the Battle of Tsushima in 1905 and such ships as the French were able to spare for the Far East from the Mediterranean, which they were covering to leave as many British ships as possible free to garrison the North Sea and the Channel. At the start of the war, the French had two armoured cruisers, the *Montcalm* and the *Dupleix*, and a handful of destroyers and other smaller ships east of Suez; the Russians had the cruiser *Askold* and the light cruiser *Zhemchug* (of which we shall hear again) and various smaller vessels based on Vladivostok on their Pacific coast. The German Squadron had little to fear from these potential opposing forces. But under 'C' the picture altered in drastic fashion. Britain was allied with Japan, which possessed a large, efficient and experienced navy including battleships and battlecruisers. British involvement brought in Australia and New Zealand: the fledgling Australian navy possessed, in HMAS *Australia*, flagship of Admiral Patey, a brand-new battlecruiser capable of destroying the entire German Squadron with its 12-inch guns without assistance. In 1914 Patey's British-built flagship was the most powerful man-of-war, not just in the Pacific but in the entire southern hemisphere. The Australian Squadron he led came under direct Royal Navy command as soon as war broke out. But Spee's principal opponent was Admiral Jerram, the British C-in-C, China, with his bases at Hong Kong, Weihaiwei north of Tsingtao, and Singapore, and his two heavy cruisers, one old battleship, two light cruisers and eight destroyers. On the other side of the Pacific the British had what amounted to a scratch force of mostly elderly ships under Admiral Cradock, based on Port Stanley in the Falkland Islands. The Royal Navy had subsidiary commands and bases in India, South Africa, East Africa and West Africa. Wherever Spee and his ships, together or separately, might decide to go, formidable enemy forces, especially British, could be mustered against him. Spee, promoted Vice-Admiral at the end of 1913, knew that one of the first moves of the British and their Japanese and Dominion partners in the event of war would be to capture all German possessions overseas, leaving his ships without coaling stations or friendly harbours, and that there was nothing he could do about it. At the same time he believed in the 'fleet in being' theory – that an undefeated naval force, no matter how outnumbered or disadvantaged, would give the enemy pause so long as it existed. He had a sporting chance of surviving a short war and a good chance of inflicting disproportionate damage and disruption for several weeks if not months; he had more than half the surface of the globe to hide in; all he needed was coal. How was he to get it?

German naval strategy, whether in home waters in the North Sea where the fleet was concentrated or in the Far East where its sole major detachment operated, was concerned above all with circumventing the world maritime supremacy of the Royal Navy. The British had bases, large and small, all over the world; the Germans effectively had none in the event of war with Britain. To counter this they had invented the naval *Etappe*, a land-based office run by a navy officer of middling rank, normally a lieutenant-commander. The *Etappe*, usually established well before the war, handled communications, intelligence, coaling and supply, and such posts had been set up wherever possible in relevant major ports round the world. Those established in neutral territory carried on functioning after war broke out and proved invaluable. On the eve of war, Müller set up an *Etappe* in Tsingtao itself to work after he left port, and he was also in touch with such posts in Shanghai and Batavia, capital of the Netherlands East Indies (now Indonesia). Once war broke out, the entire German merchant marine was at the disposal of the navy, and in the last days of peace a particularly keen watch was kept on the movements and positions of coal-ships. With the navy's needs in mind, a high proportion of German merchant vessels had been equipped with Telefunken wireless transmission equipment, to supplement and eventually replace the sparse network of very powerful shore-based transmitters on German islands and in other colonial territories. German use of wireless was distinctly ahead of British in these respects, but then their need was greater. Relatively few British merchantmen had Marconi transmitters, a fact from which the *Emden* was to benefit considerably. Finally, although so much of the Far East was under the control of Germany's enemies, there was also plenty of neutral territory, including China, the Dutch East Indies, the Philippines (then American), and other islands under the United States flag such as Guam and Hawaii. In almost all of these places, people friendly to Germany could be found in useful numbers, and with the help of *Etappe*-officers maximum use could be made of the limited time allowed for coaling and repairs to belligerent warships in neutral waters.

Winston Churchill wrote of Spee and his Squadron (in *The World Crisis*): 'He was a cut flower in a vase, fair to see and yet bound to die'. But, 'Von Spee and his squadron could turn up almost anywhere . . . we could not possibly be strong enough every day everywhere to meet him.' His own superiors left him complete freedom of action; with remarkable wisdom and forbearance they realised in Berlin that any orders would tie his hands in a predicament only he fully understood. They wrote him out of their long-term calculations and hoped he would be able to strike at least one major blow against at least one of his enemies before he met his fate. As indeed he did.

In the dying days of July and peace, Müller, as Spee's agent in Tsingtao, made his final dispositions. He detailed two gunboats and the *S90* to remain in Tsingtao, at the disposal of the governor, naval Captain Meyer-Waldeck, for local security duties. On the night of the 30th to the 31st of July he received an urgent telegram from the Berlin Admiralty, brought by one of the party of sailors he had thoughtfully stationed at the Post Office for the purpose, saying: 'War broken out Austria-Hungary Serbia. Political tension has broken out between Triple Alliance [Germany, Austria and Italy] and Great Britain France Russia.' Aboard the *Emden* the last war supplies were loaded and gear 'not wanted on voyage' unloaded. The latter included peace-time items of equipment that might cause unnecessary clutter or risk of fire but had given the ship a few elements of home comfort. Müller also earmarked ships carrying a total of more than 10,000 tons of coal to go to three points in the Pacific for the Squadron on Admiralty orders and in line with his instructions from Spee. These ships could not be sent out until after he had left port because no requisitioning could take place legally until the 'state of tension' telegram was followed by the 'war imminent' message. Müller had already chartered the SS *Elsbeth*, a coal steamer, which he was planning to send to Yap Island for the Squadron. He left it to the new Tsingtao *Etappe* to despatch the rest and relay the 'war imminent', the mobilisation and the 'war declared' messages to the Squadron, the gunboats in China waters and *Etappe* posts in Shanghai, Tokyo, Manila, Batavia and Singapore.

At 7 p.m. on Friday, 31 July 1914, the *Emden* slipped her moorings and moved slowly out of the harbour. The *Elsbeth* followed southwards for four hours until she turned away for Yap. War watches were kept on the cruiser, now prepared for action day or night, her ready-use ammunition already primed. War watches meant that the crew spent twice as many hours per day on duty as normal and slept close to or at their action stations. Further acute discomfort was caused by the necessity to darken ship in the evening, which meant closing every opening aboard, thus reducing ventilation suffocatingly by eliminating all draughts in stifling weather (this problem was soon solved by cutting out certain electrical circuits so that some portholes, air-shafts and the like could be left open without risk of an accidental outpouring of light). The ship's parting message to Berlin said she was leaving but staying within wireless range; her first ceremonial act in wartime was three cheers for the Kaiser on 2 August, a Sunday. On that day, the message was received that Germany had begun to mobilise the day before and that war had been declared on Russia. Müller told his crew that the impending war was the result of envy of

Germany's economic success and had come in spite of the Kaiser's peace efforts. The captain expected every man to do his duty to the flag and the good name borne by the ship.

Germany declared war on France on 3 August, and Britain on Germany the next day. Italy, the third member of the Triple Alliance, obliged to fight only if her partners were attacked and not if they started hostilities, stayed neutral. This news was passed to the ship from Tsingtao as she headed slowly south-east and then east, round the southern end of the Korean peninsula. Tension on board was high; there had been a near miss on the 1st when the *Emden* saw the wakes of what had obviously been a formation of warships after hearing loud and busy coded wireless traffic (Jerram's squadron heading out from Weihaiwei southwards, as Müller learned in November). While a sighting would not in all probability have led to shooting – war was still hours away – the *Emden*'s whereabouts would have been revealed, and no doubt a ship would have been detached to follow her until it became permissible to open fire. Müller was prepared to fight an equal or an inferior enemy and knew he had the speed to evade any French and Russian ships in the area if he needed to. But his plan was to intercept Russian steamers in the straits between Korea and Japan, close to the scene of the famous Battle of Tsushima nine years before. By making a nuisance of himself in the steamer lanes he hoped to draw enemy warships away from Tsingtao, before he started out across the Pacific to meet Spee and the Squadron. One of the many messages to the ship on 1 August had been from the Admiral, telling Müller not to bother with his idea of minelaying off Indo-China but to head east after settling matters at Tsingtao, to join up with the Squadron.

In the early hours of 4 August, in a rough sea and heavy rain, the alarm bells sounded on the *Emden* and the ship throbbed in tune with her accelerating engines. Between gusts of wind and rain it was possible to make out the substantial shape of a ship without lights, perhaps a warship. Müller took personal charge of the chase towards Japanese territorial waters round Tsushima Island. Through a gap in the weather a black steamer with two yellow funnels could be made out. Lauterbach reported that these were the colours of the Russian Volunteer Fleet and Müller decided to capture it. The signal flags for 'stop at once – do not wireless' were hoisted and a blank shot fired. The Russian ship ignored all this and tried to make a run for it into neutral Japanese waters (Japan did not enter the war until 23 August). Her wireless was heard sending requests for help and her call-sign, CQ. The *Emden* jammed the signals with her own transmitter. Another blank shot was ignored, and only after the firing of twelve live rounds did the *Emden* succeed in persuading the Russian to halt. The chase had lasted more than an hour, from 6 a.m.

Lauterbach was sent in a cutter with an armed boarding party of two warrant officers and twenty men to seize the ship. The rough swell almost caused a catastrophe at the very outset of *Emden's* career as a corsair. Either by accident or by design, the gangway of the Russian ship had been lowered too far down her side, so that when the cutter came alongside and the ship rolled towards it, Lauterbach's boat was almost impaled and thrust under the water – the alarmed Müller ordered a second cutter to be readied for going to the rescue of the first. The imperturbable Lauterbach solved the problem by launching his impressive bulk with impeccable timing in the direction of the end of the gangway and hauling himself aboard, whereupon he was able to adjust the position of the steps. After sending his men to guard key points on the ship, including the wireless shack and the bridge, Lauterbach questioned the master, Captain Ausan. He professed himself unable to speak German until Lauterbach laughingly reminded him that they had been drinking beer together in the club at Tsingtao only the previous month. The ship was the *Ryaezan*, as Lauterbach signalled back to the *Emden*, now lying 150 yards to windward. She was a 3,500-ton mail steamer with eighty passengers but little cargo, en route from Nagasaki in Japan to Vladivostok. She was a modern vessel built at the Schickau Yard at Danzig, with a good turn of speed for a merchant ship, as had just been admirably demonstrated. She had got up the exceptional speed of 17 knots in the chase. Müller therefore decided to convert her into an auxiliary cruiser rather than sink her, and the German flag was hoisted at her stern. Lauterbach signalled that Captain Ausan was protesting against the seizure of his ship in allegedly neutral waters. Müller replied: 'Inform captain he crew and passengers under German military law and he has nothing to protest about.' Whereupon, said the commander laconically in his report, the captain calmed down.

Reading through the *Ryaezan's* signal log, Lauterbach discovered that the ship had exchanged messages with the French squadron, which she had sighted earlier that morning, and had learned that the warships had left Vladivostok on a southerly course. Extra lookouts were posted as the *Emden* headed south-westwards, on the first half of a curved course designed to bring her back to Tsingtao with the first prize of the entire war steaming a few hundred yards ahead of her. At 5 p.m. a lookout reported the smoke of five ships on the starboard beam. It was the French squadron, and Müller immediately ordered evasive action. The *Emden* went to action stations and Lauterbach was ordered to prepare the *Ryaezan* for sinking and to swing out her boats: she would be scuttled if there was any danger of the enemy seizing her otherwise. Uncoded messages overheard on the wireless showed the Germans that the French had not only spotted the *Emden* but taken her for the outrider of the entire Spee Squadron. They decided to withdraw from the area, southwards. The German officers laughed with relief, and Sub-Lieutenant Fikentscher idly remarked to First Officer von Mücke what a pity it was that the *Emden* did not have a fourth funnel like the heavy cruiser for which she had apparently been mistaken: they would have been able to cause real panic among the Frenchmen. After the evasive action, the light cruiser headed west and later north-west on the way to Tsingtao.

The next day, 5 August, Tsingtao relayed the message that Britain had declared war on Germany. At a stroke the odds against the *Emden* and the rest of the Squadron were quadrupled. Müller, fully aware of the proximity to Tsingtao of the British base at Weihaiwei, decided nonetheless to risk a return to the German port and turn his prize into an armed merchantman. With the *Ryaezan* astern and the *Emden* cleared for action, Müller carefully approached the harbour entrance at dawn. Tsingtao was blacked out behind a belt of mines and a pinnace put out to guide the ships through it.

The naval personnel left behind on 31 July had not been idle. Three gunboats had been stripped of their armament to convert the Imperial mail-steamer *Prinz Eitel Friedrich* into an auxiliary cruiser. The *Cormoran* was afloat again after repairs, and Müller ordered her to be stripped to arm the *Ryaezan*, which was given her eight 4-inch guns and renamed *Cormoran II* (she was ready in four days and was to join Spee in the South Pacific on 27 August). The *Emden* feverishly topped up with coal until she once again had nearly 1,000 tons aboard, as she had done on 31 July. Fears of war had led to a shortage of 'coolies', which made life very hectic for the crew. The very last superfluous items were dumped on the quay and thirty-nine extra men were added to the crew, including a reserve officer and an army doctor, Ludwig Schwabe, who volunteered his services to Dr. Johannes Luther, the naval staff surgeon already aboard. All this brought the crew up to a strength of 398, plus three Chinese laundrymen. Müller was in conference most of the day, leaving Mücke in charge of preparations; Lauterbach handled the formalities concerning the *Ryaezan* in a specially convened prize court, while her holds were thoroughly cleaned (she had been carrying large quantities of distinctly assertive Japanese garlic) and work began on her conversion.

By 6 p.m. the *Emden* was as ready as she would ever be. The ship's band assembled on deck and played martial airs as the crew saluted the Governor, passing in his launch, and took what they realised was likely to be their last look at Tsingtao. With the British already in the war and the Japanese, their allies, likely to follow, an attack on the port was inevitable and a defeat no less so. The *Emden* slowly passed the harbour entrance, her crew lining the deck, singing to the band and staring at the German town spread out behind them in the low sun of evening. Outside the harbour and the minefield the *Emden* halted, as two rainbows appeared over the hills behind the settlement, until she was joined by the *S90*, the *Prinz Eitel Friedrich* and the SS *Markomannia*, a modern, British-built 4,500-ton collier (Captain Faass), allocated to Müller with a full load of first-class coal. The two warships made a sweep to northwards to find out if any enemy ships were approaching Tsingtao, then southwards to join the requisitioned merchant ships. The *S90* (*Kapitänleutnant* Brunner) signalled her farewell off Tsingtao and resumed her patrols there: on 17 October during the siege of Tsingtao she daringly torpedoed the old Japanese cruiser *Takachiho*, whereupon she was run aground and blown up by Brunner to prevent her falling into enemy hands. The crew of sixty went into internment in neutral China.

The destination of the small flotilla was the German island of Pagan, in the Marianas chain north of Guam, to link up with Spee, as arranged by wireless between the Squadron and Tsingtao. The route lay south-east, through the Yellow Sea and the eastern China Sea and then between the Japanese islands and Chinese Formosa (Taiwan) into the Pacific. During the first night and on the move, the two merchant ships put on disguises, the *Markomannia* imitating a Blue Funnel Line ship and the *Prinz Eitel Friedrich* the white and yellow of a P & O liner. With the attention to detail characteristic of the man, Müller ordered the Japanese name *Nagato Maru* painted on such items as lifebelts and life-rafts: such precautions would conceal from the enemy the sinking of the *Emden* should it come to that.

The passage to Pagan passed without important incident. A few Japanese vessels were seen but the cruiser and the disguised liner found nothing to capture. As early as 8 August, less than forty-eight hours out, the wireless operators picked up reports of unknown origin saying that the *Emden* was in the East China Sea 'with two captured steamers'. They also heard of the German advance in the west and the Russian advance into East Prussia. Lauterbach lectured his brother-officers on the science of seizing merchant ships in his new role as prize officer. 'He seemed particularly suited for this role,' Müller wrote. 'During the cruise of the *Emden* he carried out all duties devolving upon him with inexhaustible zeal and extraordinary skill.' The slower *Markomannia* was sent ahead to Pagan while the other two ships searched in vain for booty. At dusk the *Emden* anchored alongside the *Scharnhorst*, the *Gneisenau* and the *Nürnberg*, none of which she had seen for more than seven weeks. Eight supply ships were also in the bay overlooked by a smoking volcano. The *Marko-mannia* was due to arrive next day, the 13th. Only the *Elsbeth*, the coal ship which had left port with the *Emden* on 31 July, had not been heard from. She had gone to Yap, some 900 miles south-west of Pagan, to wait for the Squadron. But on the day the *Emden* reached Pagan, Admiral Jerram with the heavy cruisers HMS *Minotaur* and *Hampshire* and the light cruiser *Newcastle* arrived off Yap in the hope of finding Spee's Squadron. The *Elsbeth* scuttled herself; and the British, after warning people on the island to get clear, shelled the mast of the powerful and important German radio station until it was totally destroyed. They sailed away without landing. The British radio traffic was clearly heard, if not understood, by the Germans at Pagan, whose anchorage was busy throughout the night.

3

FAREWELL TO THE SQUADRON

Count Spee summoned his captains aboard the flagship *Scharnhorst* on the morning of the 13th, as the *Markomannia* joined the Squadron. He wanted to discuss strategy and tactics. His original plan had been to disrupt enemy, particularly British, commerce in East Asiatic waters, but he also wanted to pursue the 'fleet in being' concept to the maximum effect. He had therefore already dismissed the idea of leading his force into the Indian Ocean because it was a British lake and his coaling problems would prove insurmountable. The news from Berlin that Chile, with its enormously lengthy coastline on the western side of South America, was friendly disposed, was tempting because it meant he could rely on getting coal there. Müller ventured to disagree with some of what Spee had said, pointing out that the Squadron would make little contribution to the war on the long voyage across the Pacific and would be able to achieve very little on arrival: 'If the coaling problems were to prove too great for a deployment of the Squadron in East Asian, Australian and Indian waters, I went so far as to ask, would it not be right at least to send one light cruiser from the Cruiser Squadron off to the Indian Ocean, where conditions for cruiser warfare would be particularly beneficial, and because the appearance of German naval forces on the Indian coast would be a beneficial influence for us on the attitude of the Indian population.' The other captains and the staff officers fell in with Müller's view and Spee said he would think about it. The officers were dismissed.

After lunch, a written order was delivered to Müller by boat from the *Scharnhorst*: 'You are hereby allocated the *Markomannia* and will be detached with the task of entering the Indian Ocean and waging cruiser warfare as best you can . . . Tonight you will stay with the Squadron; this order will come into force tomorrow morning through the signal "detached". I intend to go to western America with the rest of the Squadron.' The Admiral took Müller's point that a single light cruiser would be able to go where a large force could not, because of the coaling problem. One rogue ship could both cause much damage and disruption to enemy commerce and tie down a disproportionate number of warships. At this stage, the light cruiser *Königsberg* was off East Africa on the western side of the Indian Ocean, the *Dresden* in the western Atlantic (with the *Karlsruhe* on the way to relieve her) and Spee's *Leipzig* was coming back from a visit to the west coast of Mexico. *Nürnberg* had boiler trouble and could not be detached. The *Markomannia* had 5,000 tons of coal aboard; for the rest, the *Emden* would have to fend for herself by capturing enemy colliers.

Meanwhile the *Emden* was taking on 450 tons of coal from the SS *Staatssekretär Kraetke*, Lauterbach's ship, on one side and the *Gouverneur Jaeschke*, Lauterbach's previous command, on the other. He transhipped his personal library, his wine-cellar and some deck-chairs to the *Emden*. At the same time the ships were exchanging supplies with one another while their men exchanged rumours. The *Emden* sailors learned that a wireless report had said she had been in a fight with the Russian five-funnelled cruiser *Askold* and both had been sunk; and, more accurately, that she had taken the *Ryaezan*. Small wonder they had been so fervently cheered when they entered harbour.

All Chinese ancillary personnel – mainly cooks and laundrymen – were being assembled aboard the *Kraetke* to be sent to Tsingtao and out of this Europeans' war. The three laundrymen of the *Emden*, to the consternation of the crew, were at first less than keen to stay aboard. They had tried to leave in Tsingtao, but had been persuaded, mainly with money, to stay on by a fourth Chinese known as Joseph, who had been their leader. Joseph then proceeded to desert alone as they left Tsingtao for the last time. After a while however, the trio, whose real names have never been discovered, announced that they were happy to stay after all and unpacked their possessions again. Lauterbach had taken them aside, reminded them that the *Kraetke* was his ship and said he knew for certain that it was not going to Tsingtao, nor even to China (in fact she was interned in Honolulu by the Americans). The trio, known to all as One, Two and Three (in Chinese), were to die in action. The men of the *Emden* always had clean washing on their lonely mission, and they appreciated it.

All ships were under orders to have steam up by 5.30 p.m., and at dusk on the 13th they headed eastwards from Pagan in two parallel lines, the four cruisers and one merchantman in one, led by the *Scharnhorst*, and the eight other auxiliaries in the second, led by the *Prinz Eitel Friedrich*. Overnight, two of the latter line disappeared, being unaccustomed to travelling in convoy, but they were found after a short search. At 8 a.m. on the 14th, the *Scharnhorst* hoisted the signal: 'Detached. Wish good luck.' The *Emden* replied by semaphore: 'Thank your Excellency for trust placed in me. Wish Cruiser Squadron *bon voyage* and good luck.' The collier *Markomannia* turned out of the other line and the two ships headed, in the first instance, southwards.

Müller's first priority was to infiltrate the Indian Ocean with maximum surprise, which meant every effort had to be made to avoid being sighted by any vessel, enemy or neutral, that might pass on the news of his ship's whereabouts. His second priority was to save coal: henceforward his ship would be at her most vulnerable when coaling. The steering engine was not used except when action was likely and any other energy-consuming apparatus which could be switched off, operated by hand or used at reduced power, was so treated. Of the ship's twelve boilers, four to six were used for routine sailing, eight in the steamer lanes and all twelve only in action. The course at first was south-east and the first destination the German Palau Islands, northeast of the Moluccas in the Dutch East Indies.

Once clear of the Marianas, the *Emden* changed course to the south-west and passed well to the south of Yap, suspecting, wrongly as it turned out, that it had already been occupied by hostile forces (it had only been shelled on 12 August by the British). On the night of the 18th to 19th, the cruiser picked up wireless messages from two German ships: the mail steamer *Princess Alice*, which reported herself to be close to Yap with only a few days' coal left, and the slow old gunboat SMS *Geier*, which was off the northern coast of Dutch New Guinea (now West Irian, Indonesia) and wanted news. Müller ordered both ships to join him at Angaur in the Palau Islands, which he reached on the 19th, some hours before the *Alice* (Captain Bortfeld), which arrived at 3 p.m.

From Bortfeld Müller received the portentous, if hardly unexpected, news of the Japanese ultimatum to Germany of 15 August. This required the Germans to remove all warships from East Asian waters or to disarm them, and to evacuate Kaio Chow by 9 September. Given until 23 August to accept, they did not deign to answer. The Japanese move meant that Tsingtao would be lost, either by surrender or to a siege (the Germans chose to resist). Captain Bortfeld was also able to report the details of the British attack on Yap. They had not cut the telegraphic cables, they had failed to discover the survey ship SMS *Planet* there and, although they had destroyed the radio mast, the transmitter would not be out of action for long. From the German manager of the phosphate company at Angaur, the nearest approximation there to a government representative, Müller learned that a British phosphate ship without wireless had left three days earlier before completing loading. The master did not know that war had broken out, but he smelled a rat when he failed to get an answer from Yap to his wirelessed request from Angaur for the latest news.

The *Emden* took 240 tons of coal from the *Markomannia* before dark, bringing the total aboard to 900 tons, and then led the two merchant ships out to sea. The *Geier* was ordered by wireless to proceed to a rendezvous at sea instead of Angaur. During the night the *Alice*, a 10,000-ton Imperial mail steamer owned by North German Lloyd, got lost. Müller ordered it to rendezvous with the two other ships the next day, but Captain Bortfeld replied that he had too little coal and also boiler trouble. Müller had had it in mind to convert the ship into an auxiliary cruiser, but in the end he sent it into internment in the Philippines, at Cebu. German naval men alleged later that Bortfeld exaggerated the difficulties of his ship to evade war service and protect his owner's property. Müller makes no such suggestion in his report. The mailboat carried, fittingly enough, messages from the *Emden* to the Admiralty reporting her assignment to the Indian Ocean, and to the *Etappe* in Manila to despatch coal steamers to rendezvous points in the Dutch East Indies by mid-October and mid-November; she also carried private letters from the crew.

Müller tried to pass on to the Squadron the news he had received from the *Alice* but got no answer. He never did find out if his signal got through: he guessed the Squadron was likely to be observing radio silence, so there was no ground for concern over the lack of reply.

On the afternoon of the 20th the *Emden* met the *Geier*. The puny old twelve-knot gunboat with her elderly armament had a collier, the SS *Bochum*, in tow which towered over her, a comical case of the tail wagging the dog. Müller now regretted having lost the *Alice*, which could have been equipped at sea with the *Geier*'s guns and turned there and then into an auxiliary cruiser. On the open sea in wartime the *Geier* was effectively a liability, vulnerable to the smallest modern destroyer, and too slow to catch even a middling steamer. Müller therefore ordered her captain, Lieutenant-Commander Grasshoff, to turn about and head north to Angaur and send the two coal-steamers due there on the 21st to one of the predetermined map references. He was then to proceed to Yap to examine the position there after the British raid, and to use its radio or cable-links to pass the latest news to the Squadron, after which he would stay to guard the island. If the radio station was still out of action or if he could not contact Spee he was to join the two colliers and await further orders there. Grasshoff told how he had stopped in Singapore on the way to the South Pacific. When it became apparent that war was imminent, he stole out of harbour with the *Bochum*. (Eventually the *Geier* limped into Honolulu and was interned by the Americans, who commandeered her when they declared war on Germany in 1917 and converted her into the coastal gunboat USS *Carl Schurz*. She was lost in the North Atlantic in June 1918.) She provided the *Emden* with her last poignant sighting of another German warship, as she steamed slowly away at dusk on the 20th. The *Emden* headed south to the Molucca Strait, taking pains to avoid Dutch coastal traffic. She hoisted a British flag on sighting a Japanese steamer: Müller did not know whether Japan was yet at war.

On the 25th she was off the eastern tip of the Portuguese part of the island of Timor, where a collier should have been stationed. There was no sign of her, but as it was a safely remote spot 470 tons were taken from the *Markomannia*. The cruiser was able to keep to her economical cruising speed of twelve knots, comfortably within her companion's maximum speed of fourteen. Now they changed course from south to due west, heading for the small island of Tanahjampea, where another collier should have been waiting.

They arrived there on the 27th but there was no sign of a steamer; very loud wireless traffic could however be heard in the radio room, soon diagnosed as originating from a Dutch warship. Coming out of the island's western anchorage, steam up and formidable guns trained from only 3,000 yards, was a miniature battleship of 5,300 tons. Müller ordered action stations as the two ships converged along either side of a low-lying spit of land. The Dutch ship was the *Tromp* (Captain Umbgrove) and an elaborate exchange of courtesies ensued, from which Müller gleaned useful information. As the smaller ship and junior commander, it fell to the German to call upon the Dutchman later in the day in his best uniform and a hastily scrubbed pinnace. He was told that the *Tromp* had sent the collier out of the area as she had been there too long. Umbgrove also said that the Netherlands proclamation of neutrality allowed a warship one period of twenty-four hours in Dutch waters in three months, for coaling purposes, running repairs and the like. (Despite German complaints and British pressure, the Dutch remained punctilious in their neutrality, not only for ethical reasons but also because their fabulous tropical empire in the East Indies had long been jealously eyed by the warlike, expansionist Japanese, the newest of the belligerents as Müller had learned from a Dutch radio station two nights before. The Dutch were no less vulnerable in the world's richest empire in the east as they were as neighbours of the Germans, who had just raped Belgium next door, in the west. The profound, not to say desperate, neutrality of the Dutch was not to be doubted.) Politely declining the offer of a glass of beer in the ship's stateroom, Müller was piped over the side. The *Emden* was followed for three miles out of territorial waters by the *Tromp* and headed south until over the horizon, whereupon she turned west again, passing along the north of the long chain of islands leading to Java. That night, the 27th, the Germans heard a Dutch radio station reporting the sighting of a four-funnelled British warship in the Sunda Strait on the south side of the chain of islands, identified as a destroyer.

First Officer Mücke now recalled the idle remark of Sub-Lieutenant Fikentscher after the capture of the *Ryaezan* that it was a pity the *Emden* lacked a fourth funnel. In fact her three tall smokestacks were a very distinctive identification sign for her class of light cruiser in German service. Mücke obtained Müller's consent to the construction of a crude fourth funnel out of canvas and wooden spars, painted to match the grey of the ship's superstructure. They planned to go through the narrow strait between the islands of Lombok and Bali the next night so as to be able to sail westward on the south side of Java rather than the north; such a device ought to work at night in deceiving watchers ashore. The passage was a dangerous one; British wireless traffic had been heard again during the night and anything to confuse unseen eyes would help. After dark on the 28th, with the crew at action stations and the *Markomannia* at a distance behind with orders to make a run for it if an enemy appeared, the *Emden* stole into the narrows. Nothing untoward was observed, however, and the cruiser completed the passage without incident. The ship swung to starboard to follow the Java coast, her collier between sixty and seventy miles behind, and both ships a similar distance from the Javanese, and later the Sumatran, coast.

A welcome lull ensued, during which the primitive, two-dimensional fourth funnel could be improved, boilers could be cleaned and tubes replaced, action stations and manoeuvres practised and gunnery worked up. Vigilance could hardly be relaxed, however, and any inclination to do this was offset by repeated overhearings of the call-sign QMD, identified as British but not as to name or even type of ship. She was using the Royal Navy's then normal 600-metre waveband. The volume remained the same, and it became clear that the two ships were following parallel courses at similar speeds south of Sumatra. The only difference was the *Emden*'s strict radio silence, which concealed her presence from the nameless enemy.

At the beginning of September, the second month of the war, the

Emden crossed the Equator going north-west. The usual 'crossing the line' ceremonies had to be dispensed with: the ship was now approaching the island of Simaloer (now Simeuluë) off the north-western end of Sumatra. On the north-eastern coast of the island there was the perfect coaling spot, a natural harbour with a narrow entrance. It was covered by an islet and all but surrounded by jungle. The water was calm at all times. On the morning of 4 September the cruiser cautiously entered the anchorage and soon afterwards, when the *Markomannia* arrived as prearranged, coaling began. The heat made it doubly exhausting work and it went very slowly, so that a second day's coaling was necessary. On the morning of the 5th, as this was under way, a Dutch launch arrived carrying a colonial government official who knew exactly when the Germans had arrived. He asked them to leave, as they had already had their permitted twenty-four hours. Müller summoned Chief Engineer Officer Ellerbroek and ostentatiously asked him, 'How long will it take you to get up steam?' Catching the captain's drift, Ellerbroek lied: 'Two hours, sir.' Naturally the warship had steam up in several boilers in case the lookouts spotted danger. But the Dutchman accepted a departure time of 11 a.m. and was happy to accept the hospitality of the ship in the meantime, while coaling was completed. She set off in the wrong direction until the Dutchman was out of sight and then resumed her north-westerly course, bound for the Bay of Bengal. This huge expanse of open sea now lay in front of her; all the islands of the sprawling Dutch East Indies lay astern. There was no sign of QMD, whoever that was.

Müller had concluded that coaling in the Dutch East Indies was not as attractive as had at first appeared when the Squadron was making its plans for war. The Dutch were obviously going to enforce their neutrality and were clearly alert, firm and efficient. The *Emden* had already been caught twice. Her captain had been surprised to discover that there was a cable from Simaloer to Sumatra but relieved when the Dutch official promised that he would disclose the ship's visit only to his superiors: it would not be given to other belligerents, even by accident. The promise was kept. The Dutchman also did not reveal that HMS *Hampshire* (QMD) had been at anchor off Simaloer as the *Emden* passed only twenty miles away on the 3rd! The British cruiser had been searching the coast of Sumatra and its parallel islands. Coaling on the high seas was on balance probably safer.

Now the solitary German cruiser was at large in the Indian Ocean, open for business. Sunday, 6 September was marked by the usual church service, conducted by the captain, and rough rain squalls. On the 7th the *Emden* prowled the steamer-route from Sumatra to

47

Ceylon and adjacent lanes without sighting anything more interesting than a cloud. The next day was no more memorable. Morale began to slip; the straining eyes of lookouts conjured up hallucinations; a British steamer was heard on the wireless but not seen. The cruiser spent the 9th on the Colombo–Rangoon steamer-lane. The day passed fretfully but uneventfully; the night arrived with the accustomed suddenness of the tropics. Nobody in the world knew where they were, not the Squadron, not the Admiralty in Berlin, not the growing list of Germany's enemies, not the Dutch who had been the last to see them. As far as the rest of humanity was concerned, SMS *Emden* could have struck a rock and sunk without trace. Every man aboard felt it was time she made her presence felt in this British maritime preserve.

With the *Emden* now for better or for worse on her own, not knowing but wondering if she had seen her last German ship, naval or mercantile, a number of vessels which have figured in the narrative so far now pass out of it. This seems as good a place as any to record what happened to them.

The *Prinz Eitel Friedrich* had a splendid career as a commerce raider, mainly in the Atlantic, and ran into Newport News, Virginia, in March 1915, to internment.

Cormoran II, ex-*Ryaezan*, remained at large as a frustrated commerce raider until December 1914, when she finally entered Guam and American internment.

The main body of the Cruiser Squadron under Spee found Admiral Cradock's Squadron off Coronel in Chile and virtually annihilated it. The Battle of Coronel was the first British defeat at sea in more than a century. The British armoured cruisers *Good Hope* and *Monmouth* were sunk on 1 November 1914. Appalled beyond description, the British Admiralty mobilised Admiral Sir Doveton Sturdee to avenge his colleague, who had died with more than 1,000 of his men. They gave him HMS *Invincible* as his flagship and another battlecruiser, *Inflexible*, as well as appropriate supporting ships. On 8 December he was coaling in Port Stanley, in the Falkland Islands, when Spee was sighted offshore. In a second terrible battle, off the Falklands, the *Scharnhorst* and the *Gneisenau*, now outgunned as they had outgunned Cradock's ships, were destroyed by the 12-inch guns of the avengers. Smaller British ships caught up with the *Leipzig* and the *Nürnberg* and destroyed them. Spee and all his captains and hundreds of men died. The *Dresden*, temporarily attached to the doomed Squadron, escaped, but was cornered in March 1915 and blew herself up at Juan Fernandez Island after evacuation.

4

GENTLEMAN-OF-WAR

The *Emden*'s cruise in the Indian Ocean began, strictly speaking, on 5 September, when she left the Dutch island of Simaloer for the Bay of Bengal to the north-west. But it is more appropriate to regard the 9th of the month as the real starting date, for it was precisely then that the solitary light cruiser became an influence on the course of the war in the Far East, like the first move of a knight on a chessboard. Well after dark the stern light of a ship was seen, and at 10 p.m. the alarm bells for action stations sounded. Slowly in the moonless night the shape of a single-funnelled steamer could be made out. The *Emden* crept closer and fired two blank shots. The ship stopped; a signaller on the cruiser used a lamp to send in Morse code and in English the message: 'Stop your engines. Don't use wireless.' Lauterbach took an armed boarding party to the ship in a cutter. Within half an hour their signal lamp was flashing information back to the cruiser. The first victim of the *Emden* was a neutral, the Greek steamer *Pontoporos*. The disappointment on the bridge gave way to satisfaction when Lauterbach, after examining the ship's papers, signalled that she was carrying more than 6,600 tons of Bengal coal for the British Government. This made the cargo legitimate contraband under the international rules for cruiser warfare. Müller decided to keep the coal as a reserve and made the captain of the steamer an offer he probably felt he could not refuse: to transfer to German service on a charter basis. The ship's chief engineer, Mr. B. B. Forbister, happened to be British (the name smacks of Orkney) and was made a prisoner of war. He was transferred for the time being to the *Markomannia*. With Lauterbach and a prize crew supervising the Greek seamen, the *Pontoporos*, which had been on the way from Bombay to Calcutta, was ordered to follow the *Emden* through the night as best she could with her top speed of nine knots.

Soon after dawn on the 10th another steamer was sighted, this time flying a British blue ensign, indicating that she was in government service. Leaving her two colliers behind, the *Emden* put on speed and went to investigate the oncoming ship. As the gap between them closed, strange structures could be made out on the deck of the single-funnel steamer. Just in case these masked the armament of an armed merchantman, the *Emden* trained her guns on the ship, which showed no signs of alarm at the approach of the cruiser. But when she fired a blank shot across the bows and hoisted the German ensign, the reaction was swift. The ship hove to at once and within minutes a shower of burning paper could be seen coming out of a porthole near the stern as secret orders were destroyed. The captive was the *Indus*, 3,393 tons, on charter as a troop and horse transport to the Indian Government and on her way to Bombay to load. The strange structures on the deck turned out to be stalls for the cavalry mounts, as Lieutenant von Levetzow discovered when he took an armed party aboard and put to use the lessons he had learned from Lauterbach's lectures on the art of capturing ships. The international signal flags 'M N' had been hoisted aboard the *Emden*; as soon as she was close enough, the order to heave to and not to use wireless was repeated by megaphone. The wireless aerials of the *Indus* (Captain H. S. Smaridge) showed that she was one of relatively few British merchant vessels equipped with a Marconi transmitter.

Although the ship was in ballast, she did have some useful provisions aboard which were gratefully removed. By one of those curious oversights which seem to be so common in wartime, the provisioning of the *Emden* in Tsingtao had been light in toilet soap, a shortcoming which the Squadron had been unable to make good at Pagan in mid-August. Barely a fortnight's supply was left, and First Officer Mücke had been teasing the captain about the necessity of seizing a soap-ship as first prize. Although the *Pontoporos* failed to please in this respect, the *Indus* handsomely made up for the omission by yielding large quantities of soap – 150 cases. And on 25 September, by which time the *Emden*'s name was a household word, the following curious and enterprising advertisement appeared in the *Empire*, a Calcutta newspaper, under the heading 'German cruiser *Emden*':

> There is no doubt that the German cruiser *Emden* had knowledge that the *Indus* was carrying 150 cases of North-West Soap Company's celebrated ELYSIUM Soap, and hence the pursuit. The men on the *Emden* and their clothes are now clean and sweet, thanks to ELYSIUM Soap. Try it!

Many a true word having thus been spoken in jest, it is not difficult to imagine the delight of the German sailors when one of their number came across the advertisement in a copy of the newspaper found on another prize about a month later. The text was at once signalled to the cruiser and recorded in her signal-log.

The crew still had much to learn about the art of legalised piracy upon which they had just begun. At this stage the clear, if narrow, dividing line between looting and impounding of essential supplies or contraband was not appreciated. Nor could the sailors yet foresee what would be useful or necessary rather than merely attractive. Müller comments in his report that the crew did not understand that all goods taken from captured ships were German Government property. Lauterbach having transferred from the *Pontoporos* to the *Indus* to ensure that nothing was missed on the latter, Mücke took charge of the collection of booty and drew up a plan for its distribution to ship's stores and among the men which he submitted to Müller for his approval. As was to become the custom, however, the beer found aboard was handed to the men straight away. Thus after initial confusion and wasted effort the *Indus* was systematically scoured for useful items to add to the liqueur chocolates, preserves, bath- and hand-towels and other luxuries taken first. The entire wireless installation was unshipped, and charts, chronometers, binoculars, fresh food, tobacco and cutlery were soon stacked on the warship's deck. In the end Müller ran out of patience and ordered the ship cleared of crew and German sailors and made ready for sinking (but not before a quarter of a million cigarettes and cases of wine and spirits were hurriedly salvaged). The seamen were put aboard the *Markomannia* and a sinking party of five men was sent over to open the prize's 'Kingston valves' (the patent seacocks in every ship's bottom which could not be resealed once broken). At 4 p.m. they were called back and the *Emden* fired six shells into the hull; but it was more than an hour before the *Indus* visibly began to settle in the water. Finally she turned turtle and went down by the bow, making terrible groaning and tearing sounds as she died. The near-euphoria of the looting which had gone before gave way to shivers of apprehension among the men lining the warship's deck. The deliberate destruction of a sturdy ship, even after every care had been taken to look after her crew, was no laughing matter even for the men of a cruiser at war. The busy day ended in gloom. Captain Smaridge stood on the deck of the *Markomannia* and silently shed a tear for his ship. Her lifeboats remained afloat, and after ineffectual efforts to sink them (for which they were not of course designed) they were left to drift, not being worth the ammunition that would have destroyed them.

The *Indus* was unlikely to be missed until she was due in Bombay on the 15th, which gave the German interlopers some breathing space and time to leave the area if necessary. On the 11th, with good

51

humour restored on the ship, Mücke supervised the stowing of the booty that was still cluttering the decks, ensuring amid much banter that every mess got its fair share. At about 2 p.m. a smoke-cloud was seen off the starboard bow and the *Emden* set off to investigate. It turned out to be a rather larger version of the *Indus*, a packet-boat of some 6,102 tons converted for the transport of troops and 380 horses in stalls. She was the *Lovat*, flying the 'blue duster' of the Indian Government and on her way, as the *Indus* had been, to Bombay to pick up troops. Lauterbach was once again delegated to uncovering her secrets, after she had been brought to a halt by one shot across her bows and blasts from the *Emden*'s foghorn to arouse the blissfully unaware crew from their apparent reverie. Generously permitted to take personal belongings with them, the crew were slowly tran-shipped to the *Markomannia* until, at dusk, the sinking party having done its work, the *Emden* opened fire at short range. She, too, took more than an hour to die; it was only later that the gun crews discovered exactly where to place their shells for fastest effect. The *Lovat* offered nothing not already seized in generous quantity from the *Indus*, so Lauterbach was ordered to leave everything aboard and to bring only newspapers back with him. These proved to be a mixed blessing.

The back numbers of Indian newspapers turned out to be a priceless source of intelligence, obligingly listing sailings of ships and reporting those in port. But they also contained the most remarkable brew of rumours, served up as news, about the war in Europe. Whole German armies had been wiped out, the Reich was collapsing under the strain of the war and generals were queueing up to shoot themselves for their failures. Such material, if allowed to spread unchecked among the crew of a ship wholly dependent on its own resources and what it could steal, could have had disastrous effects on morale. Anyone who has served or worked abroad in almost any capacity and experienced being cut off from news from home in times of crisis much less severe than war will understand the danger Müller and Mücke now identified. The considerable persuasive powers of the First Officer were mobilised to offset the rumour-factory found in every institution, be it a school, a factory, a regiment or a warship. His method was simple. Using as his illustrative text the Reuter report, picked up in August by wireless, that the *Emden* had been sunk in action with the Russian *Askold*, Mücke read out the war reports and then gave his sceptical and well thought-out comments upon them, armed with a pointer and a large map of Europe. These demythologising sessions soon became some of the most popular occasions of the cruise.

There was time for such a session on the 12th as the *Emden*, with her two colliers in tow, moved closer to the Calcutta lightship off the mouth of the Hooghly River on which the great Indian port stands. Müller considered destroying the lightship, which had a Marconi wireless transmitter, and also seizing the pilot boat for the Hooghly, a treacherous waterway scarcely navigable without a pilot. Such moves would have had incalculable effects on British seaborne trade in the region. Müller was lurking south of Calcutta because the two captured masters had revealed that there had been at least three other ships in the river behind them. At about 11 p.m. he sighted the lights of one and stopped her by attracting her attention with his foghorn; he then ordered her by signal-lamp to stop without wirelessing. This was the *Kabinga*, 4,657 tons, a British ship.

The cargo manifest showed that she was carrying goods from British companies in Calcutta to North American ports. They were thus neutral property and had to be left unplundered, which meant that the ship carrying them could hardly be sunk. Müller decided therefore to make the best use of her that was open to him: to transfer the crews of the two sunken prizes to her and set them free with her. Her master, Captain Thomas Robinson, who had his wife and child aboard, accepted the role thus thrust upon him of acting as what the Germans called 'Lumpensammler', which translates roughly as 'refuse-collector'. But there was no hurry. The *Kabinga*'s wireless was put out of action, and Müller waited for his next victim, confident that he would not have to wait long in this busy steamer lane.

About 2 a.m. on the 13th the lights of another ship were seen and the *Emden* went to action stations to investigate. This time it was the collier *Killin* (Captain J. K. Wilson), 3,544 tons, with 6,000 tons of Bengal coal aboard. Müller had no use for this and decided to sink the ship when convenient the next day. Now as she sailed slowly north the *Emden* was at the head of an inverted 'V' of five ships, the *Kabinga* and the *Markomannia* to starboard and the *Pontoporos* and the *Killin* to port. All five were of course blacked out, and close enough to remain within hailing distance, so that signal lamps need not be used in the darkness. The echelon formation was to guard against collision. But the weather broke, heavy rain squalls spoiled the formation and the shepherding cruiser kept in contact with them all only with difficulty.

At 10 a.m. in a heavy sea, the *Killin* was sunk by opening her seacocks and by gunfire, sinking within about half an hour, to the relief of the *Emden*'s crew, who already showed the offhand skill of veterans in their peculiar work. Lauterbach, who had been up all night on the *Kabinga*, was allowed to get some sleep in his own bunk at last, only to be sent for again at about 3 p.m. Another cloud of smoke had been spotted in rough seas off the starboard bow. As the *Emden* approached it from dead astern, the new victim revealed itself to be a large steamer which looked smart enough to be on her maiden voyage, the 7,615-ton *Diplomat* (Captain R. J. Thomson). She eventually hoisted the 'red duster' of the British mercantile marine. The cruiser's sixth victim was, as a ship, the largest and most valuable and by general agreement the handsomest prize of them all. With her cargo of 10,000 tons of tea, she was the second-largest loss inflicted on the British by the *Emden*. Müller decided she must be sunk at once, this time by the setting of explosive charges in her hull. Sub-Lieutenant Witthoeft, the torpedo officer, and his explosives party accompanied the usual seacock-saboteurs. When Witthoeft emerged from setting his charges among the tea that now would never get to London, he could not see his own ship anywhere. Lauterbach told him that another sighting had drawn her away over the horizon. When she reappeared, shepherding another, rather smaller steamer, the boarding parties got back into their cutter once it had finished helping to tranship the crew and the handful of passengers from the *Diplomat* to the *Kabinga*. When they were only 200 yards away, the first explosion blew a large plate from the ship's side into the water close to the rowing boat. Tea chests littered the sea. The ship began to sink by the bow and eventually, tilting more and more until almost vertical, plunged below the surface with a terrible roar.

As one of the finer examples of the shipbuilder's craft died railing against her fate, attention turned to the disreputable rust bucket the *Emden* had brought to join her three charges. This was the SS *Loredano* (Captain Giacopolo), an Italian and therefore neutral ship carrying no contraband and on her way to Calcutta. Müller tried to persuade the master to take some or all of the passengers and crew from the prizes to Calcutta, whither he was in any event bound, against payment and with extra food to nourish them on the way. The captain demurred, but then allowed himself to be convinced by the arguments of the *Emden*'s officers that no breach of neutrality would be involved in taking more than 200 men aboard the 'Lumpen-sammler' to a port friendly to them. But then Müller had second thoughts of his own. It was getting dark, there was a heavy swell and conditions in general argued against yet another transfer of large numbers of men from ship to ship. The *Loredano* was allowed to continue her run into Calcutta. Until the grubby Italian freighter was over the horizon, the *Emden*'s little convoy steered a false southerly course and later changed to one a little west of north.

Meanwhile, the neutral Captain Giacopolo could not wait to tell the British of his encounter with a German cruiser in the Indian Ocean. Meeting the steamer *City of Rangoon* coming away from the Hooghly, he gave the news by semaphore. The *Rangoon* passed it on by wireless, thereby saving three ships coming downstream from a possible encounter. The pilot vessel was moved to a safer station, five other ports round the Bay of Bengal were warned, and a number of leading lights for the guidance of ships were extinguished for the time being. The Royal Navy's Intelligence Officer in Colombo sent the following telegram to the Director of Intelligence at the Admiralty in London on the 14th:

> German *Emden* with four prizes sighted by Italian steamer position 18.0 north 86.16 east time not reported, estimated 8 am 13th September: I am causing inquiry to be made. I have delayed shipping at present in Bay of Bengal including Colombo–Singapore trade routes.

The message was relayed to Admiral Jerram, C-in-C, China, during the night of the 15th to 16th. In the morning, HMS *Hampshire* was sent from Singapore to search for the German cruiser once more. The next day the light cruiser *Yarmouth*, which the *Emden* sought to impersonate with the fake fourth funnel, set out from the same base. The Japanese cruiser *Chikuma* was also alerted on the 16th at sea. On the 18th, the *Yarmouth* had to put into Penang with her condensers leaking. Further south, HMS *Minotaur* and the Japanese battle-cruiser *Ibuki* were alerted. The initial reaction to the first definite sighting of the *Emden* since she had left Tsingtao on 6 August was the despatch after her of no less than five cruisers, all of them superior in armament. The value of the *Emden* as an effective diversion of enemy resources was confirmed by the cautious Admiral Jerram himself on 20 September, when he reported to London that he could do nothing about the news that Spee's cruisers had been seen off Samoa on the 14th because all his available ships were taken up by the hunt for the *Emden* and by the need to protect the first troop convoy from Australia and New Zealand. In this respect the detachment of the *Emden* prolonged the career of the German Squadron by giving it a free run across the Pacific.

Back in the Bay of Bengal, Müller abandoned his provisional plan to make for the waters off the Ganges Delta east of Calcutta to coal because the monsoon had veered south-east and might easily blow him towards the shore while coaling at sea. During the night the cruiser became separated from her convoy; she nearly collided with the *Kabinga* during the search and it was only by signalling 'full speed astern' on the engine-room telegraph that disaster was avoided. A passing ship was challenged. When she identified herself as the Italian *Dandolo* the *Emden* signalled by lamp, 'Thank you. Good voyage' without identifying herself. In the meantime, the powerful current had been pushing the ship westwards, so that at about 9 a.m. on the 14th the notable landmark of the Black Pagoda south-west of False Point and Calcutta was sighted. This was much closer to land than Müller wanted to be and he turned east and then followed the coast northwards from further out. In the afternoon he stopped the convoy to enable the last seamen from the sunken prizes to transfer from the *Markomannia* to the *Kabinga*.

As this was in progress, another smoke-cloud was sighted. It came from an unladen British steamer of 4,028 tons called the *Trabboch* (Captain W. H. Ross), on her way back to Calcutta after delivering coal along the coast. The crew was transferred to the *Kabinga*, now distinctly overcrowded, and the usual destructive measures taken. When the explosive charges went off, however, the coal dust in the holds turned the act of sinking into an unintended spectacular as a vast column of flame tinged with blue shot into the air. It was the loudest explosion for which the *Emden* was responsible on the open sea. Müller was concerned in case it had been seen, as he was close enough to the coast, which lay both to the north and the west at this most northerly point of the ship's Indian Ocean voyage, and it was already getting dark.

It was time to release the *Kabinga*. As she was being made ready for departure, with the last captives transferring from the *Markomannia* and the German guards preparing to step over the side, two remarkable gestures were made. Her master, Captain Robinson, sent a letter to Commander Müller to thank him for the way he and his family had been treated while detained. And the men about to be released gave three lusty cheers for the enemy captain. It was quite clear that these did not only stem from relief at being set free: they had all been required to sign the customary declaration that on release they would not take up arms against Germany or her allies. They were saluting a man whose concern for fair play in the middle of a campaign where, as seamen, they could see the odds were stacked against him, was highly exceptional. This is the stuff from which legends are made: hardly any of those involved actually met Müller. Once these men were back on shore and free to talk of their experiences at his hands, the legend of the *Emden* was undyingly established. The ship and her captain, whose conduct determined her reputation, became known as the 'Gentleman-of-War' to the main enemy at sea, the Royal Navy, its allies and people at home in Britain and all over the Empire in the Far East.

The *Kabinga* headed off for Calcutta. Captain Robinson and his wireless operator, Mr. A. Wesselly, managed to restore the damaged transmitter to working order remarkably quickly, so that they could put out warnings about the presence of the *Emden* and their own approach. The river steamer *Bunerwali* met her at the mouth of the Hooghly to relieve the overcrowding on board. The warning was already being justified at that very moment. Barely had the *Kabinga* vanished in the gloom before the stern light of another steamer was spotted by the Germans, to the east. Once again it was action stations as the *Emden* set off in pursuit. The ship would not respond to blasts on the foghorn or even blank shots. Only when a live round sent up an enormous fountain of water before her bow did she start to heave to. There ensued an exchange by megaphone.

'What ship?'

'*Clan Matheson.*'

'English?' Short pause. Then, with palpable irritation:

'No, British!'

Captain William Harris was a Scot, and his ship was as Scottish as her name implied. There was appreciative laughter on the bridge of the *Emden*. But the ship was to be sunk swiftly for trying to make a run for it. Lauterbach went aboard with the sinking party. He found out that the great explosion on the *Trabboch* had been seen from the *Clan Matheson*, a 4,775-ton vessel of the Clan Line, and that Harris had rightly interpreted this as bad news, which was why he had vainly tried to escape. The cargo was mouthwateringly valuable in a now useless sort of way. It included locomotives, cars, typewriters and other expensive machines, and one gleaming racehorse. The ship was on her way from Britain to Calcutta with a cargo that had obviously been assembled in peacetime. The horse was despatched with a pistol-shot to the head before the ship was abandoned to her fate. She sank within half an hour once the explosive charges went off. The crew meanwhile had been transferred to the *Markomannia* with the usual generous allowance of personal belongings.

During the night the *Emden* overheard radio signals broadcasting the *Loredano*'s report, and the *Kabinga* listing the five sinkings that had taken place before she had been sent away. Captain Giacopolo was later awarded a gold watch and chain by the Indian Government. The *Emden* had in just five days held up eight ships, sunk six, retained one as a collier and released one. Now her presence was known to all who cared to listen. It was time to move on. Coaling was now of paramount importance, and the ship headed southwards towards the Andaman Islands in search of a sheltered spot for the purpose.

Even in the best possible conditions, coaling ship was the curse of all navies until oil superseded solid fuel. The best conditions were of course in peace-time, in a naval base at home in cool weather without wind or rain, in calm water and with all the time in the world to complete the task. In port, the coal could be poured straight into some of the bunkers (but sailors had to ensure it was evenly stored, which meant work with shovels in choking dust). Practically nobody was excused from this onerous task; it was not uncommon for coal to be brought aboard in sackloads and emptied into the bunkers, backbreaking work at any time and all but intolerable in hot weather or other adverse conditions. Coaling from a steamer at sea often presented a combination of the worst possible circumstances, and became more and more difficult as the collier's supplies ran down, because the sailors had to go ever deeper into her holds and carry the coal further. At sea, the warship's coal stocks were constantly being shifted from one bunker to another as it was used up, in the interests of trim and of the most rapid availability to the stokehold. After the coaling, the ship was inevitably filthy and had to be thoroughly cleaned. Because the British had so many bases all over the world, coaling at sea was something most ship's crews did not have to become familiar with (most officers would not even have considered it a practicable possibility). The men of the *Emden* gained more experience of the ordeal than most crews before or since.

The next day, 15 September, found the *Emden* steaming south-east towards Rangoon at the southern extremity of Burma, in heavy rain. On the 16th, in totally calm water, the cruiser coaled from the *Pontoporos*. Indian seamen ('Lascars') from the *Clan Matheson* were engaged to help with the work, for payment. About 440 tons were taken on. Müller then sent the Greek collier away to a predetermined rendezvous point west of Simaloer because her maximum speed of nine knots was holding up the little convoy. The Bengal coal she carried proved to be less than a godsend. It was a good thirty-five percent less efficient than the best steamer coal, which was Welsh, it left a much thicker residue after burning and it produced enormous quantities of dense, revealing smoke. The boilers also tended to choke.

The Germans moved on to the crossing of the Singapore–Calcutta and Madras–Rangoon steamer lanes, looking for prizes, but nothing was sighted. The always diligent monitoring of wireless transmissions yielded a lot of traffic about the *Emden*. Incredulously, the operators heard one station ask, 'Who is QMD?' and another answer, '*Hamp-*

shire'. In his austere report, even Müller permits himself the comment, 'very naive', on such elementary breaches of security. At 4 p.m. another cloud of smoke was sighted, and the Germans followed at a pace slow enough to enable them to catch up after dark. It was the Norwegian (neutral) steamer *Dovre* on her way from Penang in Malaya to Rangoon. A check by Lauterbach revealed no contraband. The captain agreed to a request to take the crew of the *Clan Matheson* out of the *Markomannia* to Rangoon on payment of 100 Mexican silver dollars (Spee had often sent a light cruiser to the west coast of Mexico to show the flag, and specie was always appreciated in those days). What is more, the Norwegian master even agreed to delay his arrival until the following morning; the obviously friendly neutral mariner also reported that he had seen two British auxiliary cruisers in the Malacca Strait and the two French cruisers *Dupleix* and *Montcalm* in Penang. When Lauterbach reported his gleanings on the bridge of the *Emden*, Witthoefft suggested a raid on Penang. Müller wrote: 'I examined the possibility and suitability of such an undertaking and bore it in mind for a later time.'

During the quieter days of the cruise when there was no prize to examine and no coaling to endure, Mücke writes that Müller spent most of his time, much more than duty required, on the bridge. One of Lauterbach's wooden deck-chairs, with built-in footrest and plenty of cushions, was placed there so that he could sleep and yet always be on hand for a sudden development. These chairs should not have been on board at all: such fripperies were meant to have been disembarked before the war-cruise began, and it was Müller's good fortune that Lauterbach had both met his old ship at Pagan and decided to bend the rules. On the bridge in quiet periods, Müller studied charts, read almanacs and handbooks and analysed old newspapers, wireless intercepts and any other intelligence that came to hand. All this was intended to improve his knowledge of the hostile seas around him and to produce plans of action against the enemy, whose very domination of the region guaranteed a wide choice of targets. Much of the success of the ship's campaign resulted from this thoroughness and attention to detail. We have already seen how ideas thrown up by others would be weighed up, worked out and used (everything from the fake funnel to Mücke's idea of using rolled-up hammocks as fenders during coaling at sea). For most of the crew, except during action, Müller was a figure in the distance but quite definitely the man in charge, however remote. The men were proud of him as they were proud of the ship he led, Mücke wrote. Singing or horseplay would stop at once if someone said, 'the Captain's tired'. A word of praise or encouragement from Müller was prized like a medal and commonly led to superhuman effort during such dreadful ordeals as coaling.

No detail was too small to escape his attention. Just one example of his forethought in action is the printing in advance of a notice in three languages, to be posted up in ships likely to be under the *Emden*'s control for a considerable period, such as the *Pontoporos*. It was written in German, English and French; the English version read as follows:

NOTICE

During the occupation of this ship by a detachment from a German man-of-war, the ship's crew and passengers are subject to German martial law.

Whosoever forwards the interests of Germany's enemies or harms the German Navy during this occupation incurs death.

During this time every offence and every neglect of orders and directions issued on this ship will be punished according to the penal law of the German Empire.

Moreover every hostile movement or even the attempt of such an action by any of the crew or passengers may have the most serious consequences for the whole ship, crew and passengers.

All arms and ammunition must be handed over immediately. Whoever will be found to be in possession of arms or ammunition in the course of half an hour will be arrested and punished according to the law.

Everybody of the ship's crew is obliged to attend to his usual work till he is dismissed or expressly released thereof.

The language is not elegant but its import is unmistakable. A copy of the notice survives in British Admiralty records.

5

MADRAS, 22 SEPTEMBER 1914

Having released hundreds of men captured on his first six prizes to tell their tales ashore, and having heard the wireless traffic about his ship's doings, Müller now had it in mind to broaden the scope of his campaign against British interests in the Indian Ocean. Adopting his usual deceptive tactic, he steered south until the *Dovre* was well out of sight and then swung west. He explains why in his report:

> I intended going from the Rangoon estuary to Madras and, in the dark, shelling the oil-tank installations, which were ideally positioned. I had this shelling in view simply as a demonstration to arouse interest among the Indian population, to disturb English commerce, to diminish English prestige.

He had been looking for a spectacular target which would damage and embarrass the British without causing Indian casualties, and his poring over charts had led him to choose the coastal oil tank installation of the Burmah Oil Company immediately to the south of the harbour of the great city of Madras on the east coast of India.

The weather was so fine on the 19th that he paused to take 310 tons of Shantung coal from the *Markomannia*, a considerable improvement on the product carried by the *Pontoporos* if still distinctly inferior to Welsh coal. After that he passed through the Preparis South channel, north of the Andaman Islands. The wireless operators were once again hearing the *Hampshire*'s 'QMD' call-sign loud and clear. The British heavy cruiser was on her way north to look for the *Emden*; the six-inch Japanese cruiser *Chikuma* had been sent to Colombo to coal and was then to work with the British warship and under her orders, with the specific instruction to cover Madras. Under the influence of the enemy wireless traffic, the Germans maintained strict war-watches during their westward passage across the Bay of Bengal. Some time during 19 September the *Emden* picked up a wireless message in uncoded English recorded by Müller as saying: 'I hear from really reliable person that gunfire has been heard near Akyab.' Akyab (now Sittwe) is on the north-west coast of Burma, on the opposite side of the Bay of Bengal from Madras. The *Hampshire* (Captain H. W. Grant, RN), picked up the same message and turned north-east on a course diverging markedly from the *Emden*'s. The rumour was false, probably occasioned by a thunderstorm combined with the nervousness prompted by the unseen presence of an enemy cruiser in the Indian Ocean. Its effect was to place the *Hampshire* 300 miles away from the *Emden* on the way to Madras. The *Chikuma* took her time about coaling and then wasted more time in seeking local authorisation in Colombo for what to do next, despite Captain Grant's instructions to cover Madras. Müller learned all this only later, but he was in luck: without undue despatch, the *Chikuma* could and should have been off Madras at the same time as the *Emden*.

But she was not. On 21 September the Germans went to action stations to practise a fight with an enemy warship, using the *Markomannia* as a 'target'. It was entirely possible that an offshore venture might lead to an encounter with a patrolling enemy near such an important port. No other ship was seen all day or until dark on the next, the 22nd, when at 6 p.m. the collier was sent from the point the two ships had by then attained, some fifty miles off Madras, to a rendezvous fifteen miles east of the French enclave of Pondicherry down the Indian coastline. The orders to Captain Faass were to go to Simaloer if the *Emden* did not arrive on the next day, and if the cruiser did not appear within a few days the collier was to seek internment in any Dutch harbour.

Other preparations for the coming raid included the usual painstaking attention to detail: the canvas awnings in whose shade the men worked and slept in the tropics were stowed away in case of fire; the lifeboats were filled with seawater for the same reason (easier to empty a boat of water than sail away on its ashes); the ship's log was put in the safe; ready ammunition by each gun was doubled; the chain of command in the event of the incapacitation of captain and first officer was rehearsed in the wardroom, where officers were also briefed on the general war picture as Müller saw it; the men were allowed a fresh-water shower and ordered to put on clean clothes (all in case of wounds). After all, not only was there, as far as they knew, the danger of an encounter with an enemy warship; Madras was also a defended harbour under the protection of the 6-inch guns of Fort St. George.

At 8 p.m. the *Emden* began her approach towards Madras from the east at full speed, nearly 24 knots. The crew was now at action stations. The port's leading light had been spotted; as they drew nearer, they could tell that the city was lit up as if for carnival, so much so that the navigation lights were sometimes difficult to distinguish. The Germans could scarcely believe their own good fortune or the enemy's stupidity. Or was it arrogance that led to such carelessness in the eighth week of a war that was already global? To add to the unaccustomed festival of lights there was the not uncommon manifestation of sheet lightning out at sea in the sultry night, enough to make Müller anxious about being seen from shore, conveniently outlined for the shore battery. He need not have worried. At a point about due east of the northernmost light on the mole which formed the eastern confine of the harbour and passed beyond the entrance at the north-east corner, the *Emden* stopped about 3,000 yards out. The four great searchlights, sited in pairs one third of the way up the cruiser's two masts, probed for the oil tanks. The effect of the beams was diminished more than somewhat by the lavish background lighting, but it was not exactly difficult to locate the white-painted cylinders. The idea was to align the ship with the tanks and also with the new flashing navigation light immediately to the south-west, on top of the court buildings. Müller's studies of the layout of the city showed him that such an alignment would reduce to a minimum the risk of stray shells falling on residential areas of the city, because most of it now lay to the right of his line of fire. The captain had heard enough of the stories of German atrocities from old newspapers and the wireless not to wish to add to them (the stories were exaggerated, yet not as exaggerated as a chivalrous and gallant officer of Müller's stamp would have wished). His care was to be rewarded by the enhancement of the *Emden* legend to an unparalleled degree.

But it was time to open fire. Müller told *Kapitänleutnant* Ernst Gaede, the gunnery officer, to fire when he was ready as the ship once again built up speed. The effect of the initial handful of ranging shots was made harder to assess by the lights of the city, but as the ship turned and ran southwards parallel with the coast for ten minutes, some twenty-five salvoes were fired from the starboard broadside of five guns. On shore, according to some witnesses, the salvoes seem to have been heard as single shots; the long muzzle-flashes from the guns merged into one orange streak of flame, followed more than eight seconds later for those on shore by the deep-toned crack of the quintuple detonation, which was compounded by the closeness of the air. Between the flash and the crack the individual shells struck home.

A shell from the first salvo hit the verandah of the bungalow occupied by Mr. Ellis, the manager of the installation, a little after 9.45 p.m., causing extensive damage but no injuries. The local staff fled the site as Mr. Ellis went into action in what rapidly became an inferno. An early shell penetrated the roof of one of the six tanks and exploded inside, igniting the fumes and causing a tremendous explosion. This tank had been about one quarter full; another about one third full ignited in the same way. A third had its roof partly torn off by a shell but was not ignited; a fourth was pierced by shell fragments but also failed to explode; a fifth, containing 114,000 gallons of mineral oil, was pierced by a shell but did not catch fire; the sixth tank was not hit. The first four tanks contained kerosene. A total of 346,000 gallons of fuel was destroyed, worth 180,700 rupees (about £8,000). Mr. Ellis and two patrolling military policemen started the site fire engine. This Canute-like enterprise could not be matched by the municipal fire brigade, whose appliances approached the scene and retreated to a safe distance as soon as it became clear they could not help. Mr. Ellis calmly organised the removal of cans of petrol out of range of the flames: these would have been even more volatile than the kerosene. In fact the damage was a lot less than it might have been, but the effect was visually and psychologically sensational. It looked a lot worse than it was (*The Times* in London reported that one and a half million gallons had been destroyed).

Moored at a buoy in the harbour was the SS *Chupra* (Captain W. C. Morrison), a 3,962-ton ship of the British India Steam Navigation Co. registered in Glasgow, and loaded with more than 6,000 tons of general cargo. She had left London with her crew of 92 and 5 passengers on 15 August and had been in port about a week. A stray shell hit the bunker hatch on the boat deck at the starboard side and exploded. 'The shell burst right in the midst of five young cadets who were standing together having a little conversation prior to retiring to bed,' Captain Morrison told the *Madras Mail*. 'Of these, Joseph Saul Fletcher, aged seventeen, received no fewer than fourteen wounds and died on the spot. Cadet Wheeler was seriously wounded and had to be removed to the General Hospital.' The five merchant ships in harbour doused their lights, lowered their lifeboats and sent their crews ashore while the officers stayed aboard to take such precautions as possible against fire.

In the expansive style of the time the *Madras Mail*, among the 8,000 words it devoted to the raid in its issue of 24 September, vividly described how curiosity overcame prudence in the teeming streets of the city:

An extraordinary circumstance in connection with the whole affair was the way in which the people of Madras, especially of Georgetown, treated the bombardment. One would have thought that the moment they heard the cannonading commence they would have taken shelter in their houses, or wherever they could; but the reverse was the case. In a very short time the residents not only of Georgetown but of the suburbs were hurrying down to the beach, in every possible way that they could – in motor-cars, carriages, motor-cycles, bicycles, on foot, etc. – once they realised what had taken place, and for a couple of hours afterwards crowds of excited people were busy hurrying to and fro, trying to glean information and discussing the situation.

To judge from the paper's blanket coverage, a measurable proportion of the crowd must have been *Mail* reporters.

Merchant Navy officer-cadet Joseph Fletcher earned the sad distinction of being the only fatal casualty inflicted by the *Emden* on the merchant mariners of Germany's enemies. Three Indian policemen and one watchman at the oil installation were also killed; one officer and four cadets, as well as three of the passengers, were injured aboard the *Chupra* and four people in Madras town, a total of five dead and twelve injured. Given the street scenes described by the local newspaper, there could have been slaughter; but it was quickly appreciated in the area that the angle of fire had reduced casualties to a minimum. Including ranging shots, the cruiser fired about 130 4-inch shells during the raid. One or two of them landed close to the battery which was positioned on high ground between the high court, with the navigation light on its roof, and the harbour. Sub-Lieutenant Bonstead rallied his men and managed to organise the firing of nine shells from the elderly guns. Of these, only three were seen by those aboard the *Emden* to explode, one detonating in the water 100 yards short and the other two wide of the ship. After the first few shots from the German guns, the ship's searchlights were switched off; they were not needed once the tanks caught fire. But an offshore breeze ensured that the fire was confined to the oil tanks.

After the ten-minute bombardment, Müller turned north-west, with some of his port-side lights on to lead watchers ashore to report that he had gone northwards. After about half an hour he darkened ship and turned southwards for his rendezvous with the *Markomannia*. As they sailed through the night the crew saw a great orange glow in the sky to the west; after dawn they could see a column of black smoke from eighty miles out to sea. But the material effect of their bombardment was as nothing to the psychological. For days afterwards the trains going inland were crowded with people anxious to place themselves out of range of shells from the 'mystery ship'; this was true not only in the Madras area but all along the coast. The local economy was severely affected for many weeks, because among the most assiduous refugees were the money-lenders or 'Marwaries' who took their moneybags way inland from as far away as Calcutta. The *Emden*'s raid was the talk of the bazaars for months, and for a while the word 'Emden', meaning 'valley by the Ems (river)' came to signify in the Madras dialect of the Tamil language an 'enterprising and ingenious person'.

The British authorities in southern India were moved to initiate a campaign of counter-propaganda in the schools, the villages and the towns, at public meetings and the like. Leaflets laying down guidelines for officials to use in their briefings on the war in general and the situation in the seas round India in particular were printed and distributed in thousands. The mystery cruiser from another world became the stuff of legend in the southern portion of the subcontinent, and the damage to British prestige was immeasurable, as Müller had guessed it might be. The British Empire began to crack in the First World War, and the *Emden* made a significant contribution to the first little gusts of the wind of change with the salvoes she laid down on Madras.

The German Foreign Office would have had her do more. Dr. Robert Heindl, chief of the criminal police (CID) in Dresden, wrote a report in autumn 1914 about a visit he had made shortly before the war to the penal colony on Ross Island off the south-west coast of Burma. He suggested that the 15,000 or so prisoners from India kept there, many of them described by him as political prisoners and revolutionaries, could be unleashed to cause trouble for the British in India. He had it all worked out. All that was needed was a surprise attack by a cruiser which would shell the administration into submission, land armed sailors to overwhelm the small force of guards, distribute guns to the prisoners and evacuate them in small boats. At the end of September 1914 as the *Emden*'s exploits were echoing round the world, the Foreign Office took its scheme to the Admiralty in Berlin. They were particularly interested in freeing two named revolutionaries, V. D. Savarkar and Hemchandra Dass, of whom they entertained particular hopes. As a result, on 2 October, the Admiralty sent an order to all *Etappe* posts and naval attachés in the Far East: 'Order for SMS *Emden*: Free imprisoned revolutionaries on Andaman Islands.' But five days later second thoughts prevailed at the Admiralty about the dangers inherent in such an undertaking: 'Order no. 87 for 562 [*Emden*] concerning Andaman Islands is cancelled. SMS *Emden* to act on own assessment.' (One reason for the reappraisal may have been the apparent geographical confusion about the Indian Ocean in Berlin. *The Times Atlas* shows no Ross

66

Island in the Andamans; there is one, however, just off the Burmese coast in the Mergui Archipelago, which is now called Daung Kyun. Dr. Heindl was probably more familiar with the back-streets of Dresden than the backwaters of the Bay of Bengal.) No more was heard of the project.

Meanwhile in London Mr. Winston Churchill, First Lord of the Admiralty, was becoming increasingly frustrated, angry and concerned about the depredations of the *Emden*, which had slipped out of the Bay of Bengal without being sighted by any of her pursuers but was still sailing across the columns of the newspapers. The government of New Zealand had threatened to resign unless the protection for the first Australian and New Zealand military convoy was reinforced in case of an attack on the transports by German cruisers.

In a letter to the Secretary of the Admiralty and the First Sea Lord (Prince Louis of Battenberg), the First Lord wrote on 29 September:

The escape of *Emden* from the Bay of Bengal is most unsatisfactory, and I do not understand on what principle the operations of the four cruisers *Hampshire*, *Yarmouth*, *Dupleix* and *Chikuma* have been concerted. From the chart, they appear to be working entirely disconnected and with total lack of direction. Who is the senior captain of these four ships? Is he a good man? If so, he should be told to hoist a commodore's broad pennant and take command of the squadron which will be detached temporarily from the China Station and all other duties, and should devote itself exclusively to hunting the *Emden*. She appears to be making for a coaling place in the Maldives; but anyhow orders should be drafted which will ensure these four ships hunting her in combination and continuously . . .

The ever-combative First Lord's attitude to the capacity of just one cruiser to cause so much disruption is entirely understandable. Clearly illustrated here is Müller's principal advantage in his one-ship campaign: space. He could be anywhere between Africa, South Asia, Australasia and Antarctica, an area of hundreds of thousands of square miles. Without radar, four ships on a sweep in line could cover a maximum of 120 miles from side to side and thirty miles ahead and astern, or about 3,600 square miles, in broad daylight, fine weather and with the most alert lookouts. At night they could sweep a line just twenty miles wide, five miles ahead to astern and no more than 100 square miles in visible area. The only factor that would bring the German raider's embarrassing career to an early conclusion was luck:

an accidental encounter by a superior ship; an accident of another kind rendering the *Emden* incapable of evasion; or catching her unawares, as a result of an alert put out when a ship of greater armament and speed was close by. There was no certain way whereby the overwhelmingly superior Royal Navy and its allies could so dispose themselves in the relevant operational areas as to be sure of catching a solitary enemy ship under the command of an enterprising captain with a reasonable run of luck.

The *Emden* now turned her attention back to the business of harassing enemy commerce. All she had to do was to keep moving; the science of detection by radio direction-finding was not yet developed and would not have been of value in any case because the Germans used their wireless almost exclusively for listening. They had nobody to whom they could usefully send a message.

6

THIRTEEN UNLUCKY SHIPS

The *Emden* met the *Markomannia* off Pondicherry at 5 a.m. on 23 September, as arranged, and the cruiser followed the coast as far south as Cuddalore, keeping about fifteen miles offshore. This enabled lookouts in the crow's nest to study the coast while the ship's hull remained below the horizon, concealed from any observer on shore. But it was not a safe procedure – any smoke cloud would have the rising sun directly behind it. Müller wanted to see if there were any merchant ships in the port, but none was sighted. He considered another bombardment but abandoned the idea because the town was not fortified and military targets were not easily discernible. So a change of course to the east was ordered with a view to coaling and drawing supplies from steamers which should have been sent by the *Etappe* at Batavia to a rendezvous off Simaloer. During the night the captain changed his mind again and decided on a shift in strategy in the form of an excursion into the western Indian Ocean, west of Ceylon (now Sri Lanka). He had avoided this hitherto because he thought the *Königsberg* would be operating there, but he had gleaned nothing about her from captured merchant captains or enemy news-papers and radio (she was in fact operating off the East African coast). A few days on the steamer routes west of Colombo ought to yield some prizes, even if this entailed coaling off the Maldive Islands before going to Simaloer. The change of plan also meant that the *Emden* would have to stand and fight any enemy ship she encoun-tered, no matter how superior, because she would not have enough coal aboard to run to the nearest neutral harbours in the Dutch East Indies at full speed; further, many enemy cruisers were faster than she. But we have already seen how Müller could assume that the odds were in his favour, against his being found: the new disruption he could cause far outweighed the risk. He also decided always to keep a collier with him despite her much slower speed.

Such a course naturally entailed another risk, but it did mean that the *Emden* could protect her companion from capture by lesser enemy ships, and that she would have a reserve to cover her coal needs if no other collier were found at the fixed rendezvous points. An accompanying collier, which could always be sent some distance away for short-term safety, was also useful for carrying crews from prizes, enabling these to be sunk at once.

Galle, at the south-western extremity of Ceylon, was passed at a safe distance at lunchtime on the 25th, whereupon a ship was sighted. No doubt feeling secure so close to British Ceylon, she blithely hoisted the red duster. She was the 3,650 ton British steamer *King Lud* (Captain D. Harris) and although travelling in ballast, she yielded much-needed provisions to the boarding-party before being sent to the bottom. From thirty miles offshore searchlights could be seen playing off the mouth of Colombo harbour: evidently the shelling of Madras had galvanised the authorities into action.

At 10 p.m. on the busy steamer-lane between Colombo and Minicoy Island in the Laccadive Islands west of southern India, the *Emden* espied another steamer heading west and steered a slowly converging course to come alongside one hour later, well away from any land. This was the British steamer *Tymeric*, 3,314 tons and laden with 4,600 tons of sugar for England, which made her a valuable prize. As they were still too close to Colombo for comfort, Lauterbach was sent aboard with his team with orders to follow through the night and prepare for sinking the next day. But for the first and only time on the *Emden*'s cruise the prize officer encountered resistance from the master, Captain J. J. Tulloch, who, backed by the Chief Engineer, refused to cooperate and ordered the crew to do nothing to assist the 'damned Germans'. Captain Tulloch was apparently outraged at being stopped within sight of the Colombo searchlights. Lauterbach, reporting all this through lamp signals, recommended immediate sinking. Müller acquiesced. The captain and the chief engineer were arrested and confined aboard the *Emden* to separate them from the crew – but not before they received a dressing-down from First Officer Mücke for coming aboard in slovenly fashion, the master with a cigarette dangling from his lips. The crew were given ten minutes to abandon ship for the *Markomannia*, and were thus denied the usual time to gather more than the most readily available and portable personal belongings, a fact which did nothing to endear their captain to them. The *Tymeric* was sent to the bottom in the usual, now deadly efficient manner, and the Germans, anxious to carry on westwards, did not wait for her to disappear below the surface but resumed their journey at 12.30 a.m.

Lauterbach had not forgotten to collect a useful quantity of newspapers, many of them bought in Colombo on the morning of the 25th.

From these the effects of the bombardment of Madras were learned in detail and its psychological effects were made clear; it was equally clear that there was much admiration for the *Emden* and her captain on the enemy side, even though her presence was causing panic.

Still in the very early hours of the 26th, on course to Minicoy, the cruiser sighted a third steamer, which was ordered by the hailer to stop, boarded by Lauterbach and made to follow. She was the *Gryfevale*, 4,437 tons, travelling in ballast from Aden to Colombo, and neither her captain nor her crew made difficulties. Müller decided to use her as a 'Lumpensammler' for the crews of the two ships just sunk. When *Emden* spotted a Dutch steamer astern and also heading west in the lovely weather of the 26th she let the Dutchman slip out of sight. Shortly afterwards the wireless men overheard a British steamer asking whether the Dutch had seen anything untoward on the way from Colombo. With satisfaction they heard the tantalising reply, 'Refuse to answer on grounds of neutrality'. The Dutchman's suspicions must have been aroused by the sight of three ships travelling together; the British ship would no doubt have taken the stiff reply as a warning in itself.

In the early hours of the following day the *Emden* came across another steamer heading in the opposite direction, due eastwards. Here was a find to make a corsair's mouth water in the age of steam, perhaps one of the luckiest moments of the cruise and certainly one of the happiest. The new prize was called the *Buresk*, a 4,350-ton collier, loaded to the gunwales with 6,600 tons of first-class coal from South Wales, plus 900 tons in her own bunkers. There was special satisfaction in the fact that the coal was destined for the British China Squadron at Singapore. Before the nature of her cargo was discovered, Müller had intended to keep her in company only until daylight. To give Lauterbach a rest and to allow one of his eager pupils to gain some practical experience, retired *Kapitänleutnant* Klöpper, who had volunteered to rejoin the colours at Angaur on 19 August, was made prize officer, leaving Lauterbach in charge of the *Gryfevale*, which was still in the convoy.

The master of the *Buresk*, Captain F. J. Taylor, surprised the Germans by offering the services of himself, his officers and his crew to go on working their ship. In the end Müller allowed the master, the chief engineer, the first mate, the second engineer, a British steward and a Norwegian cook to stay aboard for the time being. Some Arab hands were retained for wages, as were some of the *Tymeric*'s Chinese seamen. Klöpper was given Sub-Lieutenants Roderich Schmidt and Eugen Gyssling as officers of the watch, together with nine specialists from the *Emden*, to look after the new fuel supply.

71

The faithful *Markomannia* was still on hand but was approaching the end of her usefulness as a coaler. What was left in her holds now lay deep enough to make coaling from her slower and more difficult each time and much worse for the sailors. Thus the *Buresk*, the twelfth enemy-owned ship to be stopped on the Indian Ocean cruise but the thirteenth capture of the *Emden*'s war career if the *Ryaezan* is included, was a most timely piece of good fortune.

An excess of good cheer also broke out on the *Gryfevale* this fine Sunday morning of the 27th. As planned, most of the crews of the sunken *King Lud* and *Tymeric* had been transferred to her from the *Markomannia*. Immediately after a fervently thankful Evangelical-Lutheran church service conducted on deck by Müller, Lauterbach signalled with a report of drunken disorder on the 'Lumpensammler' and asked for reinforcements to restore order. The *King Lud* men had been liberal with the whisky they had been allowed to bring with them and fights broke out between British seamen and Chinese hands involving the use of fists, a soup tureen and finally knives. The German guards broke up the fighting and the worst offenders were put in irons, the rest being locked up in the forecastle. The *Gryfevale*'s officers helped to restore order and Müller ordered Lauterbach to have all the spirits aboard collected and destroyed.

After lunch, another smoke-cloud appeared dead ahead. It was the *Ribera*, 3,500 tons, on the way from Alexandria to Batavia in ballast. Her crew was transferred to the *Gryfevale*, her provisions to the *Emden*. Her valves were then opened and a few shells fired into her hull to send her to the bottom. Just after dark, a new victim fell into Müller's hands, although he wanted to interrupt his campaign to top up with coal, now a matter of some urgency. As it was late, a prize crew and the expert saboteurs were sent aboard the *Foyle*, a British steamer of 4,147 tons on her way from Aden to Colombo in ballast. Her crew, too, was put aboard the *Gryfevale*. While all this was going on at something approaching record speed, the cruiser went to investigate one more wisp on the horizon, a Dutch mail steamer which was left to go on her way. After she was clear of the scene, the *Foyle* was despatched and left to sink.

The 'three-ship Sunday' which had been one of the busiest days of the cruise so far was not over yet. The captain and chief engineer of the *Tymeric*, whose hostility had become passive aboard the *Emden*, were told to prepare to move to the *Gryfevale*. The cruiser moved to a position alongside the steamer and trained some of her guns on her to cover Lauterbach's evacuation, but there was no recurrence of unrest as the prize crew withdrew and the grim-faced *Tymeric* officers went in the opposite direction without a word of farewell. Instead, under the blaze of light thrown by the cruiser's searchlights, the assembled British seamen from six victims of the *Emden* gave three rousing cheers for the German captain, three more for his officers and three for the crew. The 'Lumpensammler' pulled away towards Colombo and the *Emden* zig-zagged for a while until Müller was sure that his new course, due south for the Maldive Islands, would not be observed by the departing British seamen.

Approaching the Equator down the eastern side of the long chain of atolls which make up the Maldives, Müller searched for a sheltered spot at which to coal. There were only 320 tons left aboard, the lowest level since the cruise began and less than a third of the ship's capacity in war conditions. On the 29th, using the Miladunmadulu Atoll as a shield against the strong south-westerly swell, the *Emden* took her last load of coal from the *Markomannia*. It was time to bid farewell to the collier, which had proved so reliable for eight weeks since the two ships sailed from Tsingtao on 6 August. Her radio, taken from the *Indus*, was transferred to the *Buresk*, as were her accumulators, originally from the *Kabinga*, and all the engine oil and water she could spare. The coaling went on all day and was resumed at daybreak on the 30th, until 645 tons had been loaded. Captain Faass, who had 'carried out all requests with skill and also accustomed himself quickly to new tasks such as sailing without lights' (Müller wrote in his report) was detached. His orders were to go to Simaloer to meet the *Pontoporos* and take as much coal as possible from her, together with her prize crew and then to pay off the Greek ship. Any other German coal steamers found in the vicinity were to be sent to a rendezvous in the Cocos (or Keeling) Islands, and Faass was also asked to try to organise food supplies for the *Emden* from the port of Padang in Sumatra. He also took the mail. It was an emotional parting for all concerned.

Thanks to the riches represented by the *Buresk*, Müller was in a position to abandon his plan for an early visit to Simaloer for the time being in favour of crossing the Equator and sailing to the Chagos Archipelago (later known as the British Indian Ocean Territory) due south of the Maldives. The captain realised that the almost frantic activity of the past ten days or so would have the double effect of increasing the number of enemy warships and reducing merchant marine activity in the Bay of Bengal (he had already read in a newspaper that the price of rice had gone up in anticipation of shortages and disruption). New pastures beckoned. He had read of shipments of troops from India to France and he deduced that Australia and New Zealand would also be sending troops; it was entirely likely that the ships used for the Indian soldiers would be sent back via Aden and onward to Australia. Empty troop-ships were unlikely to be escorted by warships, and it would be very useful to disrupt them en route. If he patrolled off the Chagos islands he could also interfere with the route from Cape Town to Colombo and Calcutta. Before embarking on this new campaign he would, having left the scene of his 'crimes' thus far, find a quiet place to carry out running repairs for which there had been no time. Having sailed south without incident until 4 October, the *Emden* prowled the shipping lanes on either side of Chagos, reaching the westernmost point of her cruise on the 7th (69°30′E). At nightfall on the 8th, having sighted nothing, Müller decided to find a lair and lay up for a few days for repairs.

In far-off London, Churchill as First Lord had become anxious and furious about the elusive German raider which was getting so much publicity and making the Royal Navy look silly. In a letter to the Secretary of the Admiralty, the Chief of Staff and the First Sea Lord, of 1 October he wrote:

> Three transports, empty but fitted for carrying cavalry, are delayed in Calcutta through fear of *Emden*. This involves delaying transport of artillery and part of a cavalry division from Bombay. The Cabinet took a serious view, and pressed for special convoy . . . but I should be very sorry to interrupt the offensive operations against *Emden* for the sake of convoying three empty transports . . . Let me have your proposals at once. It is clear that the transports have got to go, and India is very sticky and nervous.
>
> I am quite at a loss to understand the operations of *Hampshire*'s captain to catch *Emden*. He has apparently started eastward from Colombo on the 26th, and is now marked on the chart nearly opposite the Andamans. *Emden* was, however, reported on the 27th near the Laccadives. Did *Hampshire* get this information? If so, what did she do? What has happened to *Yarmouth*? Her movements appear to be entirely disjointed and purposeless . . . I do not think these desultory movements ought to continue . . . I must be satisfied . . . on a sensible and concerted scheme.
>
> [Churchill then proposed concentrating two British, one Japanese, two Australian and two Russian cruisers in a coordinated hunt for the *Emden*, now it was clear that Spee was heading for the Americas – he had shelled Papeete in French Tahiti on 22 September, the day *Emden* shelled Madras.] This will give seven ships searching for *Emden* and avoid the necessity of moving one of

the three light cruisers now hunting *Königsberg*. Numbers are everything; and the extirpation of these pests is a most important object . . .

[Three 'P'-class cruisers should join the *Emden* hunt later from New Zealand waters] . . . if the *Königsberg* is caught, the three light cruisers hunting her should turn over to the *Emden*. We must without further delay take measures which will give reasonable prospect of a decisive result. It is no use stirring about the oceans with two or three ships. When we have got cruiser sweeps of eight or ten vessels ten or fifteen miles apart there will be some good prospect of utilising information as to the whereabouts of the *Emden* in such a way as to bring her to action. Such large and decisive measures are much the cheapest and most satisfactory in the end.

I wish to point out to you most clearly that the irritation caused by an indefinite continuance of the *Emden*'s captures will do great damage to Admiralty reputation (*sic*).

W.S.C.

There is no better illustration of the effectiveness of Müller's lone campaign in the Indian Ocean than this letter of the First Sea Lord, marked 'Urgent' in his own hand above the typed text.

At daybreak on 9 October SMS *Emden*, somewhat the worse for wear, arrived off the coral island of Diego Garcia, near the geographical centre of the Indian Ocean at latitude 6°34'S and longitude 72°24'E, one of the loneliest places on earth, and one of its prettiest.

'There soon came aboard an Englishman, head of the local coconut plantation company, and a Creole, his principal employee. From what they said, I soon observed that they had no idea of the outbreak of the World War. As I did not know when they would next have the chance to pass information, I thought it better to suppress the war situation.'

Müller allowed himself no more than this brief entry in his report about what was surely the most surreal incident of the cruise. Diego Garcia was near to, but not actually on, one of the great maritime crossroads, as described above. Having searched the area without sighting anything at all, Müller decided that he was unlikely to find a better time or place to halt for twenty-four hours to complete some pressing business. The wireless was quiet and the natural harbour, guarded by coral reefs except for one navigable entrance, offered the right kind of shelter. The crew had not set foot on land for some two months, and had seen it from afar only once or twice since leaving the Dutch East Indies. To go ashore, however briefly, in a place like this,

75

a lovely island in sapphire-blue water with coconut trees all around, was an exciting and, alas, deceptive prospect. There was too much to do. The hated process of coaling had to be undertaken once again – the cruiser had by this time used up half her load – and the first use was about to be made of the stolen Royal Navy coal aboard the *Buresk*, which had also entered the anchorage once the *Emden* was satisfied it was clear. There was no radio station or cable relay on the island, nor even a ship to be seen anywhere. Since there was virtually nothing between Diego Garcia and Antarctica, any ship visiting it would be doing so by intent and not casually or accidentally. The steamer-lane crossing was well to the north-east. The island was beyond the end of the nearest branch line, as it were, and was as safe as could be imagined.

Well inside the anchorage, compartments below the waterline on one side of the cruiser were flooded and she began to list. Men on ropes from above and in the ship's boats from below began to chip and scrape at the barnacles and marine vegetation revealed as she leaned over. Once one side had been washed and scrubbed as low down the hull as was practicable, the process was repeated on the other side of the ship. This was as much as could be done without going into dry dock; but it was highly necessary to do what was possible in this respect because marine growths slowed the ship down and might easily cost her the half-knot that could enable her to escape danger one day. There had been no opportunity to do this for more than two months. The loading of 475 tons of coal was integrated with the scraping, so that nearly all the crew found themselves working very hard in their borrowed tropical paradise, under the firm control of First Officer Mücke. Below deck boilers and engines which had performed excellently so far were receiving care and attention as well.

Hardly had all this work begun when a man of indeterminate age, nationality and race came alongside in a rowing-boat, chattering excitedly in what was eventually recognised as French. He was taken to the captain (whose mother was French). It was scarcely breakfast-time, but the officers hurriedly cleared up the ward-room of items like captured newspapers as the visitor was ushered in for a whisky and soda of suitably numbing proportions. The time of day did not discompose the man, who turned out to be the under-manager of the coconut plantation which was the island's sole economic asset. He was a Creole from Madagascar, and it was soon very clear that he did not know there was a war on. He explained that the island was visited every three months by a schooner which brought supplies (and news) and took away the copra to Mauritius. The last call had been late in

July. He apologised for his poor English and was politely informed that it would be perfectly acceptable if he adhered to his mother-tongue. His happy chatter died away when his eyes lit upon a sepia-tinted photograph on the bulkhead. It was an unmistakable portrait of Wilhelm II, the German Emperor, in the uniform of a Grand Admiral. Certainly it was a German warship, the officers said; had they tried (or indeed had the chance) to pretend otherwise? The under-manager did not seem too put out; the last time he had seen a German warship, he recalled, sipping his whisky, was the *Bismarck* in 1899 . . . As he gratefully accepted another drink, his superior, the manager, the only European on the island and indeed the ex-officio representative of His Britannic Majesty's Government, arrived aboard and was conducted to the ward-room. It took a little more than whisky and soda to satisfy his rather keener curiosity. What was a German ship in such a tattered condition doing in a place like this? Why had it come here of all places to coal? Could the bottom not be scraped in harbour? Improvising ingeniously if desperately, the officers spoke, with a nice, and probably unintended, irony, of 'worldwide joint manoeuvres' with the British and the French, of putting down a native rising in German East Africa and of being damaged in a storm, plying the whisky the while. The manager's anxiety was assuaged; it vanished altogether when Müller detailed two men to go ashore and repair the broken-down engine of his official motor-boat. When he asked for news of the outside world, Müller dried up after reporting the death of Pope Pius X. No matter. Shortly afterwards a boatload of fresh fruit and vegetables, a live pig and a collection of fish arrived with a covering letter of thanks for the work on the boat and the hospitality: would the captain care to join the manager for breakfast the next morning? Müller politely declined on the grounds of having too much to do, but sent back wine, *Sekt* and whisky and some boxes of cigars. The war was exactly ten weeks old and it was time the *Emden* returned to it.

Having completed the shipping of 475 tons of coal early the next morning, the 10th, the cruiser and her collier left Diego Garcia at 11 a.m., sent off with friendly waves by the plenipotentiaries of the coconut company. The ship had plenty of fish, caught by the crew during breaks as well as supplied by the manager, which promised a change of diet; coaling was over for a few days; repairs were complete and the ship clean (even her paintwork had been touched up). The course was NNW until out of sight of shore, then NE, running eastward of the Chagos Archipelago in the hope of a prize, then NW and finally northwards on the western side of the Maldives towards Minicoy. On the 11th, 'QMD' could be heard all day at fairly close range. HMS *Hampshire* was, in fact, searching southwards and east of the Maldives as the *Emden* sailed northwards to the west of them. Captain Grant had been in Colombo when the *Gryfevale* arrived there with the released crews, guessed that Müller would probably head south because the Bay of Bengal had become too hot for him, and went after him, encouraged by reports of sightings from a number of islands on the way. Grant went as far south as the Chagos islands; the auxiliary cruiser *Empress of Russia* was sent ahead to check Diego Garcia on 12 October. The reaction of the coconut company managers can be imagined. For all Churchill's strictures, Grant consistently and on several occasions read Müller's mind better than anyone else; had he not been obliged to check false reports as well as true ones he might well have accounted for his quarry.

The story of the *Emden*'s courteous call at Diego Garcia was soon out and the British at once saw the funny side of it, even though it added to the ship's legend; newspapers spoke of 'high comedy on the high seas'.

Müller thought that the north-east monsoon had been blowing long enough for him to be able to top up with coal west of the Maldives, but a strong swell was still running from the west. So he cut across to the eastern side, passing north of the Miladunmadulu Atoll and taking 280 tons from the *Buresk* east of Thiladunmathi Atoll on the 15th. He wanted the ship to be full to the gunwales for a sweep off Minicoy Island just to the north, with its great lighthouse so familiar to all mariners in these waters. Sure enough, not long before midnight a steamer was sighted, heading towards Minicoy from the west as the *Emden* approached from the south. It was the *Clan Grant* (Captain Norman Leslie), displacing 3,948 tons and carrying 4,000 tons of valuable mixed cargo, bound from England to Calcutta via Madras. A prize crew was sent across with orders to have the ship follow through the night. An accumulation of smoke behind the steamer and a trick of the light caused alarm aboard the cruiser; for a moment it was thought that a warship was trailing the merchantman and the torpedo tubes were loaded before it was realised that nothing was there. At daybreak, the *Clan Grant* was searched for provisions. A large and very welcome stock of beer and cigarettes, of which the Germans never seemed to have enough, was discovered with no less generous quantities of food, including live cattle. Engine oil and firebricks for boilers were also taken. The crew, meanwhile, was transferred to the *Buresk*. After about three hours of this profitable work, Lauterbach was called back to the *Emden*. Another column of smoke had been seen to the west. The collier was left to take aboard the rest of the booty while the cruiser set off to investigate.

As she closed in on the new victim, a single mast with a yardarm was made out, swinging quite markedly from side to side even though the sea was far from rough. It could be a small destroyer or a torpedo-boat. The alarm bells rang for action stations; within minutes the order was cancelled. Incredulously the men on the bridge made out the peculiar shape of a dredger, perhaps the last vessel likely to be encountered under its own steam on the open sea. Lauterbach got himself and his party aboard – warily, as its pitching motion made this unusually awkward. The vessel was the *Ponrabbel*, displacing 478 tons and capable of four knots at full speed. The men of the *Emden* were now quite accustomed to being cheered on the departure of captured crews: but it was an unlooked for pleasure to be welcomed with open arms at the moment of capture. Captain Edwin Gore and his men could hardly wait to become prisoners. More than one memoir of the *Emden*'s cruise has the captain actually jumping for joy (a not inconsiderable feat, apparently, on the deck of a vessel which tended to roll over in sympathy when it saw a wave coming). By the time Lauterbach's men got aboard, the crew had their bags packed and lined up on deck. For them it was the end of a nightmare which had been going on as long as the war. They represented the second attempt to supply the port of Launceston in Tasmania with a new dredger. The first had to be abandoned in a sinking condition. Captain Gore had wisely managed to obtain payment of £500 in advance for himself and his crew, so all they had to lose was discomfort and boredom. For them the transfer to the *Buresk* was the start of a pleasure cruise, and they lined the rails and applauded when the *Emden* fired a couple of shells into the dredger. It turned turtle so quickly that the air in the hull did not have time to escape, and it stayed afloat upside down for an unconscionably long time during the sinking of the *Clan Grant*. Then, as Müller resigned himself to wasting another shell or two on the dredger, it just as suddenly sank out of sight.

The day's work was not yet complete, however. An hour before midnight, as the *Emden* and the *Buresk* sailed slowly eastwards, limiting themselves to the collier's maximum speed of ten knots, another steamer was sighted, the *Benmohr* (Captain J. D. Sarchet), 4,806 tons. She was carrying full cargo of 6,700 tons of valuable piece-goods, including a large and elegant motor-boat, from London to Penang and Japan. The crew was transferred to the *Buresk* and the ship rapidly sunk by explosive charges.

Such ships as had been sighted so far on this phase of the cruise were all heading east. Nothing at all had been seen coming west-wards, from Colombo. Müller deduced from this that his recent exertions in the Bay of Bengal had led to counter-measures: either a convoy was being formed or ships were being urged to use a route off the regular shipping lanes. So from his position south-west of Minicoy he sailed east through the Eight Degree Channel, south of the island, and then turned north on its eastern side. At 4 a.m. on the 18th, a Sunday, a ship was at last sighted heading west. But as it was a Spanish one, she was sent on her way.

There was enough leisure for a church service, but no sooner had it ended than a cloud of smoke was once again seen on the horizon. By this time the cruiser was about thirty miles north of Minicoy, some way off the regular routes. The latest catch was the Blue Funnel cargo-liner *Troilus*, 7,562 tons, on her maiden voyage. The master, Captain George Long, was furious with the naval intelligence officer in Colombo who had told him that if he passed thirty miles north of Minicoy he would be safe. His rage was compounded by the fact that his splendid ship was on her first voyage, westward bound from Japan, China and Singapore to Rotterdam and British ports with an extremely valuable cargo of rubber, copper and tin, and other items. The 10,000 tons in her holds and her own value as a ship made the *Troilus* by far the most valuable catch of the *Emden*'s piratical career. The loss she represented probably quite comfortably exceeded £1,000,000, which in the monetary values of the period was a spec-tacular sum – enough, for example, to build three light cruisers.

As Lauterbach examined the new prize he discovered a handful of passengers aboard. From behind him there came a woman's voice which said, 'Hallo, Captain Lauterbach, how are you?' The lady, whose name is not recorded, had been a passenger aboard one or other of the prize officer's peacetime commands. She had been trying to get home to England since the war began but had been held up for weeks in Hong Kong and then Singapore, largely for fear of the *Emden*. Now she had been caught by the German cruiser after all, but unlike her apprehensive fellow-passengers she took it very well and handed out chocolate and cigarettes to the startled members of Lauterbach's prize crew.

The *Troilus* was ordered to follow the cruiser for the time being, with Lauterbach keeping a watchful eye on Captain Long on the bridge. Müller was now heading east to see what he could find on the new steamer-lane. At 9 p.m. he found the *St. Egbert*, 5,596 tons, a British ship carrying 6,600 tons of piece goods for the neutral United States. There was no contraband aboard, so it was decided to use this quite larger steamer as a 'Lumpensammler'. In the same area, between midnight and 1 a.m. on the 19th, the British steamer *Exford* was brought to a halt by loud-hailer. This was a 4,542-ton collier, laden with 5,500 tons of the best Cardiff coal. With this and the *Buresk*'s cargo, the *Emden* had enough coal of the finest quality to keep going for the best part of a year, all of it originally destined for the Royal Navy. Now, however, the *Emden* had a total of four ships in tow, and it was time to get out of the shipping lanes to settle their fates.

The crews of the *Clan Grant*, the *Ponrabbel* and the *Benmohr* were transferred from *Buresk* to *St. Egbert*. To the same ship went the crews and passengers from the *Troilus* and the *Exford*. A prize crew under the navigation officer, *Kapitänleutnant* Gropius, took over the latter with some Chinese seamen and stokers from the captured ships as hired hands. The captain, first mate and chief engineer of the *Buresk*, who had stayed on their own ship until now, were also put aboard the *St. Egbert*, leaving the British steward and the Norwegian cook as sole representatives of the legitimate crew. The Arab seamen were replaced on the *Buresk* by more efficient Chinese. All the food and medicines, machine oil and other useful items found on the prizes were distributed among the *Emden*, *Buresk* and *Exford*. In the absence of Gropius, Lauterbach was to act as navigation officer.

As all these complicated arrangements were being made on the morning of the 19th, another column of smoke was sighted to the north. The *Emden* rapidly hoisted one of her cutters back aboard and steamed off to check. Her thirteenth victim since the shelling of Madras turned out to be the SS *Chilkana*, 5,140 tons, with a valuable cargo of piece-goods and on the way to Calcutta from Britain. The ship had wireless but did not attempt to call for help when signalled to stop. Her principal value to the Germans lay in the large quantity of provisions and medicines she carried, which were distributed among the cruiser and the two colliers. Her crew went to the *St. Egbert* and her radio to the *Exford*. Nearly all the officers and a high proportion of the crew of the cruiser worked all day for eleven hours on plundering and the transfer of prisoners. The Kingston valves on the *Troilus* were opened and she began to settle in the calm water. Many passengers and seamen on the *St. Egbert* lined the rails to watch, but the splendid ship would not go down. The other ships were sent clear and several shells were fired into her hull. She stayed afloat however for another three hours, until a second salvo finally sent her to the bottom. The *Chilkana*, subjected to the same double assault on her seacocks and her hull, went to the bottom long before the *Troilus*. The *St. Egbert*, with nearly 600 people aboard, was sent off with orders to go to any Indian port except Bombay or Colombo (Müller wanted to spread unease). She promptly set off in the wrong direction, westwards, to the amazement of Müller, who chased after her. His orders had been misunderstood as meaning that the ship should not call at *any* Indian port. She put about and headed for Cochin. The *Emden* executed a double bluff of two false courses, before heading southwards in the dark at the end of her busiest day as a commerce-raider.

7

PENANG, 28 OCTOBER 1914

After five hectic days when seven British ships had been held up, of which five were sunk, one became a 'Lumpensammler' and one was kept for her coal, the *Emden* left the profitable steamer lanes. The prizes which had been heading east for Colombo would soon be missed and an increase in enemy patrol activity could therefore be expected. Müller felt it was now time to head east again, back to the Bay of Bengal. But first it was necessary to take a wide sweep round the great island of Ceylon. The southerly course adopted on parting from the *St. Egbert* became south-easterly and eventually easterly. Progress was slow, at less than nine knots, so that the two colliers would not be left behind. Müller wanted their crews to learn or improve the working of the two ships while under his protection. As the *St. Egbert* would reach Cochin on the 20th, it was important to get out of the potentially dangerous waters west of Colombo. So whereas during the preceding days the cruiser had chased after every light seen after dark or wisp of smoke in daylight, at this stage she altered course to avoid them.

On land nothing was to be heard for nine days from or about the *Emden*, except rumour and speculation and the legend-enhancing tales of the prisoners she had set free. At the end of that time, a new and terrible dimension was to be added to her reputation: the knight in shining armour would set aside his mercy; or, more bluntly, the Dick Turpin of the sea was to become a hit-and-run killer.

Meanwhile, there was time to bring some semblance of order to a ship which was perforce far from shipshape and a living challenge and disgrace to the German passion for neatness and cleanliness. Her condition often astonished captives. In addition to the inevitable rust from a long period afloat and the ineradicable dirt left by coaling at sea, to say nothing of the dents and scrapes this process caused, the ship sometimes resembled a floating farmyard. Prizes often yielded cattle, sheep or pigs on the hoof which were kept as a welcome change of diet and looked after by some of the farm-boys among the crew.

There were usually chickens, sometimes ducks or geese; there were always six cats, the ship's cat having produced five kittens at sea (named after prizes). Weather permitting, the men slept on deck in hammocks under awnings. Also rigged up on deck were many salt-water showers. Whenever a rain-squall was sighted and circumstances allowed, the officer of the watch would step up speed and steer for it while all those free to do so would strip naked and wash themselves in the rainfall; if the ship ran out of the squall or the rain simply stopped too soon, men would be caught covered in soap. The only other source of fresh water at sea was prizes and it was treated like gold. On the afternoon of a quiet day the ship's band turned out to play, one of the few pleasures the ever-vigilant lookouts could also enjoy while at work. The band also played during coaling, to distract and encourage. Just like the British, the Germans in uniform attached enormous importance to martial music and a good band as aids to morale. Unlike the British, the Germans seized every opportunity to have a sing-song, even when entirely sober. The lustily roared strains of *Die Wacht am Rhein*, the German soldier's song, often echoed across the emptiness of the Indian Ocean from the grubby decks of the solitary cruiser in those early weeks of the war. On October 22 there was a formal parade in honour of the Empress's birthday, complete with best uniforms, the national anthem and a twenty-one gun salute, confidently fired 100 miles south of Ceylon.

Because the *Exford* was even slower than the *Buresk* (barely eight knots compared with nine), she was sent away to a rendezvous thirty miles north of North Keeling Island in the Cocos (or Keeling) group, with instructions to wait there until 15 November unless contacted before then. If she was not contacted by then she was to withdraw to the Dutch East Indies and internment there, with instructions to any other German steamers that had been sent out with supplies to do likewise. The *Exford* was sent on her way with three cheers on the afternoon of the 21st. The crew by this time knew something was in the wind. Their ship was now running away from potential prizes instead of rushing to investigate everything that moved. The captain seemed even more remote than usual. The men were put through one drill after another, including damage control, firefighting, range-finding, action stations, torpedo evasion . . .

The *Buresk* towed a target for the gun crews, whose weapons could be adapted by a special attachment fitted inside the barrel to fire a rifle bullet. This enabled accuracy to be tested without wasting ammunition. On 25 October the entire ship was put through her paces at action stations to simulate a fight with an enemy warship, something the *Emden* had so far been spared but could hardly hope to avoid forever. It went very well. The next day, off the Nicobar Islands, the ghastly business of coaling from the *Buresk* had to be faced again, with 480 tons being loaded by 4 p.m. After that, the *Buresk* was also sent away, to a rendezvous forty miles west of Simaloer, with instructions to wait there until contacted or until her supplies ran out, in which case she was to go into Dutch internment. During the coaling, the *Buresk* had her name painted out and her colours changed – it was well known to the British by now what had happened to her.

The new target was Penang, an island just off the north-west coast of the British colony of Malaya, at the end of the Indo-Chinese Peninsula. Müller, having caused panic five weeks before on the western side of the Bay of Bengal, now wanted to do likewise on the eastern shore, to cause alarm all the way from Singapore via Rangoon to Calcutta in the north of the Bay. In doing this, Müller was taking up the suggestion of Lieutenant Witthoefft in response to what they had learned from the captain of the Norwegian SS *Dovre* on 16 September about the use of Penang by enemy warships. As usual, Müller had allowed the idea to germinate, assisted by painstaking study of all available information. The north-eastern corner of the island is a tongue of land ending in a point, where the harbour of George Town stands. The tongue of land cuts halfway across the narrow strait between the island and the mainland and offers natural shelter, with approaches from both north and south. The southerly approach is shallow and suitable only for small vessels; the northerly one is both deeper and shorter. The plan was to race into the harbour, select a target or targets, destroy them and dash off again. It was a bold scheme, depending for its effect completely on surprise. There was no way of telling what was in the harbour. If there were a superior enemy warship or ships they would have to be immobilised while at anchor. There was always the chance that a warship might just be coming out as the *Emden* went in, something which would reduce the surprise advantage considerably.

At dusk on the 26th, Müller set course due east for Penang, at the economical cruising speed of twelve knots. He aimed to be steaming into the harbour at dawn, torpedo-tubes and guns cleared for action and ready for a split-second choice of target. The moon would be up until 2 a.m. on the morning of the 28th, the chosen date, so that the *Emden* would still have to be out of sight of the elevated observation post overlooking George Town at that time. The fake fourth funnel, making the cruiser resemble HMS *Yarmouth*, a regular visitor to Penang, was put up, steam was got up in all boilers and at 3 a.m. the order 'three-quarter speed' (18 knots) was rung down on the engine-room telegraph. The cruiser was now running ESE, bearing down in a straight line on the northern mouth of the channel. On drawing level with the illuminated navigation buoy outside the harbour she turned SE without exciting the suspicions of the pilot-boat stationed nearby, and shortly after that, SSE. The normal harbour lights had confidently been left burning, which was a great help to the Germans as they passed into the anchorage in an excruciating state of tension.

No less helpful than the harbour lights, the forged fourth funnel and the grey paint which had long since been adopted in place of peacetime tropical white was no doubt the British white ensign which the German raider now sported at the moment of going into action. The ruse may appear to be a borderline matter, but it raises questions which go to the heart of the nature of the First World War and what it was to become. The German General Staff's Rules of War, which applied also to the navy, specifically stated: 'The donning of enemy uniforms and the use of enemy or neutral flags or insignia with the aim of deception are declared permissible.' Unfortunately, Article 23 of the Hague Convention on the rules of war, to which Germany was a signatory, specifically prohibited such deceptions. The accord supplemented the original Geneva Convention. Grey paint was a form of camouflage (invented by the Germans in 1902) exactly comparable with the British Army's adoption of khaki towards the end of the nineteenth century and was no more exceptionable than other devices meant to save lives on the battlefield. The fourth funnel was designed to mislead the casual observer into thinking that the cruiser without flag that was passing must be British because German cruisers had three funnels, or to lead experts to whom such sightings were reported to think so. It was commonplace for warships not to fly a national flag at sea; in port it flew at the stern, in action in the tops. To fly the enemy's flag in the enemy's port, which the ship is entering with intent to sink vessels at anchor, is questionable. The *Emden* hauled down the Royal Navy's ensign and hoisted the German war-flag before opening fire. One wonders whether anything would have been lost by entering port with no flag at all; one also wonders how much further Müller might have bent the rules had he served in Hitler's navy rather than Wilhelm's. Flying false colours is of course a device as old as colours themselves; but the civilising conventions of the nineteenth century whereby the principal powers attempted to regulate war like a game of chess or cricket were pushed into the background by the First World War, the 'total' nature of which far outstripped the decent utopianism of the convention-makers. Müller's general chivalry outweighed this particular lapse; but the deception at Penang belongs on the same side of the balance sheet as a number of other incidents during this war which illustrate the 'all's fair in love and war' approach of the Germans in 1914, and to which we shall have to return in evaluating the performance of the *Emden*. Until now, 28 October 1914, the cruiser not only showed punctilious chivalry; she could afford to. All the encounters so far had been completely one-sided, even if her strategic position remained wholly adverse. Now there was a danger of somebody her own size shooting back, of a fight with a worthy, even a superior, opponent. These points need to be made at this juncture in the interests of balance, in case what now follows is simply seen as an aberration from an otherwise unremittingly gallant history. What the *Emden* did in Penang harbour conformed with the rules of war, the matter of ensigns apart; so, by the same token, did her own fate, when it came. The matter of flags was to play a role in the latter incident no less than in the former.

From the bridge of the *Emden* at the first glimmer of dawn just after 5 a.m. a forest of masts showed dimly through the early morning mist, with a bewildering collection of hazy lights below. Four particularly bright ones were discerned at equal intervals from one another – the stern lights of four destroyers? From 1,300 yards it became clear that they all came from the quarterdeck of a cruiser about their own size. It was the 3,050-ton *Zhemchug*, a Russian light cruiser of antiquated design, completed in 1903 and armed with six 4.7-inch guns. The *Emden* pulled away so that her already loaded starboard torpedo tube could fire deeper below water-level. The missile struck directly below the after funnel (of two). Gaede was then ordered to open fire with his guns, and the enemy ship was 'soon holed like a sieve' all along her hull, as Müller wrote in his report. The first torpedo was fired at 5.18 a.m. The interloper came up against a line of merchant ships and executed a fast turn under the desultory fire of one of the Russian's 4.7-inch guns, the bow piece. Just twelve rounds of ammunition had been brought up onto the deck of the *Zhemchug* in case of emergency, six for each of the two guns cleared in case of need, the after-gun and number two starboard gun. The after-gun was put out of action when a ship's boat fell on it as a result of the *Emden*'s shooting; number two starboard gun was on the wrong side of the ship, facing the island and not the channel to port, where the *Emden* was. So the twelve shells were dragged to the forward gun. Müller says the *Emden* was not hit at all and that the Russian shells

87

passed over her to hit a merchant ship. Returning past the Russian cruiser, in case of an attempt by her to get off a torpedo, Müller ordered Witthoefft to fire the port tube. At 5.28 a.m. the second German torpedo went home directly under bridge and conning tower. A 'monstrous' explosion tore the ship apart and within a minute only the top of her single mast showed above the water. Müller considered attacking the twelve merchant ships at anchor, but decided against this in case other warships appeared out of the inner harbour and because there was no time to clear them of seamen and sort out the neutrals from the enemy-owned ships. If a superior enemy was in the offing inside or outside port, the more time *Emden* spent in the narrow space, the greater the danger for her. The psychological impact of the sinking of the Russian cruiser would be lost if the *Emden* were then to be despatched herself. So Müller piled on steam and went up to top speed for the escape run.

Watching helplessly as the *Emden* went into the attack were two professional witnesses, one French, the other British, and both naval officers.

> I was awakened by a deafening detonation resembling a distant clap of thunder, followed almost immediately by several others, the character of which could only be defined as a vigorous gunfire. When I went on deck it was scarcely dawn, the ships at their moorings being vaguely outlined in the mist, on a calm sea. A mile away from us, bearing NNE, the Russian cruiser *Zhemchug*, to which my attention was immediately drawn, was disappearing in a cloud of yellowish smoke which enveloped her right up to the masthead. A few degrees on her right appeared the vague silhouette of a four-funnelled man-of-war which seemed to be making for the usual anchorage to the east of Cornwallis Light

wrote *Capitaine de Frégate* (Commander) L. Audemard, the officer in charge of the small French flotilla based on Penang, to Admiral Jerram in his capacity as C-in-C, Allied Fleets in Indo-Chinese waters.

Reporting to the same authority, Lieutenant G. Maund, RN, liaison officer attached to the *Zhemchug*, wrote:

> When about half to three-quarters of a mile off the *Zhemchug*, [the incoming ship] hoisted German colours and very shortly afterwards discharged a torpedo which took effect on the port quarter of the *Zhemchug*, flooding the aft engine-room. When nearly abreast of the *Zhemchug*, and at a range of about 400 yards, the *Emden*

88

opened fire, exploding some twelve rounds which, however, did a great deal of damage, more particularly by splinters and fragments . . . Fire was opened by the *Zhemchug* when the *Emden* had passed her, and about twelve rounds in all were fired, two hits being obtained but unfortunately on the superstructure only. The *Emden*, having passed clear of the *Zhemchug*, turned sixteen points, during which time Commander Macintyre [RNR, harbour-master of Penang] went alongside the *Zhemchug* in his launch and did all in his power to exhort the men to greater exertions at the guns . . . *Emden* next proceeded on a northerly course, firing at and passing close to the *Zhemchug* whom she again torpedoed, with the result that the foremost magazine exploded. A huge column of flame, smoke and debris was thrown up, accompanied by a violent detonation, and in about one minute the ship sank, this being about fifteen minutes after the first shot was fired.

Fortunately for Maund, he had taken up temporary residence at military headquarters in George Town because he was very disturbed by the slackness prevailing aboard the cruiser to which he was attached (and aboard which he had a cabin). The Lieutenant knew that any sighting of a suspicious ship approaching the harbour would be reported to headquarters first; he also kept a launch with steam up in its boiler hard by, 'and by this means I hoped to be able to reach the ship in time to warn them.' The terrible fate of the *Zhemchug*, the only ship in the undefended harbour with guns heavy enough to give the *Emden* pause, was largely the result of the Russians' incorrigible carelessness, which had reduced the British officer to the desperate expedient of supplementing the sailors on watch on the ship herself by keeping a boat ready to *sail over to her to deliver a personal alarm* in the event of danger. The *Zhemchug* might have survived the attack on her in port but only if her guns had deterred the *Emden* from firing the fatal second torpedo from point-blank range, which they pathetically failed to do. A well-run ship would have got off a broadside within minutes.

The *Zhemchug* had arrived at Penang on 26 October to clean her boilers. The captain, Baron Cherkassov, a Captain, Second Grade (Commander), said the process would take a week. Jerram thought this an unconscionably long time and asked through Maund for it to be speeded up. Cherkassov replied that he could not reduce the process by more than a day and this was accepted. On 27 October Commander Macintyre asked to see the captain with Maund. 'We impressed upon him the necessity for special precautions, owing to Penang being an undefended port and the consequent liability (*sic*) of an attack on the *Zhemchug* from the sea . . . so as to command the entrance with the whole broadside, as was done by HMS *Yarmouth* when at Penang recently,' Maund reported. The Russian captain agreed, but the cruiser 'was not hauled up but lay up and down the tideway' instead of across it. 'Knowing that a poor system of look-out was maintained aboard the ship, I felt some doubt as to the alarm signals being seen,' Maund added: hence his withdrawal to head-quarters and his despairing reliance on cleft-stick methods of warning in the event of attack.

Meanwhile, Commander Audemard had ordered all available small boats into the water to pick up survivors. As he recalled it:

Scarcely had this order been carried into effect when a violent detonation, similar to the first one, was heard; at the same time, the unknown cruiser, completing her turn towards the open sea behind several merchant ships which had momentarily hidden her from our view, showed her four funnels, of which the foremost one was visibly a dummy . . . This tragic action, or rather this carnage, was accomplished in less than fifteen minutes.

Aboard the all-but-helpless, slovenly Russian ship eighty-eight men and one officer died, 120 men and three officers were wounded, many of them horribly mutilated by the shelling, and only 133 men and ten officers, including the First Officer, Senior Lieutenant Kulibin, were unharmed. The captain was not aboard at the time; having ordered the torpedoes disarmed, the ready ammunition stowed except for the twelve rounds, and the fires out in all but one of the sixteen boilers, and having failed to set extra watches or darken ship, he left the *Zhemchug* at 6 p.m. on the 27th to spend the night with a lady-friend ashore. (In August 1915, Cherkassov was sentenced to three and a half years in a 'house of correction' and Kulibin to one and a half years for gross negligence of duty. Both men were stripped of their rank, their decorations and their status as members of the Russian nobility by a naval court in Vladivostok. The dead were buried at George Town and a memorial was later erected there by the Russians.)

There were indeed other warships in and around Penang harbour, as Müller had guessed, and they were all French, under the command of Audemard. In port were two small destroyers, the *Fronde* and the *Pistolet*; on patrol outside was a third, the *Mousquet*; and also in harbour, protectively hidden among the merchant ships, was the large gunboat or third-class cruiser *D'Iberville*. Both the *Fronde* and the *D'Iberville* had boiler trouble and were effectively out of action;

the *Pistolet* had developed bearing trouble, yet was under one hour's notice to get up steam (but she was tied to the crippled *Fronde*). There was, however, a moment when the *D'Iberville* could have opened fire with her subsidiary 1.8 and 2.5-inch guns (the main, 4-inch guns could not be brought to bear), just as the *Emden* turned round. The smaller guns, Audemard says, would not have been effective:

Under these conditions, could I give the order to fire? I did not think so. To open fire would have been for the enemy, already triumphant, but the signal for another easy victory; for us, the useless sacrifice of our 300 sailors and the final annihilation of the Allied forces assembled at Penang. For all these reasons I did not hesitate in keeping silent, at the same time holding myself ready to reply vigorously to any attack by the enemy. On board the torpedo-boats [i.e. destroyers] . . . the situation was just as full of anxiety . . . There prevailed there the same indecision concerning the motives of this inconceivable aggression, and each one attempted to penetrate this mystery which, as on board us [*D'Iberville*], was elucidated only on the *Emden* leaving, the cruiser then being outside the range of their torpedoes.

(The quotations are taken from the official English translation of Audemard's report in the Admiralty records.)

But the *Pistolet* got up enough steam for 20 knots and left port in pursuit at 6.35 a.m.

The *Emden* had spotted the *D'Iberville* among the merchantmen; but she went after a column of smoke that appeared to be coming from a grey-painted ship north of the harbour entrance. It could well have been a destroyer, a dangerous prospect in the narrow confines of the channel. The cruiser opened fire at 6,000 yards, whereupon the vessel turned broadside on and headed for the Penang shore north of George Town. It could then be seen for the first time that it was a small, unarmed patrol boat and firing ceased. The vessel made harbour in a sinking condition without casualties. Müller blamed the severe refraction (the mirage effect) for his error. As they continued northwards Mücke, on Müller's orders, told the crew that they had sunk a Russian cruiser comparable with their own. There were three cheers for the Kaiser. Near the navigation buoy, the *Emden* halted the British steamer *Glenturret* and Lauterbach and his boarding party went aboard with the despatch now second nature to them. Before anything much could be done, the party was recalled. Lauterbach, on Müller's orders, told the captain as he left that he had been instructed to apologise for the fact that the *Emden* had fired in error on an unarmed patrol boat, and to explain that the *Emden* had not stopped to pick up survivors from the *Zhemchug* because large numbers of boats had been seen heading towards her. The ship was then set free.

The boarding party had been recalled and their cutter hastily hoisted back aboard because another dense cloud of smoke had been sighted bearing down on the harbour from the north. It was after 7 a.m. by now. From 7,000 yards the new arrival was identified correctly as a small destroyer; it was, in fact, the French *Mousquet*. The *Emden* piled on full speed again and hoisted her war-flags, which she had taken down with the dummy funnel on leaving harbour. The funnel was put up again too. At 4,500 yards the cruiser opened fire with her 4-inch guns. The small enemy vessel ran up the tricolour and then turned broadside on, apparently in an attempt to run for the coast to her port side. The third or fourth murderous salvo struck the engine-room, stopping the Frenchman, who managed to get off at least one torpedo and have one gun fire back. After this, as the range closed, the *Emden* systematically demolished the destroyer, which showed no inclination to strike her colours. She was already going down by the bow within ten minutes of the unequal fight starting, and she had ceased fire. The little ship's stern rose almost vertically at the last and she disappeared. The *Emden* lowered two boats to pick up the men in the sea. Müller wrote in his report that some of them tried to swim away at first because they had heard that the Germans shot their prisoners. One officer and thirty-five men were picked out of the water, seven of them badly and eighteen lightly wounded. Forty-two men had died with their ship, including *Capitaine de Corvette* (Lieutenant-Commander) Théroïnne, the captain, who had lost both his legs in a shell-burst but insisted on being strapped to his bridge and going down with his command. The destroyer, of 310 tons, had come in response to the gunfire in the harbour; she had not seen the *Emden* on her way in, the prisoners said. The captain, Müller quotes the survivors as saying, went down with his ship 'because he did not wish to survive the shame of men of his crew having jumped overboard' after the first salvo. In fact, they appear to have been *blown* overboard by the blast from the exploding shells. Dr. Luther and Dr. Schwabe, who had so far had to cope with one case of pneumonia and one broken leg on the cruise, now worked round the clock treating the Frenchmen.

The *Pistolet* was sighted following at a distance which grew steadily greater as the *Emden* pulled away near her top speed. Throughout her escape run, the German cruiser was jamming the wireless wavelengths used by the Royal Navy; when this was given up at noon, the operators heard the message, '*Emden* at Penang . . . *Emden* at

Penang' repeatedly. The *Pistolet* lost the trail when the *Emden* disappeared into a rain squall and a swell slowed the smaller ship down.

Müller sailed northwards to the Singapore–Rangoon steamer-lane to look for prizes, and also a neutral or suitable enemy merchantman to take the French sailors off his hands. Nothing had been sighted by 10 p.m., so he turned west to try the Sabang–Colombo lane. During the ensuing night, two of the French sailors died from their wounds. They were buried at sea with full naval honours after daybreak. On the morning of the 30th, the Germans stopped the British steamer *Newburn*, carrying a cargo of salt. Her captain agreed to take the French sailors to Sabang in Sumatra. He also accepted a letter from Müller to the German consul-general at Batavia reporting the Penang raid, for forwarding to the Admiralty in Berlin. It was delivered. A third prisoner had died during the night of the 29th and was buried in the same way, leaving the *Newburn* one officer, his leg amputated, and thirty-two men to take ashore. The officer and warrant and petty officers expressed their thanks to Müller for the way they had been treated. They arrived at Sabang on the 31st: the Germans heard about it from a monitored Dutch radio station soon afterwards.

8

'STRANGE SHIP IN ENTRANCE'

Part of the *Emden* legend arose from the apparently uncanny knowledge of shipping movements she seemed to her victims to possess. It led the more fanciful to suggest that her captain must be in league with the devil. A neutral Danish correspondent in London summed up the British view of Müller and his ship as seeming 'to combine the properties of the Flying Dutchman with those of the *Alabama*'. Certainly, the *Emden* was a ship of ill-omen to enemy merchantmen and was also the most famous commerce-raider since the Confederate cruiser's spectacular one-year campaign against the trade of the North in the American Civil War; but her quasi-magical reputation resulted from excellent staff-work and was inflated by false sightings all over the Indian Ocean. Lauterbach, inevitably, did his best to help by saying on more than one occasion to a British captain, 'You should have been here hours ago,' or words to that effect, or asking about a particular ship still in port at Calcutta. We have already seen how Müller devoted much of his time to planning and how Lauterbach's mercantile experience and knowledge of Far Eastern waters was part of the intelligence at his disposal. The obliging lists of ships carried by the Indian press were no less useful, and captured masters often seemed prepared to indulge in loose talk about ships they had followed or preceded out of harbour. Mücke, the First Officer, never a man to praise the British when there was a chance to execrate them – they were the enemy, after all, and the enemy was there to be loathed – put the latter phenomenon down to commercial motives. He wrote that a captain about to lose his ship wanted the same fate to overtake the property of other owners he knew to be in the area. The loose-tongued condition of one or two captains can more realistically be put down to shock and ignorance. The Royal Navy, confident in its overwhelming superiority, did not do very much to protect merchant ships in the Indian Ocean at the start of the war. Naval intelligence officers said they had advised masters to steer clear of the shipping lanes by thirty to fifty miles and to sail without lights at night;

captured captains usually said they had received no such advice. There was no attempt to organise convoys except when troops were being transported. But it was difficult to avoid regular steamer lanes at the approaches to a port such as Calcutta, where half a dozen converged off the mouth of the Hooghly.

Nonetheless the suspicion grew and persisted that the *Emden* was getting help from somewhere. The Dutch in the East Indies were accused several times of allowing, or at least failing to prevent, German merchant ships wirelessing information to the *Emden*. Governor-General Idenburg was obliged to spend time in correspondence with the British consulate-general in Batavia and with the Colonial Ministry in The Hague, where the British envoy made a *démarche* on the subject. The Dutch denied collusion and carelessness. Indeed, only one of the *Emden*'s victims, the *Tymeric*, had called at a Dutch colonial port before being caught just outside Colombo. Admiral Jerram reported that wireless operators in Australia had heard German merchantmen broadcasting information. The SS *Roon* in particular was accused of signalling to the *Emden* and the *Geier* from Dutch ports. The Dutch said that belligerent ships were made to take down their aerials to put their wireless out of action; the Germans were accused of running a wire up their masts at night as a substitute. In the case of the *Roon* a Dutch East Indies Army field wireless station was set up in the vicinity to monitor, and picked up nothing. Lacking proof, the British accepted the Dutch denials. But there was some truth in the allegation after all. In October a secret transmitter was found aboard the SS *Preussen* in the Dutch port of Sabang; the Dutch authorities said they would prosecute the captain and the wireless officer for a breach of neutrality regulations. A year later, the two men were acquitted; but a higher court overturned this verdict in March 1916 and sentenced them to one year's imprisonment each. It was the only case of its kind.

A level-headed appraisal of the *Emden*'s sources of information was made by the intelligence officer of the Royal Navy at Colombo, Royal Marine Artillery Captain A. W. Caulfried, in December 1914:

There is little ground for supposing that *Emden* had any sources of information other than what she obtained from her opponents. With the possible exception of the attack on *Zhemchug* at Penang, none of her movements require to be accounted for by the possession of special information. She attacked the eastern trade routes at their most vulnerable points, and at the time of her first appearance in the Bay of Bengal there was no British man-of-war within 1,800 miles of Calcutta. The wireless station of Calcutta is reported to have made her task easier by announcing the departures of ships from Calcutta and calling them up from time to time. [The master of the *Buresk* had been in her company for three weeks and reported that a very careful watch was always kept on the wireless . . .] She soon learned the secret call signs of the Allied warships, and judged their distance by the strength. The *Hampshire* call was changed on that account. At one time the Ceylon papers published the names and destinations of ships arriving and departing, and on capturing the first ship one of these papers was found. This accounts for the knowledge of the names and destinations of vessels which so impressed the masters of captured ships. At the same time she did not depend on this kind of information. Her method was to go to an area that offered a chance of a good bag and chase smoke, and on two occasions she spent over twenty-four hours in such an area without seeing anything . . . A certain amount of information was probably given away by 'chatty' operators both of wireless stations and merchant ships . . . [The important fact of the fate of the *Pontoporos* and the *Markomannia* had not been discovered by the *Emden* until sixteen days later . . .] On the whole it is considered that the movements of the *Emden* are such as would naturally be made in a carefully planned attack on the eastern trade routes by an active and enterprising commander who took advantage of every opportunity that came in his way.

Admiral Jerram, in a report of his own of similar date, concluded: 'Generally speaking, I do not consider that the Dutch *authorities* [his emphasis] ever gave *Emden* any assistance in any way whatever, but I believe that wireless signals were made to other German men-of-war by German merchant ships in Dutch waters.' He thought, however, that Dutch wireless operators must have known of the secret signals sent by the *Roon* and the *Preussen*, and that *Emden* had made use of press telegrams picked up on her wireless from Dutch transmitters. Müller himself in his own report makes it clear that he used German merchantmen to pass on information, orders and requests for him but he makes no mention of receiving intelligence from them.

Müller also knew, because it was common knowledge, that troops had been shipped by the British from India to Europe in this opening stage of the war and he had rightly guessed that contingents would also be going from Australia and New Zealand. We have already seen how he made a fruitless sweep off the Maldive Islands in the hope of catching troop transports on their way east for this purpose. But he had no knowledge at all of the convoy which brought the first major

SMS *Emden*

Captain Karl von Müller

First Officer Hellmuth von Mücke

The morning after at Madras

Victim number fifteen: SS *Clan Grant*

Nemesis: HMAS *Sydney*

The wreck of the *Emden*

Direction Island: the transmitter mast

The station office

The severed cable to Perth

Captain Glossop's letter to Müller

In reply please quote
No.

H.M.A.S. "Sydney",
at Sea,
9th November 191 4.

Sir,

I have the honour to request that in the name of humanity you now surrender your ship to me. In order to show how much I appreciate your gallantry, I will recapitulate the position.

(1) You are ashore, 3 funnels and 1 mast down and most guns disabled.

(2) You cannot leave this island, and my ship is intact.

In the event of your surrendering in which I venture to remind you is no disgrace but rather your misfortune, I will endeavour to do all I can for your sick and wounded and take them to a hospital.

I have the honour to be,

Sir,

Your obedient Servant,

John C.T. Glossop
Captain.

The Captain,
H.I.G.M.S. "Emden".

Official praise for the cable station staff

The German landing party embarks . . .

and leaves Direction Island . . .

in the *Ayesha*

The Australians close the stable door

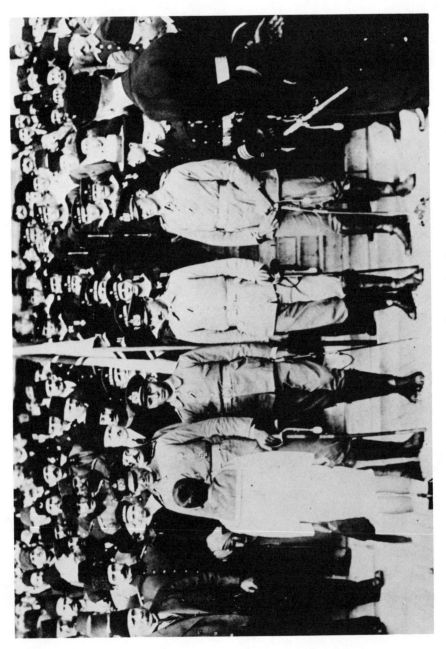

Welcome to Constantinople

reinforcement for the Allies from the two distant Dominions, and which was Admiral Jerram's major preoccupation for the first three months of the war. The German captain's ignorance on this subject was to prove his downfall.

On the outbreak of war, Australia and New Zealand promptly offered Britain troops. The Australian Expeditionary Force assembled for this purpose eventually amounted to 20,000 men, made up of one infantry division (three infantry brigades plus field artillery) and one brigade of light horse, as well as support troops; the New Zealand Expeditionary Force consisted of some 8,250 men of one mounted rifle brigade (three regiments) and one infantry brigade (four battalions) with their supply columns and a divisional headquarters. Also to be transported were 1,050 Imperial troops and reservists. Altogether, some 30,000 men were to be shipped halfway round the world to help 'the Mother Country' in her hour of need, to be followed by regular shipments of reinforcements and replacements. Horses, weapons, ammunition and supplies were also to be shipped. Transport and protection of these forces was initially and in the main the joint responsibility of Vice-Admiral Patey, commanding the Australian Squadron (integrated into the Royal Navy in wartime), and Vice-Admiral Jerram, C-in-C, China, until they passed into the area guarded by Rear-Admiral Peirse of the East Indies Station. Patey was also responsible for capturing the German islands in the Pacific and for helping to contain Spee's Squadron; Jerram, also concerned with the latter task, had to cover the British contribution to the mainly Japanese blockade and capture of Tsingtao (it fell on 7 November 1914) and hunt the *Emden*.

But the convoy was the main concern of the two British admirals in the eastern Pacific. It was originally due to sail on 22 September, the day Spee shelled Tahiti and Müller shelled Madras. But problems with ships and fears of raids by German cruisers, to say nothing of logistical problems on land, caused one delay after another. The nervousness of the New Zealand Government, which threatened to resign unless the convoy received maximum protection (their contingent represented one eighteenth of the male population between 20 and 40 years of age), also caused delay. The New Zealand Expeditionary Force finally left Wellington on 16 October in ten ships, bound for Albany at the south-western extremity of Western Australia where twenty-six transports were assembled for the Australian Army. On the morning of 1 November, these thirty-six ships set out in convoy under the protection of the heavy cruiser HMS *Minotaur* (Captain E. B. Kiddle), Jerram's most powerful ship and his flagship when he was not based ashore at Singapore, and, from Patey's

Squadron, HMAS *Melbourne* and HMAS *Sydney*, a matching pair of light cruisers. From Fremantle on the south-west coast of Western Australia two more transports and the Japanese battlecruiser *Ibuki* joined and completed the convoy, which headed for Colombo at a speed of nine and a half knots.

All four protecting ships outclassed the *Emden*, their main preoccupation, decisively in guns, armour and/or speed. There were no German submarines east of the Mediterranean (they had no bases), Spee was known to be heading towards the Americas and the *Königsberg* was also accounted for, locked up in East African waters. Apart from the convoy escorts, Jerram had one other heavy cruiser, another light cruiser (*Hampshire* and *Yarmouth*), a Japanese cruiser squadron, several armed merchant cruisers and destroyers of the Royal Navy and assorted Russian and French warships looking for the *Emden*. 'There were thus reasonable grounds for hoping that in a few days the force in the Indian Ocean would be sufficient to bring the *Emden* to account,' Jerram wrote modestly in his report to the Admiralty of 13 November.

A week after the convoy set sail with its overcrowded ships, Jerram sent a message to the *Minotaur* via the cable and wireless station on Direction Island in the Cocos (or Keeling) group, detaching the big cruiser from the convoy and sending her at top speed to South Africa. This was done on orders from the Admiralty in London for which there seem to have been two reasons. The order to the ship read: 'Join *Albion* off South-West Africa in view of probable raid by *Gneisenau* and *Scharnhorst*.' South-West Africa (now called Namibia) was a German colony, on the other side of the Atlantic from South America, towards which Spee had crossed the Pacific in October. After his triumph at the Battle of Coronel on the day the convoy set sail (1 November), there was in theory nothing except coaling problems to stop Spee moving in support of the colony against the invading troops from the Union of South Africa whose territory bordered upon it. The old foes of the British in the Boer War, Generals Botha and Smuts, had intervened on the side of the British Empire against the Germans. The second reason for detaching the *Minotaur* was the rising against that decision led by another Boer War veteran, General de Wet, and other Afrikaner commanders, which eventually involved up to 10,000 men and lasted a few months before it collapsed. At any rate, the convoy was now protected by just three cruisers, of which the *Ibuki* was the most powerful and the *Melbourne* was the leader. The Admiralty in London was keeping its options open. The destination of the convoy at this stage was Colombo: from there it could be routed via Suez for service in the Middle East or Europe or via the

Cape for deployment against the Germans in South-West or the rebels in South Africa. The escort was reduced to just two when HMAS *Sydney* was detached to investigate a call for help from the Cocos Islands.

The tiny flecks of land which the *Emden* was approaching from the north-east and the convoy from the south-east in the first week of November 1914 are about 840 miles south of the Equator and some 2,300 miles west of Darwin, Australia. They have a total land area of five and a half square miles; there are two atolls about sixteen miles apart. The northerly atoll culminates in one small island called North Keeling, the southerly in twenty-six islands and islets grouped round a shallow lagoon ten miles wide at its widest, with an entrance at its northern end. The climate is healthy and sub-tropical, although the area is subject to cyclones and earthquakes. The islands were discovered by William Keeling, a mariner with the English East India Company in 1609, who gave them his name, but were settled, if that is the right word, only in the 1820s, by one Alexander Hare, an adventurer by profession, who arrived with a private harem and a retinue of slaves from the Malay Archipelago. Exhausted no doubt by his idleness, Hare made way for John Clunies Ross, a Shetland Islander by origin, who had settled on Direction Island with his family in 1827. He developed coconut plantations on which he employed the resident Malays. His descendants stayed on. In 1857 the islands formally came under the British Crown and were 'administered' from Ceylon from 1878; in 1886 George Clunies Ross formalised the family's possession of the islands by obtaining from Queen Victoria a grant in perpetuity. In 1903 they were reallocated for bureaucratic purposes to the Straits Settlements. ('Perpetuity' lasted until 1978 when another John Clunies Ross gave up the family's title and sold the islands to Australia, whose flag had flown there since 1955.) The more recent name of the islands, Cocos, derives of course from the coconut trees which grow there in profusion – there are 350,000 of them there to this day, and on Direction Island there is still a cable station owned in 1914 by the Eastern Extension Telegraph Company Limited. It was an important junction of three cables, to Fremantle and the Australia–New Zealand network, to Batavia and the Dutch and British networks in south-east Asia, and to Rodriguez Island and nearby Mauritius, which was linked in turn to South Africa and via the Seychelles to East Africa. It was a key point in one of only two direct cable connections between Britain and Australia passing through exclusively British Empire territory. (The other went across the Atlantic and then Canada to Vancouver and from there across the

Pacific via Fanning Island, Fiji, Norfolk Island and New Zealand. On 7 September 1914, the German light cruiser *Nürnberg* of Spee's Squadron raided Fanning Island and cut the cable to such effect that it took some seven weeks to repair. Restoration of service was reported on 1 November.)

On the last day of October 1914 the *Emden* sighted the *Buresk* precisely on station at the rendezvous given her off Simaloer. There was rejoicing on both ships, not least because the men of the *Emden* had learned from their French prisoners that the *Pontoporos*, sent away on 16 September, and the *Markomannia*, released on 30 September, had been caught together in the same area by HMS *Yarmouth* on 12 October. The German collier had been loading coal from the Greek ship when the British cruiser found them a few miles north of Simaloer. The *Pontoporos* did nothing; the fourteen *Emden* sailors aboard led by a petty officer (Deputy Coxswain Meyer) threw their weapons overboard and were detained by the boarding-party. The *Markomannia* tried to make a run for it, despite a blank shot across her bow; a live six-inch shell brought her to a halt after a very short chase. Her crew of 46 men, including Captain Faass and one man from the *Emden*, were taken off and she was sunk on the spot. The Germans claimed the two ships were seized inside the Dutch three-mile limit. Captain H. Cochrane, RN, of the *Yarmouth*, reported that he had established by rangefinder that his ship was four and a quarter miles offshore at the time. There were no casualties. The *Pontoporos* was allowed to proceed to Singapore and the *Yarmouth* took her sixty German prisoners to Penang, which is why the Frenchmen knew the story.

On 1 November, a Sunday, Müller promoted about forty men who had performed exceptionally well during the cruise. After church, the officers drank a glass of *Sekt* in their mess with the captain to celebrate their success. Later on that rare Sunday of relaxation at sea, Müller pondered his next moves. He developed a grand design for drawing off some of the swelling numbers of his pursuers by giving the impression that he was moving his area of operations to the waters west and south of Australia. Having thus drawn some of the enemy out of the Indian Ocean, he planned to run to its far north-western corner, off Socotra Island and the Horn of Africa, to raid commerce on the Aden-Bombay route. He calculated that a landing on Direction Island and a raid to destroy the cable station and its adjacent wireless transmitter would draw off at least some of the British forces in the desired direction. It would also disrupt sea transport to and

100

from Australia as well as her cable and wireless communications. So after completing coaling on 2 November, Müller first ordered a course south-eastwards along the southern coast of Sumatra as far as the Sunda Strait between Sumatra and Java, in case this was being used by diverted merchant traffic. For more than twenty-four hours until noon on the 5th, he patrolled south of the Strait within sight of the volcanic island of Krakatoa, a point he had last passed on the night of 31 August to 1 September. From there the *Emden* headed south-west to the Cocos Islands. Apart from a polite visit by a Dutch colonial army captain during coaling off Padang on the 2nd, to make sure the cruiser was outside territorial waters, the Germans saw nothing of interest.

The captured British collier *Exford* had been sent to wait at a rendezvous point thirty miles north of North Keeling Island while the cruiser made her fruitless diversion to the Sunda Strait. So quiet did things become on this first week of November that at dusk on the 6th, when Lauterbach was officer of the watch, he thought it worthwhile to send a runner to the wardroom to announce the landing on the bridge of an alcatras or large tropical seabird, known to German mariners, somewhat confusingly, as a *Döskopp* (in the northern landsman's Low German from which it comes, the word means simply pigeon). This time the joke was on the irrepressible Lauterbach. The German word literally means 'sleepyhead', so when the runner announced to the wardroom that there was a sleepyhead on the bridge, Mücke, no less boisterous in character and not much of an ornithologist, said: 'Our compliments to the officer of the watch, but we've known that for ages.' The strange bird, unaccustomed to taking off from a solid surface, stayed for a few hours, ate a large meal of scraps, beat its wings and pecked at anyone coming too close and finally, fortified by its rich feast, managed to stagger into the air and disappear into the darkness, to general applause. Sailors are said to be superstitious; this little incident, recalled in more than one account, no doubt encouraged any such tendencies.

On the night of the 7th, the *Emden* arrived at the rendezvous given to the *Exford* but saw no sign of the collier. By an oversight, her chronometers had not been corrected before she parted company. The cruiser therefore sailed slowly in ever-increasing circles round the meeting point until 8 a.m. on Sunday the 8th, when the collier was sighted. The raid planned for that day was put off for twenty-four hours. The navigational error caused by the unadjusted chronometers was to prove fatally costly. Overnight the *Emden* had heard on the wireless a coded message, preceded by the English word 'urgent' in plain language, being repeated again and again. At dawn it was acknowledged by a ship with a call-sign 'NC' – unknown to the *Emden* – in fact the *Minotaur*, a heavy cruiser. The operators reckoned from the strength of her signal that the enemy ship was 200 miles away. Müller deduced with uncanny accuracy that it was a ship being sent to the Cape of Good Hope to tackle the de Wet revolt of which he must have read in captured newspapers or heard on the wireless. The ship sent no message to any other vessel; the exchanges were apparently confined to her and the Cocos station sending the message to her. The convoy as such did not give itself away. Müller considered putting off the impending raid for another day to the 10th, but he was wasting coal and the enemy ship seemed to be heading into the distance at a great rate, as indeed she was. So he ordered a change of officers on the *Exford*, with Gropius resuming his duties as navigation officer on the *Emden* and Lauterbach taking his place, under orders to make his way to a point in the vicinity of Socotra and wait until the end of November. If not contacted by then he was to go back to Sumatra and internment. There were sixteen *Emden* men aboard. The *Buresk* was now sent to a point about thirty miles north of the South Keeling atoll, to await a wireless call to rejoin the *Emden* the next day, after the raid.

The *Emden* headed slowly towards the South Keeling group, steam up in eight boilers, dummy funnel in position, cleared for action. She increased speed in the last hours of darkness and circumvented a sudden squall. Müller planned to arrive off the mouth of Port Refuge at Direction Island at first light, a little after 6 a.m. It took about half an hour to transfer Mücke, Sub-Lieutenants Schmidt and Gyssling, six petty officers and forty-one ratings to the steam pinnace and two cutters and for them to enter the harbour, with orders to return if they saw the island was defended (Müller would then have shelled the communications and made off instead). Seeing that the lagoon was an excellent place for coaling, Müller summoned the *Buresk* by wireless just after arriving, rather than later. The transmitter on the island reacted almost at once: 'What code? What ship?' The *Emden* began jamming, but the message 'Strange ship in entrance' was morsed several times. Shortly afterwards the text was changed: 'SOS, *Emden* here.' Some time later an unidentifiable warship whose call-sign was not known aboard the *Emden* tried to contact the station, unsuccessfully as by this time its mast had disappeared, blown down by Mücke. The warship appeared to be 200 or more miles away, to judge by the strength of her signal. The cable station was also sending messages in all directions, to Australia, Singapore, South Africa, reporting it was under attack.

Early on the morning of 9 November in Singapore, an anxious

Admiral Jerram was still worrying about the convoy, now eight days out. He sent this message to the Admiralty in London: 'As the Australian convoy will be passing within the limit of 100 miles from Cocos or Keeling Islands today *Emden* may detect their presence and possibly attack.' In fact it was the convoy that was to do the detecting, with the aid of the forewarned wireless station crew, and to send HMAS *Sydney* from the escort into the attack.

9

THE BATTLE OF THE COCOS ISLANDS

The staff of the cable and wireless station, warned by Jerram after the Fanning Island incident to be prepared for a raid, behaved with exemplary sang-froid when it happened. The report that they were under attack was sent down all three cables for fifteen minutes. The wireless call for help was addressed to HMS *Minotaur*, with which they had been in touch over the diversion of the ship to South Africa. The operators knew she would still be within range of their transmitter, even though they had no idea that she had been sailing with the Australian convoy, which was maintaining radio silence. The *Minotaur* relayed the emergency call to HMAS *Melbourne* (Captain Mortimer Silver, RN), now in charge of the convoy, because she knew the remaining escorts were much closer than she was. It was this transmission that in all probability was picked up by the *Emden* and led Müller's men to believe that the only enemy warship in the area was 200 to 250 miles away, to judge by the strength of the signal (in those days, radio direction-finding still lay in the realm of theory, although it was to be developed by the British before the end of the war). There is some confusion in the various accounts about the intercept which led Müller to think he had a good eight hours to evade an enemy so far away, whereas the *Sydney* was in fact just fifty-two miles, or two hours' steaming at maximum speed, from Direction Island when she was detached. She had also heard the call for help.

But before that fateful event, there were ructions within the escort force. Captain Kato of the Japanese battlecruiser *Ibuki* insistently argued to Captain Silver that his ship, by a considerable margin the most heavily armed with the convoy, should be sent to tackle the interloper at Direction Island. Kato had four 12-inch and eight 8-inch guns to deploy against the 4.1-inch pieces of the lightly-armed German cruiser: would not the safest course be to send the strongest ship to overwhelm the enemy? The Japanese sailors were also spoiling for a fight. Silver was not convinced, because he rightly suspected that the *Emden* might have the edge in speed over the heavily armoured Japanese cruiser, whereas the *Sydney* could produce twenty-six knots to the *Emden*'s twenty-four and was also sufficiently superior in armament (eight 6-inch guns) and armour, and possibly because he wanted a British Empire ship to do the job. The Japanese officers wept in frustration when the decision fell against them and the *Sydney*, under Captain John Glossop, RN, was ordered to investigate.

Lieutenant C. R. Garsia, RN, was in the bath aboard the Australian cruiser when a colleague burst in to tell him that the ship was on her way to tackle the *Emden*. Attached like the captain himself to the fledgling Royal Australian Navy which was short of experienced officers, he had been recalled home in the middle of October at the 'first convenient opportunity'. No such opportunity had arisen, however, so that he became a participant in the drama now about to unfold. His subsequent excited letter to his father reveals some interesting details about the battle and its aftermath: it was even published in the British press at great length five weeks after the event. He heard the news of the ship's mission with 'great elation', he wrote.

There was a terrible inevitability about what followed the despatch of the British-built *Sydney*. For about a century, from the displacement of sail by engines and the concomitant technological leaps in guns and armour until the deployment of airpower and missiles on and against warships, the outcome of almost any naval engagement was predictable unless unfathomable luck tipped the scales. A superior ship or formation should not be defeated by an inferior one where the commanders were competent and the superiority lay in two out of three crucial areas – speed, guns and armour. The British would surely have defeated the Germans at the Battle of Jutland had that engagement been pressed to a conclusion because they had more and heavier guns: they would have won by attrition (even though their world maritime domination might have been lost as a result). At least as inevitably, a 6-inch cruiser firing 100 lb. shots would defeat a 4-inch firing 30 lb. shots unless her engines broke down, her captain proved unequal to the task or a freakish mishap occurred. As between ships of similar age and type, bigger guns almost always implied thicker armour and at least equal speed. Captain Glossop was no genius, on the contrary, but he was a competent officer in the world's greatest navy. Commander Müller was no magician, and the luck which had run his way for three months was now about to desert him: the inevitable superior enemy was on her way.

The twice-repeated summons to the *Buresk* by wireless was not acknowledged by the collier, but if she had heard, her smoke would be visible before nine, by which time the landing party, having been allowed two hours for its mission, would be back aboard. The lookout in the crow's nest reported smoke to the north towards 9 a.m. The smoke was exceptionally heavy, but this could have been due to the fact that the *Buresk* was doubtless making her best speed. There had also been a fire in her bunkers on the previous day which would have affected the way her coal burned after being doused with water. The smoke could also be from a mail-steamer on the Colombo–Australia run: a captured newspaper suggested this possibility. Then the lookout reported that the approaching ship had two masts and one funnel, which was right for the *Buresk*. Nonetheless, the approach seemed rather fast . . . But Sub-Lieutenant Guérard, Müller's adjutant, went aloft and confirmed the sighting. The landing party should by now have been on its way back, but there was no sign of the fifty men or their boats. Müller ordered a signal by flag: 'Speed up work.' At 9.15 the lookouts reported that the approaching ship had two masts and several funnels, which had become visible as she turned. Flags were run up signalling 'return at once', then the ship's horn was sounded repeatedly to recall the detachment. Finally the international code flag 'A' was hoisted to half-mast, signifying that the anchor was being weighed; the alarm bells rang, as did the engine room telegraph; the ship began to move. Astern the pinnace with the two cutters in tow could now be seen coming away from the landing-stage, with men waving urgently. The *Emden* appeared to take no notice as she ran her colours up the foremast and put on speed, heading north with only 314 men aboard. The landing party had been put together by Mücke out of thirty-two men from the seaman branch and fifteen technicians and stokers, all of whom had distinguished themselves during the raid on Penang eleven days earlier. Sub-Lieutenant Fikentscher had expressed concern to the adjutant the previous day, as he transferred to the *Buresk*, that the already announced names of the detachment included those of all ten gunlayers, whose absence would be a serious loss in the event of a sudden action. As Fikentscher stepped over the side, Müller himself reassured him that the landing would be a short affair and the risk was minimal. But forty-eight other men had also been put aboard the various colliers.

Müller, never a man to use two adjectives where one would suffice, says in his report: 'The following events now developed extraordinarily quickly as the enemy warship was approaching at very high speed – twenty to twenty-five knots.' He issued a stream of orders: steam up in all boilers, weigh anchor, clear for action, action stations, full speed ahead . . . Now it could clearly be seen that the

106

approaching enemy had four funnels and her masts were raked. This meant a British light cruiser; Müller, perhaps misunderstanding the oft-heard call-sign 'NC' of the past day or so, guessed it might be HMS *Newcastle*. The identity of the oncoming ship scarcely mattered: all modern British light cruisers had bigger guns, stronger armour and greater speed than the *Emden*. At 9.17 the German cruiser left the mouth of the lagoon, accelerating agonisingly slowly as the stokers and engineers slaved below to build up pressure in all twelve boilers, and heading NNW. The enemy approached from the north, steering SSE; at 9.30 he turned westwards, to starboard. On the *Emden*, the rangefinder operators read off the reducing range until, at 9,500 metres (10,500 yards) and 9.40 a.m., Müller ordered *Kapitänleutnant* Gaede: 'Open fire.'

Captain Glossop's account of the fight in his 'Letter of Proceedings' to Captain Silver and the Admiralty verges on the laconic:

I . . . sighted land ahead and almost immediately the smoke of a ship, which proved to be HIGMS *Emden*, coming out towards me at a great rate. At 9.40 am fire was opened, she firing the first shot. *I kept my distance as much as possible to obtain the advantage of my guns.* [Author's emphasis] Her fire was very accurate and rapid to begin with but seemed to slacken very quickly, all casualties occurring in this ship almost immediately, my foremost [range-] finder in centre of main control position being dismounted quite early and the after control being put out at about the third salvo. First the foremost funnel of her went, secondly the foremast and she was badly on fire aft, then the second funnel went and lastly the third funnel and I saw she was making for the beach on North Keeling Island, where she grounded at 11.20 am. I gave her two more broadsides and left her . . .

By the time the shooting started, the two ships were on roughly parallel courses, heading north. 'I had to attempt to inflict such damage on the enemy with the guns that he would be slowed down in speed significantly before I could switch to a promising torpedo attack,' Müller reported. He knew his only hope was the Great Equaliser, the torpedo, which the enemy also possessed, and to be able to use that he had to close the range. The enemy cruiser had two knots on him, so the first salvoes had to be good.

They were. As Lieutenant Rahilly, the *Sydney*'s gunnery officer, reported: 'If the German shell had burst properly, both our forward and after [firing] controls would have been put out of action in the first few minutes; in the *Emden* both their control positions were shot away, all the personnel being lost.' The first two five-shot salvoes from the *Emden* missed, which was quite normal; the third scored several hits, which was decidedly good or fortunate shooting, especially since the gunlayers were all absent with the detachment. The enemy momentarily disappeared in the ensuing smoke. But Müller knew his guns would do little damage at that range, and he ordered two points to starboard to get closer to the target. The eighth German salvo struck the guns on the *Sydney*'s starboard, unengaged side but failed to explode: had they done so, the 'lucky hit' Müller was hoping for might have caused a major explosion of ammunition. But the 'enemy's shell seldom burst,' Rahilly wrote, 'and owing to the large angle of descent . . . never ricocheted. Only their shrapnel burst on impact with the water.' He added that the *Sydney*'s 2-inch side armour was of 'enormous value . . . entirely defeating 4.1-inch guns at 8,000 yards and probably much less'. With the main and the reserve fire-direction centres temporarily out of action thanks to hits from the *Emden*'s unexploded shells, the *Sydney*'s shooting slowed down, with each gun of the six-gun broadside (two at the bow, two at the stern and two on the port side) having to fire individually using its own sights. But it was still devastating, even if it took the Australian ship twenty minutes to score her first major hit, destroying the wireless cabin and causing the first casualties on the German ship.

From then on the *Sydney* shot the *Emden* to pieces. The funnels collapsed when hit (rather than being holed) because the stays which normally steadied them had been detached from the deck in preparation for coaling. The dummy funnel had been lowered before the shooting began. Debris soon cluttered the deck. Another hit destroyed the electric intercommunication system for the guns, whereupon voice-pipes had to be used to direct the firing; both main fuses were destroyed; the steering telegraph was knocked out, then the steering gear itself, so that the auxiliary, manually powered steering aft had to be used (until that too was knocked out). The destruction of the funnels reduced the speed, but Müller turned sharp right in an attempt to get close enough to fire his guns more effectively before they were completely silenced, and then sharp left as the enemy did likewise to the north, to try to fire a torpedo. But the torpedo flat was a shambles by this time and the range never closed enough. The *Sydney* fired one about one hour after the battle began, but it missed. By this time the *Emden* was reduced to using her engines to steer, which of course further reduced her speed. The *Sydney* kept her distance and steadily pounded her opponent to destruction. The fact that the German ship was still afloat and moving was a tribute to her designers and builders. The worst hit was among the ready-use ammunition of number four port and starboard guns, which exploded, killing large numbers and setting the after portion of the ship on fire. At 11.15 Müller was forced to cease fire: none of the crippled main armament could be brought to bear.

By this time the *Emden* had fired about 1,500 shells, almost every round on board at the start of the unequal contest. Rahilly reported that nearly all the casualties on his ship had occurred in the first fifteen minutes and on the disengaged side at that. Had one of the early shells exploded, Captain Glossop himself would have been killed instead of merely losing his main fire-control apparatus. As it was, the *Sydney* lost four killed (including one wounded man who died later), four severely wounded and four lightly wounded. The ship had a few burns, dents and holes in unimportant places on her upperworks, from some sixteen hits. *Sydney* on the other hand, as Glossop reported, 'expended 670 rounds of ammunition nearly all of which were lyddite, the effect of which was appalling and could I have known it, I might have left her after the first half-hour.'

The death throes of the *Emden* turned her into what can only be described as a floating hell. Engine-room Chief Warrant Officer Leicht wrote:

After the first enemy shells struck us, the motor for working the fans broke down. The temperature was 67° C (152° F). About fifteen minutes after the action opened, hits were felt near the engines, noticeable by violent concussions, by the ship listing to port, by floor-plates starting and scattering in all directions, by objects on the walls being torn from their fixtures . . . and by the breaking of the glass on the clock and pressure gauge . . . During the whole engagement the danger from smoke was very serious, in fact at times so much so that nothing could be made out . . . at the first explosion the emergency lighting system went out.'

Engine-room Chief Warrant Officer Keller was on the other side of the ship in the starboard engine-room hatchway:

From the beginning we suffered from the effects of gas fumes which penetrated into the hatchway from the main and auxiliary engine-rooms on opening the bulkhead doors . . . When the armoured hatch was opened for the purpose of giving an order to the men below, a shell struck the ship above us, causing such a violent concussion that I was thrown into the hatchway and wounded by a splinter on the right side of the head . . . Only being able to move with difficulty, I remained in the hatchway. Here I helped to keep down the steam with the firehose from the auxiliary engine-room, and to transmit orders from the port engine via the armoured grating to the starboard engine. When the order was given, 'All hands on deck,' the armoured grating could not be opened. I tried to get up through the auxiliary engine-room, where the temperature was so high that the handrails burnt the palms of my hands.

Conditions on deck were no more comfortable, as Leading Signalman Lindner also recalled afterwards in captivity, at his captain's request:

At the start of the action I was under the lee of the conning tower . . . When the first shell struck the forecastle . . . and some of No. 1 port gun's crew were disabled, Yeoman of Signals Limming, Signalman Gräve, Seaman Zeidler and I sprang forward and threw the empty shell-cases and boxes overboard to make room round the gun . . . On the forecastle the supply was still being kept up with the help of Seaman Reich II and Baker's Assistant Franz. We returned under the lee of the conning tower. Shortly afterwards a second shell killed Seaman Reich II . . . Yeoman of Signals Limming and I ran aft . . . the whole deck under the poop was on fire. Thereupon we ran back to our station. On the way Limming was killed . . . As I was the only man remaining of the signalling personnel, I went into the conning tower where I was occupied in transmitting orders by voice-pipe to the transmitting station and the guns. When the foremast fell overboard the smoke in the conning tower was rather dense, so I had to relieve Seaman Werner for a short time.

Lieutenant Garsia recalled: 'We had the speed on the *Emden* and fought as suited ourselves.'

From 11 a.m. both ships were heading WNW with the *Sydney* to the north and the *Emden* approaching North Keeling Island. Müller ceased fire at 11.15 and ordered a change of course to NNW, straight at the island. The bow was pointed at a stretch of surf between two outcrops of land, indicating the presence of a reef just below the surface at the south-western extremity of the island. Müller ordered both engines stopped, and the shattered ship slid onto the reef under her own momentum. When the scraping and jolting showed that the hull had started to run aground, Müller ordered for the last time, 'Full speed ahead.' The last gasp of the engines drove the ship firmly aground, but the stern section remained afloat over deep water, the reef being almost vertical, like most coral reefs.

As I no longer had the capacity to damage the enemy, I then decided to put the ship, thoroughly shot to pieces and burning in many places, on the luff side of North Keeling Island in the breakers on the reef, to reduce it completely to a wreck in order not to make a useless sacrifice of the survivors

Müller explained in his report. But the ordeal of his ship was far from over, even after the cautious Captain Glossop fired two more broadsides just after she ran aground with water pouring into her boiler and engine-rooms. The flooding in the torpedo flat had forced Müller to give up a last despairing attempt to launch an underwater missile, and the personnel came up on deck as the ship began her run onto the rocks. Müller shouted on deck: 'Those who want to can jump overboard and save themselves by swimming to the island.' It was 11.20, and the survivors on the deck of the German cruiser saw their enemy drawing away round the far side of the uninhabited island.

I gave her two more broadsides and left her to pursue a merchant ship which had come during the action. Although I had guns on this merchant ship at odd times during the action, I had not fired, and as she was making off fast I pursued and overtook her at 12.10, firing a gun across her bows and hoisting international code signal to stop, which she did. I sent an armed boat and found her to be the SS *Buresk*, a captured British collier . . . The ship unfortunately was sinking, the Kingston knocked out and damaged to prevent repairing, so I took all on board, fired four shells into her, and returned to *Emden*, passing men swimming in the water for whom I left two boats I was towing from *Buresk*

wrote Glossop in his helter-skelter English.

During the night of the 8th to 9th, the collier had drifted about twelve miles to the north-west on the current. Receiving the wireless call from the *Emden* but unable to respond because of a transmitter fault, the ship made her best speed; at 8.30 a.m. when she was about five miles north of North Keeling Island, a large smoke-cloud was seen to the east. About an hour later, the collier was some five miles south-east of North Keeling Island, and the crew saw the *Emden*, her colours set, steaming north at a great rate. The *Buresk* slowed down and turned north to await the result of the battle; when it became clear the *Emden* would not escape *Buresk* headed north, hoping to be able to slip away, but at about 11.50 it was realised that the enemy warship had turned in pursuit of her. *Kapitänleutnant* Klöpper therefore gave the order to scuttle. The seacocks were opened, small arms

111

thrown overboard, documents burned, the wireless smashed and the boats swung out with rations aboard in case the enemy did not pick up the crew. When the warship fired her warning shot, the *Buresk* signalled by lamp: 'There are Englishmen aboard.' There was in fact only one, the perhaps eccentric English steward who had stayed aboard with the Norwegian cook, the eighteen Chinese and the *Emden*'s prize crew of sixteen. *Sydney* ordered: 'Haul down your flag,' and a boarding party arrived with orders to have the *Buresk* follow to pick up survivors from the *Emden*. When it was clear that the *Buresk* was about to start sinking, her crew was ordered to transfer to the *Sydney* in the two lifeboats. These were taken in tow as the Australian cruiser slowly returned to North Keeling. The lifeboats were released to pick up *Emden* survivors who had been blown overboard by shell-blast before the German cruiser ran aground.

While the *Sydney* was away, the survivors of the battle on the *Emden* set about making her of as little value as possible to the enemy. Her log was destroyed, her magazines flooded and the guns spiked by the removal of the breech-blocks and the smashing of the gunsights. The torpedo-aiming equipment was also thrown overboard and all secret documents destroyed. Most of the fires still burning were put out with seawater. The wounded were assembled on a cleared area of the forecastle where Dr. Luther worked on them.

Several sailors swam the 100 yards through the breakers to the island, but the treacherous water proved too much for some and they drowned; others who had jumped overboard before the *Sydney* ceased fire were dragged back onto the hulk. Repeated attempts were made to rig a breeches-buoy between the ship and the island, but these all failed. The coral was so sharp that every rope was cut on contact with it.

At 4 p.m. the enemy cruiser was seen to be coming back to the scene of her victory, and the *Emden* survivors assumed she would now pick them up, as she had two boats in tow. But these were released in the distance. The ship passed the stern of the grounded *Emden* at a distance of about 4,500 yards, hoisting signal flags.

On arriving again off *Emden* she still had her colours up at mainmast head. I enquired by signal, international code, 'Will you surrender,' and received a reply in morse, 'What signal, no signalbook'. I then made in morse, 'Do you surrender' and subsequently 'have you received my signal,' to neither of which did I get an answer; the German officers on board [from the *Buresk*] gave me to understand that the Captain would never surrender, and therefore, though very reluctantly, I again fired at her at 4.30 pm ceasing at

4.35 pm as she showed white flags and hauled down her ensign by sending a man aloft. I have given these details very exactly as subsequently I heard they were indignant, saying I fired on a white flag

Captain Glossop reported, unmistakably hurt at the very idea.

Back aboard the wreck, according to Müller again, the message 'No signal-book' was sent because it was true; the book had been destroyed with other documents. The exhausted survivors were absolutely shattered by the resumption of shelling, which caused more deaths and injuries and started new fires. Müller once again gave permission to his men to swim for it, with the same mixed results as before.

As *Emden* was no longer a ship capable of fighting but a helpless wreck lying on a coral reef, I caused a white flag to be shown as a sign of the surrender of the residue of the crew and simultaneously the war ensign which was still flying at the maintop to be hauled down and burned, whereupon *Sydney* ceased fire.

Müller was very angry about the resumption of firing but is not totally logical about his reaction in his report, which was addressed to the Kaiser: the monarch was considering whether to confer Germany's highest award for gallantry, the Order *pour le Mérite*, on Müller later in the war. The captain wrote that he was not convinced by Glossop's case, when they met the next day. The Englishman had fired after twice sending, 'Do you surrender' and getting no answer. But the *Emden* had not been firing during the last stage of the battle just before she ran aground, says Müller, she was a wreck on the reef and her signal 'No signal-book' was a sign of readiness to negotiate. But he does not say whether Glossop's later requests by signal were received, understood or answered, without denying that any were sent. Given that his ship was *hors de combat*, should he not have hauled down his colours while the *Sydney* was away, after deliberately grounding the *Emden* to save what was left of her crew? Müller does not deal with this question: it could be deduced that he simply forgot to take down his ensign and was not disposed to admit it. Had he done so, he might not have needed the white flag. He wrote: 'I also had the impression that the affair was *very embarrassing* for Captain Glossop *afterwards* and that he had let his First Officer chiefly determine the action' (of reopening fire). The words in italics in the foregoing quotation were underlined by the Kaiser in red ink as he read Müller's report.

So concerned was Glossop on seeing the German war-flag still flying over a demonstrably crippled foe that he actually sat down and wrote his enemy a letter, which read as follows:

Sir,
I have the honour to request that in the name of humanity you now surrender your ship to me. In order to show how much I appreciate your gallantry, I will recapitulate the position.

(1) You are ashore, three funnels and one mast down and most guns disabled.

(2) You cannot leave this island, and my ship is intact.

In the event of your surrendering in which I venture to remind you is no disgrace but rather your misfortune [sic] I will endeavour to do all I can for your sick and wounded and take them to a hospital.

I have the honour to be,
Sir,
Your obedient Servant,
John Glossop
Captain

This remarkable missive was dated 9 November 1914 and written on Royal Australian Navy letterhead with the address, 'HMAS *Sydney*, at sea,' and addressed to 'The Captain, HIGMS *Emden*.'

In the late afternoon of the 9th, the *Sydney* sent one of the *Buresk*'s boats to the wreck with Sub-Lieutenant Fikentscher (captured on the *Buresk*) and a message. Glossop said he felt it necessary to go back to Direction Island to find out what the landing-party had done there and to round up prisoners. The ship would return the next day to pick up survivors. Müller doubted this because he expected Mücke to put up a fight. Fortunately the weather remained friendly for the beleaguered survivors on the ship and ashore.

'It was desirous,' wrote the almost literate Glossop, (who in fact was probably let down by an indifferent naval Writer) 'to find out the condition of cables and wireless station at Direction Island. On the passage over I was again delayed by rescuing another sailor (6.30 pm) and by the time I was again ready and approaching Direction Island it was too late for the night . . .' By the time he sent men ashore the next morning, there was not a German to be seen on the island, so 'I borrowed a doctor and two assistants and proceeded as fast as possible to *Emden*'s assistance.'

I sent an officer on board to see the captain, and in view of the large number of prisoners and wounded and lack of accommodation etc., in this ship and the absolute impossibility of leaving them where they were, he agreed that if I received his officers and men and all wounded, 'then as for such time as they remained in *Sydney*, they would cause no interference with ship or fittings, and would be amenable to the ship's discipline.'

The emissary was Lieutenant Garsia, who is said by secondary sources (but not by himself or by Müller or Glossop) to have handed over Glossop's unusual, and also by now irrelevant, invitation to surrender. Garsia approached Müller and saluted. 'You fought very well, sir,' the British lieutenant said. Müller, surprised, simply said, 'No,' and walked away. Garsia, still writing to his father, went on: 'Presently he came up to me and said, "Thank you very much for saying that, but I was not satisfied. We should have done better. You were very lucky in shooting away all my voice-pipes at the beginning."' (There appears to be some confusion here on Müller's, or more likely Garsia's, part – what was lost was the internal telephone system controlling the guns, for which voice-pipe communication had to be substituted.)

The lieutenant then went for a walk round the wreck. 'She is nothing but a shambles and the whole thing was most shocking.' Work began on rescuing the wounded from the forecastle; Garsia helped with the extremely delicate and difficult task of moving fifteen badly injured men into the bucketing boats. The men who had managed to swim to the island were left there overnight without water because by the time the *Emden* herself had been cleared of wounded, it was dark. 'I was the last to leave the *Emden*,' Müller wrote without comment. New fires had been deliberately and clandestinely started in the forward two-thirds of the ship on the reef which burned through the night without completing the work of destruction. The captain's gig took Müller to the *Sydney* despite his request to Garsia for no special treatment. Aboard the 5,600-ton cruiser some German officers made the allegation that Glossop had fired on a white flag; others did not agree. Garsia thought the German officers were of high calibre: 'Captain von Müller is a very fine fellow,' he wrote. They talked about the battle and the war: 'In fact we seemed to agree that it was our role to knock one another out, but there was no malice in it.'

During that night Dr. Schwabe died on the island of head injuries received on the coral as he swam across from the ship to help the men stranded there. The stern of the *Emden* was awash at high tide and was generally expected to disintegrate; only her excellent construction held her together. Some twenty men were rescued from the island after dawn the next day, the 11th, the dead were abandoned on the *Emden* and ashore, and the *Sydney* left after 10.30 a.m. Glossop's report concluded:

> I have great pleasure in stating that the behaviour of the ship's company was excellent in every way, and with such a large proportion of young hands and people under training it is all the more gratifying. The engines worked magnificently and higher results than trails were obtained, and I cannot speak too highly of the medical staff and arrangements on subsequent trip, the ship being nothing but a hospital of a most painful description.

Müller wrote:

> I believe I can state that in this battle too, which sadly led to the destruction of Your Majesty's light cruiser *Emden*, every officer, warrant officer, petty officer and rating under my command did his duty.

In the margin, in red ink, in the manner of the Kaiser's 'All-highest marginal observations,' is the single word, *Ja*.

There died for Kaiser and country aboard *Seiner Majestät Schiff Emden* on 9 November 1914, or of wounds subsequently, seven officers, one chief paymaster, four warrant officers, twenty-five petty officers, ninety-two ratings, one civilian cook, one civilian barber, and three Chinese laundrymen. Among the survivors were, seriously wounded, one warrant officer, three petty officers, and seventeen ratings; lightly wounded, two officers, two warrant officers, nine petty officers and thirty-one ratings. The captain, five other officers, five warrant officers, thirty-nine petty officers and sixty-seven ratings were unscathed. This represents a casualty rate of sixty-three per cent, and takes no account of the men detached to the colliers and the landing-party. Four of the dead expired from their wounds on the way to Colombo and were buried at sea with full naval honours. Glossop had the forethought to wireless ahead of his arrival on 15 November that *Sydney* should not be given the traditional greeting afforded to a victorious warship entering port. As Garsia put it, referring to the Germans' reaction to this:

> It quite shook them when they found out that the captain had asked that there be no cheering on entering Colombo, but we certainly

did not want cheering with rows of badly wounded men laid out in cots on the quarterdeck.

At Colombo an early visitor to the *Sydney* and her most honoured prisoner, Commander Karl von Müller, was the man who had spent more time searching for the *Emden* than anyone else: Captain Grant of the *Hampshire*. They amazed each other with the 'near misses' which prevented an encounter between them. The wounded were taken ashore to hospital; later forty-nine of them were taken to a prisoner-of-war camp in Australia. Those not wounded were transferred to the armed merchant cruiser *Empress of Russia* and were later redistributed among a number of transports, when the convoy reached Colombo soon after *Sydney*. Müller, Dr. Luther, Prince Franz Joseph von Hohenzollern, Sub-Lieutenant Fikentscher and thirty-two men were put aboard the *Orvieto*. The convoy set off for Suez on 17 November. At Suez on the 28th, after an insufferably cramped and hot voyage through the Red Sea, all the prisoners except those on the *Orvieto* were transferred to the *Hampshire*; the latter moved to the heavy cruiser only at Port Said the next day. In London there was some confusion about where they were to be imprisoned. Churchill wanted them brought to England, and an order to this effect was sent to *Hampshire*. Admiral Oliver, the new Chief of Staff, disapproved: 'There seems no object in bringing them to England, where the captain of *Emden* will be a nuisance, as all sorts of ill-balanced people will want to write to him and visit him,' he complained in a minute. But on the 28th, Field Marshal Lord Kitchener, Secretary of State for War, had already staked a prior claim by ordering the despatch of the prisoners to Malta. The 100 Australian officers and men guarding the Germans simply could not be spared to bring them all the way to England, whereupon transport would have to be found to take the troops back to the Middle East, where the forces the convoy had brought were to remain for the time being. When Churchill found out about this, he had the order to *Hampshire* appropriately countermanded, and she took the prisoners to Valletta. Captain Grant slept on a bunk in his chartroom to leave his cabins free for the *Emden* officers, now equipped with civilian clothes. They landed on 7 December and passed into the care of the British Army.

On the voyage into captivity, Müller wrote his third letter of the war to his parents in Blankenburg in the Harz Mountains, reflecting on the loss of his ship.

Although I am a fatalist, the awareness that the loss of the *Emden* would have been delayed had I behaved differently troubles me . . . You can imagine that for me it was no pleasant feeling that I had to come unhurt out of this battle in which my beautiful ship was destroyed, and in which so many of my crew lost their lives . . . I thought at first whether I should not seek a grave on my ship, but I had the duty to look after the rest of the crew first. I would not have helped my Fatherland in that way.

Müller said he had to fight because he knew at once that the enemy had the advantage of speed; he was also particularly upset by the death of his adjutant, Guérard:

I shall never forget the enthusiastic, combative look on his face when he saw that there was to be a battle. And I also lost my servant, the brave Zeidler . . . I am not quite sure how the running of the *Emden* onto the reef and the final surrender of the rest of the crew will be judged. But I believe that, faced with the same decision a second time, I would behave no differently under the same circumstances.

The infuriating thing about this letter is that it was written in full knowledge of the fact that it would be read by British officers before being forwarded. Even here there is no clue to the innermost workings of Müller's mind and the nature of the man, who reveals nothing of his inner self in anything known to have been written by him.

From the *Hampshire*, Müller was allowed to report briefly on his defeat and the attendant casualties to the German Admiralty, via, successively, the British Admiralty, the Foreign Office, the American Embassies in London, Copenhagen and Berlin, and the German Foreign Office! The Kaiser awarded Müller the Iron Cross, First and Second Class, and all *Emden* officers and fifty men from the crew, to be chosen by the captain, the Iron Cross, Second Class; in addition, Müller was awarded honorary citizenship of the towns of Emden and Blankenburg: all this was decided before the *Emden* undertook her last raid, but became known after the ship was destroyed.

It fell to the sloop HMS *Cadmus* (Commander H. D. Marryat) to bury the dead at North Keeling Island amid the 'appalling stench from decomposing bodies'. Surgeon G. D. G. Ferguson and four men removed them from the wreck 'working under the most objectionable circumstances'. Of the nine days in November spent in the vicinity of the wreck, they were able to board it only on two. They also buried the bodies on the beach of the island. 'The paymaster's chest was very difficult to get at owing to torn and twisted iron all around it. It appears to contain a certain number of dollars, all of which were melted,' Marryat reported to Jerram. A number of items from the few left aboard were taken from the *Emden* as mementoes for the proud new Australian navy to treasure; they can still be seen in the city of Sydney, where there is also a memorial to the ship that was named after it and brought the *Emden* to book.

Vice-Admiral Sir T. H. M. Jerram summarised all these events with understandable satisfaction in his own report to the Admiralty. He found time to commend the cable station personnel: 'The promptitude with which the officials of the Eastern Extension Telegraph Company acted when the emergency arose is deserving of the highest praise.'

As the survivors of the *Emden*'s last battle went into captivity, they could look back upon a voyage of 30,000 miles during which the engines had delivered ten million revolutions and the ship had burned more than 6,000 tons of coal and had coaled at sea eleven times, all since leaving Tsingtao on 6 August. They had sunk sixteen British merchantmen in the Indian Ocean, seized three colliers loaded with British coal and plundered two other British merchant ships before using them to release prisoners; they had sunk one Russian cruiser and one French destroyer; and as an *hors d'oeuvre* they had captured a Russian liner and converted her into an auxiliary cruiser. The official British valuation of the direct losses in shipping and cargo caused by the *Emden* produced a total bill of somewhat more than £2,000,000; the highest German estimate on record seems to be Lauterbach's, at a cool 250,000,000 marks (£12.5 million), not counting the cost of the damage at Madras. A realistic figure would lie in the region of £5,000,000, or about fifteen times the cost of building the *Emden*. To this must be added the intangibles: the panic, the embarrassment, the economic disruption, the rise in the cost of rice and other essentials in the Indian Ocean region, the effect on insurance, ship and troop movements and the fact that this one German cruiser had been sought unsuccessfully by a total of seventy-eight warships from four navies. Spee's orders to Müller had been carried out with panache and dedication. Müller and his men did not know this at the time, of course, but their celebratory Sunday on 1 November came in a most spectacular week for the German Navy. It was the day Spee destroyed Admiral Cradock's squadron in the Battle of Coronel; two days earlier, HMS *Chatham* had located the *Königsberg* in her coal-less refuge up the Rufiji River in East Africa

119

(the attempt to destroy her from the sea was abandoned by the British only in January 1915 after the most extraordinary efforts); just three days later, the third and last of the independent light cruisers, the *Karlsruhe*, blew up and sank off Barbados, having captured 17 ships worth £781,996 by British valuation. This was and remains the most glorious chapter in the brief history of German seapower, and the *Emden* had made an outstanding contribution to it. The High Seas Fleet could not breach the British Grand Fleet's blockade which proved Germany's undoing; the infinitely more deadly German submarine campaign, which might have won the war, was not pursued ruthlessly enough to finish the British before it irritated the Americans sufficiently to bring them into the war on the Allied side, whereon their belated military contribution soon became the last straw. All this (and the invention of radar) leaves the *Emden* with the distinction of being the most successful undisguised commerce-raiding surface warship, or cruiser, of modern times. Her achievement was a remarkable individual *tour de force* in the history of the war at sea. It was undoubtedly good for German morale, but that commodity was far from being in short supply at this spectacularly successful stage of the war for the German armies on the eastern and western fronts in Europe.

The legend of the 'Gentleman-of-war' provided by the *Emden* and her resourceful captain was of greatest benefit to Germany as propaganda. On 29 October 1914, an unnamed French naval officer told the Penang correspondent of the *New York Times*, one day after the *Emden*'s shattering raid on the port with the loss of forty-five French lives: 'Well, he [Müller] "played the game" and he has made me, for one, feel extremely doubtful whether the much talked-of German "atrocities" are true, except where the exigencies of war have made them unavoidable.' It is entirely possible that the source was Commander Audemard. Even Churchill was moved to say of Müller, 'He did his duty,' and he personally ordered that the men of the *Emden* be afforded the honours of war if taken. The British press went so far as to mourn the ship's destruction and to celebrate Müller's survival. The *Daily News*, the *Daily Telegraph* and even *The Times* vied with each other in the fulsomeness of their editorials. The ultimate achievement of Müller's *Emden* was to counter, for a while, the hatred of Germany understandably and reasonably aroused by the conduct of the German Army in Belgium. Civilian hostages were taken there and shot in thousands in reprisals for acts of defiance by *francs-tireurs* and others who unaccountably took violent exception to the invasion of their country. The rape of Belgium culminated in the systematic destruction by arson of the city of Louvain and its irreplaceable ancient library by drunken German soldiers on the orders of their generals in the last week of August 1914. The press of the neutrals and of Germany's enemies alike at that time sang a tune rather different from the one they adopted in assessing the career of a single ship on the fringe of the war. The same Rules of War which permitted Müller to use a British flag at Penang also said that 'War cannot be conducted merely against the fighting men of an enemy state but must seek to destroy the total material and spiritual resources of the enemy'. While German statesmen put their signatures to the conventions that sought to contain the horrors of war, German officers were being taught in academies and staff colleges that terror was a legitimate weapon of war in order to shorten it: Clausewitz said so. It was the Kaiser who first used the word 'Hun' to refer to his own people in arms; Belgium made it a pejorative term which was carefully not applied to Müller, any more than it would have been applied to Luther, Goethe or Frederick the Great. The German conundrum lay in the distance between A and B, when A is Attila and B is Beethoven, a distance even greater than that between Belgium and the Bay of Bengal in autumn 1914. Anyone seeking an assessment of Müller's service to his country need look no further.

PART II

ESCAPE TO GERMANY

One crowded hour of glorious life
Is worth an age without a name.
Thomas Mordaunt,
Verses Written During the War, 1756–1763

10

SMS *AYESHA* – THE KAISER'S SMALLEST WARSHIP

'Beg to report, landing party numbering three officers, six petty officers and forty-one men disembarking,' First Officer Hellmuth von Mücke had said, standing to attention before Captain von Müller on the quarterdeck of the *Emden* at 6.30 a.m. on Monday, 9 November 1914. The men were still arranging themselves in two cutters along-side as he spoke and as the cruiser's steam pinnace was prepared for lowering into the water to tow them into Port Refuge. Their orders: to destroy the wireless transmitter, disable the cable station and seize all available intelligence material such as codes and signal books. As the Germans had assumed that such an important communications junction would be under some kind of guard, the vast majority of the small arms aboard the cruiser had been distributed among the strong landing party, including all four Maxim machine guns. Two of these were in the pinnace and one each in the cutters; each gun had 2,000 rounds of rifle ammunition already loaded into belts and ready for use. Twenty-nine of the men had standard German Army issue bolt-action Mauser rifles and bayonets and sixty rounds per weapon. The officers and seven of the senior ratings each had a Mauser parabellum pistol with twenty-four rounds. The officers also had their swords. The ratings wore tropical white uniforms with khaki solar topis, while the officers had white topis and khaki tunics. Even though they expected to be on Direction Island for only about two hours, they took with them the Kaiser's white naval ensign with the black cross, the eagle in the centre and the black, white and red flag of the Reich, embellished with the Iron Cross, in the top left-hand corner. Thus prepared with typical thoroughness for all eventualities except the one which eventually happened, the detachment, as we shall now refer to it, drew up alongside the wooden jetty at Direction Island about 3,000 yards from the *Emden*. They saw the *Ayesha*, and on the way in noted the sun-awning over her deck suggesting she was occupied. There being no sign of life aboard the white-hulled schooner, however, they did not pause.

As they approached, they saw a generally flat island thick with coconut palms. The roofs of one or two buildings could be seen among the trees, and towering over all was the mast of the wireless station, which they used as a landmark. Passing the schooner, Mücke was asked by his two subordinate officers, Sub-Lieutenants Roderich Schmidt and Eugen Gyssling from the *Gneisenau*, whether they were also to destroy her. 'Of course,' he answered. 'She's sailed for the last time. Detail a man now to have explosive charges ready.' Mücke intended to sink the little ship on the way back to the cruiser. The detachment landed without challenge or sighting anyone and the men ran in the direction of the mast, by which they found the wooden buildings of the station in a small cluster. Dividing into three sections, each led by an officer, the Germans stormed the wireless hut and the cable station and began to search the surrounding area and bungalows. No resistance was offered and no panic shown. Mücke buttonholed one of the Britons and told him in strongly accented but confident English to go and fetch 'the director'.

Mr. Farrant, the manager, duly came to the spot where Mücke stood. He seemed to be fully in command of himself. The German officer said: 'I have orders to destroy the wireless and telegraph station. I warn you not to resist. Further, it is in your interest to give me the keys to the individual buildings at once, to save me having to open the doors by force. All firearms in your possession are to be given up at once. All Europeans are to assemble on the square in front of the telegraph building.'

Mr. Farrant produced a large bunch of keys from his pocket and said there would be no resistance. He then offered Mücke his congratulations. The German stared.

'What for?'

'For the Iron Cross. The Reuter message came through a short while ago.' Farrant mentioned the mass award of the decoration to the *Emden*. At this stage of the war, an Iron Cross still meant something; later, as Barbara Tuchman recounts in her *August 1914*, it became possible for a cynical Austrian to remark that the only way a German could avoid the Iron Cross, Second Class, was by suicide. On this occasion, the Captain had been awarded the Cross First and Second Class, all the officers the Second Class, and a further fifty Second Class Crosses were to be awarded at the Captain's discretion. One begins to see what the Austrian meant: what if there had been only forty-nine gallant men among the crew? Worse, what if there had been fifty-one? But *Emden II*, when she was launched in 1916, and even *Emden III*, launched in 1925, bore the Iron Cross at the bow like no other German ships before or since. Mücke at least was very moved and proud. It was the Kaiser himself who cheapened his own awards.

Meanwhile, working flat out, the Germans completed their work of destruction. They even smashed the station seismometer. Any papers with writing on them, including newspapers and books, were bundled into sacks. A corrugated iron hut with some spare parts and other equipment in it was blown up. The cutting of the cables took much longer than expected and indirectly saved the men's lives.

When the lookout posted on a rooftop told Mücke that the *Emden*'s signal lamp had passed the message, 'Speed up work,' the First Officer gave the order to return to the boats and decided to give up the idea of sinking the schooner for lack of time. Piling weapons and captured papers into their boats and not forgetting their flag, the detachment's fifty men scrambled into the cutters and the pinnace slowly began to tow them away from the jetty. The *Emden* was already pulling clear and soon began positively to race away to northwards, hoisting her colours as she went. The men in the boats speculated feverishly about what was happening as they gave up the chase. Perhaps the cruiser had sighted a tempting merchantman and rushed off in pursuit. But as they put about to head back to the jetty, they heard the first broadside from her guns. Something serious was obviously afoot, more serious than anything so far encountered on the war cruise: the only other broadsides fired had been the planned ones against Madras and Penang.

So the detachment made its second, unplanned landing on Direction Island. The German ensign was run up the flagpole and Mücke told the station staff that they were under German martial law, warning them not to attempt to send any kind of signal. In the event of a landing from a victorious enemy ship Mücke intended to resist, though what he thought he could gain by such a course he never made clear. He agreed to Farrant's request for permission to move his staff to another island in the event of such a fight. The Germans were in no doubt that their ship was hardly likely to emerge the victor: it was clear that the enemy was a superior cruiser. Soon the lighter crack and boom of the *Emden*'s guns became not only fainter but also more intermittent. Grief and fear clutched at the marooned sailors of the German detachment as it dawned on them that they would most probably never see their ship again. They also knew that their presence on the island must be known: they had caught the operators in the act of telling the world. The *Emden*'s opponent or some other enemy ship might arrive at any time.

The choice appeared to lie between death in a hopeless battle against a British landing on the island – even if they beat off the inevitable attack, the enemy ship's guns would determine the final outcome – or resignation and an honourable surrender in the face of overwhelmingly superior force. The resourceful opportunist Mücke rejected both and fixed his gaze upon the white schooner lying in the harbour. Without discussing what was in his mind with anyone at first, he had the steam pinnace take him over to the *Ayesha*, which he boarded alone. His excuse for going was to see if the ship had arms aboard. On the schooner he found her master, Captain J. Partridge, and one seaman. Also aboard were Edmund and Cosmo Clunies Ross, sons of the owner of the islands. Mücke brought the four men back with him on the pinnace to join the other prisoners ashore. He then told Farrant he had no choice but to commandeer half the rations. He punctiliously took down the address of the telegraph company's office in Singapore and promised to try to get word to it to have the food replaced.

It was clear to the station staff that the German commander planned to make a run for it before the British cruiser arrived. They tried to dissuade him, saying that the schooner was old and rotten, her pumps were defective and she was no longer seaworthy. Mücke's brief tour of the ship led him to believe that the British were exaggerating, and considering that the *Ayesha* was only eight years old at the time, he was understandably dismissive of the warnings. The German sailors set about making the little schooner ready for sea. The island was stripped of potentially useful items and the staff even offered gifts of pipes, tobacco and other comforts, as well as advice on local climatic conditions and the best course to sail, which turned out to be usefully accurate. As some of the sailors brought the stores down to the wooden jetty, others loaded them into the cutters and transferred them to the schooner, a process which consumed most of the rest of the day. A cheerful camaraderie and unabashed fraternisation between the marooned Germans and their prisoners for a day developed rapidly, and they lunched together. The British were captives, but they knew they would soon be free and that they were in no danger from their honourable captors; the Germans' weapons gave them command of the island and all it contained for the time being, but they knew they might not get away at all, and that if they did their flight might be short-lived before the Royal Navy caught them. It was an amiable stalemate, and for the British it became something of a sporting occasion and a most absorbing interruption of the isolated routine in a tropical outpost of Empire. The Germans seemed filled with the infectious enthusiasm and determination of their leader, and their natural fears for the fate of their ship took second place to the will to defy the odds and escape.

Finally, as the sun dipped towards the horizon, all was as ready as it ever would be. The British brought out their cameras again as the Germans got into the two cutters and the pinnace for the last time and moved out towards the *Ayesha*. The rowing boats were made fast to her stern while the pinnace took station ahead of her, ready to tow her out into the open sea. The war flag was run up on His Imperial German Majesty's latest and tiniest warship, SMS *Ayesha*, and Mücke himself climbed up her foremast with a bosun's whistle to signal to the pinnace any alterations of course the reefs and shallows round about might make necessary. As the small steamboat took up the tow, the German sailors and the British station staff exchanged three cheers in the brief gloaming. There was just enough light left to complete the passage out of harbour, even though Mücke had to come down to deck level on the port side to be able to look for obstacles below the surface. In the few moments between the near-equatorial sunset and darkness, he could see every rock and tendril of vegetation on the shallow bottom, but the schooner passed through the offshore surf without incident until they were on the open sea. The sails began to fill and the pinnace was allowed to slip back alongside so that her crew could come aboard, a manoeuvre made difficult by a strong swell. The vessel was allowed to drift off to her fate and was never seen again. The two cutters remained in tow.

While still ashore, Mücke had speculated aloud in the hearing of Farrant and his staff about the idea of crossing the Indian Ocean and making for German East Africa, but he had no such intention. He calculated that the *Emden* might well have lost her fight, but that she might still just escape total destruction and seek internment in the Dutch East Indies, where her casualties could be attended to. So, as the *Emden* had so frequently done in the past, the *Ayesha* steered a deceptive westerly course until Mücke was certain that she could not be seen from land, and then turned north-eastwards. He hoped, though not very strongly, that he might run across the *Buresk*, but in vain. In the Dutch East Indies, his choice of destination lay between Batavia (now Jakarta) to the north-east and Padang, due north. To reach the former he would have to negotiate the Sunda Strait between Sumatra and Java, a passage likely to be closely watched by the enemy, whereas Padang lay on the south-west coast of Sumatra and could be approached from the open sea, even if it was considerably further away. In the end, wind and swell took over. The south-east monsoon and the equatorial current together drove the slow-moving little sailing ship more or less due north, towards Padang willy nilly. The ship lacked a chronometer journal, the chronometers were wrongly set and therefore there was no means of calculating longitude for navigation purposes. It was in any case a good idea to go north in order to reach the area of the north-west monsoon which should blow at this time of year around the 8° southerly latitude mark.

During the first night at sea there was trouble with the two cutters still in tow. They persistently struck each other, and despite the long tow-line hit the *Ayesha* from astern because the schooner was travelling so slowly. Considerable damage was being done. 'The ship seemed to be pretty rotten,' said Mücke in his *Ayesha* journal. So one of the two boats was cast adrift. The rest of the explosives they had taken to the island for demolition purposes, some of which they had intended to use to destroy the *Ayesha*, were thrown overboard. Every inch of space was needed, and there was nowhere cool enough to store them at a safe temperature.

The first day at sea was spent putting the little ship in order to reduce discomfort for the fifty men aboard to a minimum. The sailors were divided into two watches, each under a sub-lieutenant. There was crew space for just five men aboard, so the rest slept in the hold while the petty officers crowded into the navigation cabin aft. The officers used two tiny cabins built into the deckhouse, with the chartroom as their mess. Information from a nautical almanac found aboard and some careful dead reckoning enabled the officers to guess a setting for the chronometer accurate enough to be of use. Strict rationing of food and the four weeks' supply of fresh water taken from Direction Island was instituted, with petty officers appointed to supervise distribution. The officers examined the ship's bottom carefully from inside and found that it was tolerably seaworthy. The pumps were in usable condition and were able to keep the hull dry on two pumpings a day. The rigging and the larger sails were discovered to be in good condition, although many of the smaller sails were worn and weak.

11

SS *CHOISING* TO THE RESCUE

The few charts aboard covered only the route from the Cocos Islands to Batavia which the schooner used to ply, so the Germans had to make do with a small-scale general chart. Also found were an old sailing handbook containing information going back to the latter half of the eighteenth century, a nautical yearbook, a patent log for measuring distance travelled and a sextant. The latter two items were put to immediate use.

Depending on the wind, the *Ayesha* seemed to make between three and eight knots, sometimes a fraction more, with maximum permissible sail. When it rained, every conceivable receptacle was used to catch the rainwater – pots and pans, the ship's scuppers and life-boats, spare sails, the deckhouse roof – while the crew took alfresco showers and washed their clothes. They never lacked for water aboard the schooner as a result. The weather in this region close to the Equator proved hopelessly erratic, and the detachment experienced squalls, calms, storms, breezes, sun and rain at unpredictable intervals, sometimes almost all of them on the same day. The crew were unused to sail but the officers had had sail-training and the hard work of hoisting and lowering sail, sometimes several times in a day, soon went smoothly. Progress was slow, slower still when the currents worked against them and they had to pile on sail to stay in the same place. On quiet days the crew were taught all aspects of sailing a ship. Mücke led a religious service from time to time when the weather permitted. On 21 November a ship's smoke cloud was seen, but the vessel stayed below the horizon. The *Ayesha* was becalmed in the doldrums and could do nothing about it. Later the same day a strong north-easterly wind got up and they thought they were being picked up by the north-west monsoon, but it was not the steady monsoon wind that they had been hoping for. A storm blew up, and for fifty minutes the Germans watched a breath-taking display of sheet lightning, the like of which none of them had seen before.

131

Mücke, meanwhile, had firmly decided to make for Padang come what may. He knew there was a German consul of German nationality, a professional foreign service officer, stationed there, a certain Herr Schild; his two sub-lieutenants had been there and knew their way around; there were German ships there, perhaps including the modern steamer *Kleist* with a top speed of 17 knots; and the *Ayesha* was not known in Padang, whereas she was in Batavia, the only practical alternative. The one real advantage the latter harbour, serving the Dutch colonial capital, had to offer was the German naval *Etappe*, and for all he knew it could have been wound up. So Padang it had to be, and on 23 November land was sighted for the first time since leaving Direction Island. Mücke calculated that this must be one of the islands strung out in a long chain parallel to the south-west-facing coast of the great island of Sumatra. He guessed it was the island of Siberoet (now Siberut) and decided to go ashore to investigate and get a precise navigational 'fix' of their position at last. Having long since cut loose the second cutter from the *Emden* because it was taking in water and slowing them down, the Germans went ashore in one of the *Ayesha*'s little boats. All the detachment's weapons were made ready in case of trouble. 'I intended,' Mücke wrote matter-of-factly in the *Ayesha* journal, 'should I come across an enemy destroyer lying at anchor or coaling etc, to go along-side to board (her).' Having established that he had found Siberoet and precisely where he was, Mücke knew Padang lay almost exactly due east on the Sumatran mainland. On the 24th they passed into the Seaflower Channel between Sumatra and its flanking islands without sighting anything indicating human activity. That evening the patent log showed the Germans that they had been sailing for 800 miles. The next day gave them a view of the Sumatran coast. They had to proceed with extreme care in case of hidden hazards of the kind shown only on a proper, full-scale chart.

On 26 November both lifeboats were lowered and manned to tow the *Ayesha* towards the tantalising shore, from which the adverse current was driving them slowly away. There was hardly a breath of wind to help them. While this was going on, a flag, a mast and finally the hull of a ship became visible from the schooner. Eventually the vessel was identified as the Royal Dutch Navy's destroyer *Lynx*, which permitted herself a detailed examination of the schooner, particularly the stern, where the raised letters of her name could be made out under a coat of fresh paint. The *Lynx* then withdrew to a distance of nearly three miles, turned and followed at the snail's pace set by the Germans. 'Apparently the schooner was expected,' Mücke wrote. Nearly all the Germans stayed below deck. They had their war-flag ready but did not hoist it. The Dutch destroyer eventually vanished, but reappeared after dark, revealing her presence by the signal lamp with which she was conversing with an unseen ship or shore-station. Then she switched on her navigation lights and resumed her following position. The *Ayesha* signalled by lantern in English and German, 'Why are you following?' which was acknowledged but not answered by the Dutchman, who carried on as before, eventually taking up a position ahead and to one side of the schooner's agonisingly slow approach to land. Calculating that he was by now inside Netherlands territorial waters Mücke, on the morning of the 27th, raised the Kaiser's ensign. A pilot boat was sighted and Mücke accepted pilotage (for a fee of twenty-five guilders). The *Lynx* suddenly put on a turn of speed and came up close to the schooner. German sailors summoned by pipe stood to attention along the port side as Mücke, with his usual punctilio, had the ensign dipped in salute. The Dutch ship returned the salute. Mücke then signalled his intention of paying a call on the destroyer. In full uniform with sword, he went aboard by means of one of the *Ayesha*'s boats to explain to the Dutch captain his plan to enter the Padang harbour of Emmahaven. The captain said he had orders to escort the schooner into port, where the civil authorities would take over: there was no objection to the Germans entering harbour, and the captain assumed they would be staying. 'I replied that I was a warship and said jokingly that I hoped we would not come to blows with one another when I left,' Mücke recorded.

The Dutch captain at first gave the impression that he knew nothing of the fate of the *Emden*, but later in the conversation he thought better of it and told Mücke the bad news he had been half-expecting to hear. Having dropped anchor at the harbour mouth, Mücke awaited the visit from the harbourmaster which he had requested through the Dutch destroyer. Sub-Lieutenant Schmidt accompanied this official ashore to call upon the Dutch 'neutrality officer' whose task it was to secure strict observance of regulations on treatment of belligerents on Dutch territory. Mücke's message to this functionary was that he desired to enter harbour on grounds of emergency at sea, namely the deteriorating condition of the ship and need of food and fresh water; as soon as these matters had been dealt with he would set out to sea again. Meanwhile, he would like to see the German consul. That evening Mücke accepted an invitation to dine aboard the Dutch gunboat *Assahan* with the captain, from whom he learned nothing new. All evening the *Ayesha* was surrounded by ships' boats from German steamers in the harbour, which brought gifts, beer, spare clothes, written greetings and even laudatory poems – and the long-missed German newspapers, welcome even though they were very old by now. Nobody was allowed aboard the schooner in case her position were compromised.

But at 9 a.m. on the 28th the Dutch told Mücke that his ship would be treated as a prize. The ensuing row lasted all day, with the Dutch neutrality officer, a naval lieutenant-captain, sympathetic but the harbourmaster, a Belgian by birth, doing his best for his embattled mother-country by trying to strangle the Germans in red tape. Mücke, supported by his two sub-lieutenants and eventually the visiting Consul Schild, insisting on the legitimacy of the *Ayesha* as a commissioned warship, demanded the right to spend twenty-four hours in Dutch waters and then to leave. All the Dutch officials, including the Admiral commanding naval forces in the East Indies who sent a telegram from Batavia, tried to persuade the Germans to stay and go into internment. There were Japanese warships in the vicinity; there was nowhere for the Germans to run to; they had done enough aboard the *Emden* and on their own account to satisfy the most demanding considerations of honour. Meanwhile, the harbourmaster was still doing everything he could to deny the Germans anything that would 'strengthen their military potential', including even soap, clothes and nautical reference books and charts. Mücke, as might be expected, stuck to his guns, insisted that only a superior German officer could order him to give up his intentions and eventually demanded direct, secret contact by telegraph with Berlin to settle the matter. The Dutch gave in and let him have his supplies. Herr Schild slipped Mücke such currency as he had, including 190 marks, £7 10s and 200 French francs, despite the closest Dutch supervision. Schild and Mücke secretly agreed on a rendezvous point out at sea, to be written on a slip of paper and passed later to one of the German steamers in harbour, which was to be asked to keep station there (3°20′ S, 99°20′ E, roughly 200 nautical miles SSW of Padang) until 20 December, and wait for the *Ayesha*.

At 8 p.m. Mücke gave the order to weigh anchor. One of the steam-powered launches sent with supplies of food gave the schooner a tow towards the harbour mouth from her isolated anchorage well away from the quays. The food aboard included ten live pigs and many other items which promised an improvement on the monotonous diet of the past three weeks. Just before 9.30 as the towline was cast off by the harbour mouth, the German sailors lined the deck and cheered the consul, who had come on the launch to see them off. They sang *Die Wacht am Rhein* on parting and vanished into the darkness. At 2.30 the following morning, the 29th, they were hailed by a rowing boat, from which Reserve Sub-Lieutenant R. Willmann and Leading Machinist's Mate R. Schwaneberger, also of the naval reserve, came aboard to offer their services. They had been aboard the German steamship *Rheinland* in Padang. Mücke felt free to take them aboard as they were now all outside Dutch territorial waters. But on the following day, 30 November, they were back in Dutch waters, as they once again passed close to Siberoet – by design. The Germans had seen two warships exchanging signals by lamp in the early hours and went close into shore in case they were hostile. But they were Dutch: one of them was the East Indies flagship, *De Zeven Provincieën*, a small battleship, which escorted them at a distance until, later into the morning, the Germans were once again on the open sea and clear of Dutch possessions. The detachment was in fine fettle, despite confirmation of the fear that the *Emden* was lost and the undiminished uncertainty of the fifty-two men now aboard the *Ayesha*. The schooner sailed south.

The Royal Navy and its allies in the Far East were no less vigilant in their search for the *Ayesha* than they had been for the *Emden*. So high was the reputation of the crew of the destroyed cruiser that it was widely assumed that the tiny, two-masted schooner stolen by her landing-party would seek to carry on the fight, even though the *Ayesha* would have needed a tow from a tug to catch up with the slowest steamer afloat. Admiral Jerram's General Letter number 32 to the Admiralty, dated 17 December 1914, warned: 'She is a menace to trade until captured.' By that stage of course the British were aware that the schooner had passed in and out of Padang. This explains the change of tune from Jerram's previous General Letter of 27 November, which reported the details of the elimination of the *Emden*. The *Ayesha* 'may never be heard of again . . . I am informed that she makes four feet of water a day when sailing, and that both her pumps are out of order.' The British consuls-general in Manila and Batavia were asked by Jerram to press for the internment of Mücke's detachment should it appear in their areas of responsibility. Jerram heard on 2 December of *Ayesha*'s call at Padang and sent two armed merchant cruisers, *Empress of Japan* and *Himalaya*, to scour the long south-west coast of Sumatra for the schooner and the missing collier *Exford*.

In his December letter, Jerram reported that the French destroyers *Fronde* and *Pistolet* 'still remain at Penang for the defence of the harbour'. Very faintly in the margin of the top copy in British

Admiralty records is the neatly pencilled and sardonic query, 'against what?' Jerram's remark is odd, since every German ship which could have posed a threat to Penang or anywhere else in the Far East was now accounted for. The *Ayesha* was not, but even the cautious Jerram could, on reflection, hardly have believed that she threatened anything on any coast.

The schooner's southward progress to the rendezvous point, left with Consul Schild for forwarding to a German steamer among those in Padang, was painfully slow, through the unhelpfully variable and unreliable weather typical of the equatorial regions of the Indian Ocean. The log of the *Ayesha*'s last voyage is extremely laconic, often with only a couple of lines per day. But the entry for 9 December 1914 is expansive and significant: it concerns the sole recorded occasion on which she was sighted at sea after she left Direction Island. It reads:

At dawn, steamer in sight. Course was held on her, however no flag shown. When the steamer sighted the schooner, she suddenly turned away sharply and ran in a large, unnecessary curve round the schooner. Machine guns and rifles on deck. Clear for action. Signal: 'request longitude.' Reply: '99°22'.' The steamer added: 'Show your distinguishing signal.' The *Ayesha* hoisted a random distinguishing signal 'HBCZ' with obscured flags so much hidden behind sails that the steamer could see nothing. Who the steamer was could not be made out. She then sailed out of sight. Light winds during the day. All sails set.

Mücke wrote his log on cream notepaper supplied by the steamer *Kleist* in Padang at his request. The paper naturally bore that ship's letterhead, and it is to be seen in the German archives. Mücke's choice of stationery led to an amusing error eventually. His account of the *Ayesha* escapade was forwarded by mail to Germany by the captain of the ship which was to take the detachment on the next stage of its long trek home, and was promptly used for propaganda purposes. The publicity eventually led the British Admiralty to send out the following misleading message to its intelligence officers in the Far East and the Australian Navy Board in Melbourne on 23 January 1915: 'German press states that the schooner *Ayesha* is now called *Kleist*'! Even at that stage the whereabouts of the missing residue of the *Emden* was causing acute anxiety. Mücke's request to the steamer on the 9th for the longitude, which he now knew with complete accuracy, having sorted out his navigation instruments in Padang, was intended to give an impression of the carelessness common among small sailing ships on short voyages. No steamer would be surprised by such a query. In his December letter, Jerram records being informed that a British steamer, which he does not name, had sighted a sailing vessel which conformed closely with the description of the *Ayesha* that had been circulated to all friendly merchantmen. She had been spotted at 6 a.m. at a spot 3°24′ S, 99°38′ E, steering eastward. The schooner was said to have wireless (untrue) and to have failed to show her recognition sign when asked.

Mücke had approached the steamer because he was close enough to the secret rendezvous to have reason to hope that she had come to his relief: he did not know what ship to expect. It was only on Monday, 14 December that a new sighting was made, of a steamer, at 1.40 p.m. The ship disappeared an hour later – the *Ayesha* having failed to get close enough by tacking. At 3.20 p.m. when the ship hove in sight again, Mücke piled on sail. She was the German collier *Choising* (Captain F. Minkwitz): 'Fired red and white double star [from signal-pistol],' says *Ayesha*'s log. 'Steamer turned towards schooner which had set war-flag. Steamer showed German flag. It was *Choising*. First aim of *Emden* landing-crew was achieved.' The actual point of contact was 3°23′ S, 99°28′ E, quite within a reasonable margin of error (even today a meeting between ships at a predetermined point at sea is no simple matter). Now the weather proved unhelpful again – it was too rough to transfer from the schooner to the steamer. The *Ayesha* therefore ran before the fresh wind and the *Choising* followed. At daybreak on the 15th the *Choising* signalled that she was unable to maintain her course in the strong-running swell and what had become a force nine gale. They agreed a new rendezvous and took the risk of parting again. The weather chopped and changed between calm and strong winds overnight. At 8.40 a.m. the two ships sighted each other once more, and within two hours the steamer took the sailer in tow to a position to the leeward of the Palai Islands (south-west of Sumatra and due south of Padang) but out of sight of land. Everything worth keeping was transhipped while a handful of ratings bored holes in the *Ayesha*'s hull to hasten her sinking. She duly went down at 4.48 that afternoon, 1,709.6 nautical miles showing on her patent log – the distance the battered little vessel had covered since the Germans commandeered her at Direction Island. Her last voyage served to make her immortal. She was despatched with three rousing cheers from the deck of the *Choising*.

*

137

In transferring from the *Ayesha* to the *Choising*, the detachment soon discovered that it had exchanged a sponge for a firetrap. The new getaway vehicle was a small freighter of 1,657 tons with a, by now, theoretical maximum speed of ten and a half knots. She had been launched at Geestemünde in 1901 under the name *Madeleine Rickmers*, and was bought by North German Lloyd of Bremen in 1906 to ply in East Asian waters. At the end of July 1914, on the eve of war, she put into Singapore, hastily unloaded her cargo and put out to sea again on 1 August, three days before Britain entered the war, bound for Batavia. Captain Minkwitz first patrolled the steamer lanes off Singapore for a day to warn off any other German merchantmen that might appear, and duly arrived with one such at Batavia on 5 August. Minkwitz quietly delivered some confidential letters handed to him by German agents in Singapore. By the 15th, having taken on 1,000 tons of coal, shipbuilding materials and provisions, she anchored in the roads to avoid harbour dues, under orders to remain at the disposal of the local *Etappe*. But on 10 September smoke was seen rising from the coal from two of her holds, whether as a result of spontaneous combustion or of carelessness with a cigarette end was never established. The two holds were soaked in water and the fire appeared to be dead.

After the shelling of Madras on 22 September, Captain Müller wirelessed a message to the Batavia *Etappe* (it was relayed by the steamer *Ulm* which happened to pick it up), asking for a ship with 5,000 tons of coal and supplies for 400 men for three months to be sent to a point off the island of Simaloer by 1 October. Minkwitz was told on the 25th to go to the rendezvous and on the 27th, his papers cleared for Lourenço Marques (now Maputo) in Mozambique, he set sail, duly arriving on time. But during the voyage the cargo of coal started to burn a second time, much more seriously than at Batavia. A desperate battle ensued which Minkwitz could win only by filling the two affected holds to the brim with water, which left his little ship nearly eight feet down by the bow. Despite the difficulties occasioned by the consequential pumping operations the captain kept his ship on station, as work went on round the clock. On the morning of 8 October smoke started to come out of a third hold, which was flooded in turn; the next day the exhausted crew sighted a British warship in the middle distance which, however, did not sight them among the islets off Simaloer. Then a French coal tramp was sighted. Minkwitz thought the area was getting too lively and decided to move on, even though the smouldering was still intense in hold number three. He chose Padang as his emergency harbour and anchored off Emmahaven on 11 October. Two hours after the *Choising* lay safely at anchor, the crew saw the British heavy cruiser *Minotaur* pass by menacingly, just outside the three-mile limit. Minkwitz decided to pour water into all holds to a depth of five feet to prevent another outbreak of fire. Müller, as we know, had changed his plans and headed towards the Maldives long since.

The *Choising* stayed at Padang and saw the *Ayesha* arrive on 27 November and leave again just over twenty-four hours later. Early on the morning of the 29th, a messenger brought a note to Captain Minkwitz, who promptly set off by boat to see Consul Schild ashore. He was given the rendezvous point of 3°20′ S, 99°20′ E with a margin of error of twenty miles in any direction. On 7 December Minkwitz formally notified the astonished Dutch authorities of his intention to resume his voyage to Mozambique despite the fire damage. Two days later he entered the inner harbour to collect water. The authorities watched carefully to see to it that he took no more supplies aboard than were consistent with his own crew's needs for the advertised trip. But during the nights preceding the entry into port the *Choising* had been quietly stocking up with everything her captain could persuade his obliging colleagues on such ships as the *Kleist* and the *Rheinland* to spare him, in readiness for picking up the detachment. So, on the afternoon of 10 December, shadowed, and overshadowed, by the Dutch small battleship *Koningin Regentes*, which disappeared only the next day at first light, the *Choising* put to sea. The rendezvous point was reached that same afternoon. The *Choising* circled the appointed spot for the next five days until the *Ayesha* kept the tryst and the detachment was able to change ships. The fire-blackened collier dipped her flag in salute as the white schooner sank out of sight.

In her dreadful condition, the *Choising* could barely make eight knots. Mücke therefore decided, there being little choice in the matter, to try to reach the nearest friendly territory. This meant crossing the Indian Ocean in a north-westerly direction to Turkish-ruled Arab land. He could only hope that nothing hostile would be sighted on the way because the *Choising* could do nothing about it. But for the first few days of the tense crossing the collier bore a Dutch disguise, later exchanged for the livery of an Italian steamer, the *Shenir*, which resembled her rather more closely, according to the *Lloyd's Register of Shipping* aboard. The Germans kept well clear of the steamer lanes, and also of the areas of the Indian Ocean north of the Equator where bad weather was most likely to be encountered. The limping collier was in no condition to cope with anything untoward. Thus, steering a devious course, the *Emden* detachment crept across to the mouth of the Red Sea without sighting anything more alarming than the very occasional column of smoke in the distance which entailed a precautionary change of course. They reached the Perim Strait at the end of the first week in January. The detachment was now poised to make its third landing, two months after the first.

12

THE AMAZING ADVENTURES OF
JULIUS LAUTERBACH

Apart from the detachment landed on Direction Island, which had apparently vanished into the blue, the British were, for a long time after the destruction of the *Emden*, unable to account for another section of the cruiser's crew – the party aboard the captured British collier *Exford*. The *Sydney*, it will be recalled, had caught up with the *Buresk* after the battle, in time to watch the ship succumb to the scuttling action of the Germans; on 12 October the *Yarmouth* found the *Markomannia* and the *Pontoporos* off Simaloer, sank the former and eventually released the latter, taking the German sailors found on them prisoner.

The *Exford* had been sent away on the eve of the battle, 8 November, with instructions to wait for the cruiser until the end of the month off Socotra at the north-western end of the Indian Ocean. In command was Lieutenant of the Reserve Julius Lauterbach, erstwhile master with the Hamburg–America Line, erstwhile prize-officer and temporary navigation officer of SMS *Emden*. Under him was a scratch crew of 16 sailors. They carried out the first part of their orders without hearing from the cruiser or anyone else, and also without being sighted by a hostile ship. Stoically enduring the tedium of sailing slowly round the empty sea in circles off the Gulf of Aden, the crew was eventually reduced to a diet of potatoes. They spent some of their time boring holes in the sides of the ship below the waterline and plugging them, to be ready to scuttle her immediately if captured. With only smilingly uncomprehending Chinese seamen and rats for company, the Germans stuck it out until well into the first week of December. Just once, on hearing a sudden flurry of wireless traffic which may well have emanated from the Australian convoy, did they risk trying a call to the *Emden*. There was, needless to say, no reply of any kind. Finally, Lauterbach gave up the waiting game and ordered a course eastwards towards Sumatra. Müller had ordered him to seek a neutral harbour there in the event of no contact. The experienced merchant navy skipper headed without difficulty for Padang even though there were no relevant charts aboard, and arrived off the port on the 11th.

Meanwhile Admiral Jerram, having learned on the 2nd that the *Ayesha* had called at Padang a few days before, detached two armed merchant cruisers, the *Empress of Japan* and the *Himalaya*, to search the south-western coast of the island of Sumatra for the schooner and also for the missing collier. The *Empress of Japan* (Commander M. B. Baillie-Hamilton, RN), was passing south-west of Padang on the 11th when she sighted the *Exford* and sent a boarding party to investigate. The British reported that their position at the time was 25 miles SW of Padang; the Germans maintained that they had been inside Dutch waters when boarded. When Lauterbach complained to this effect to the British prize officer, he was told: 'Tell that to my Captain. I have orders to seize your ship.' And so it was. The 17 Germans were taken aboard the *Empress of Japan*, which took the *Exford* to Singapore to discharge her coal into Admiralty bunkers and handed the captives over for internment as prisoners of war.

Having digressed, we ought now to digress further and complete the story of Lauterbach's subsequent doings, even if it takes us out of chronological order. At this point a merchant marine captain with large appetites, a larger-than-life physique and manner and an unimpeachable claim to have done his duty for Kaiser and country might have been expected to bow gracefully before *force majeure* and accept the more than generous conditions of an honourable captivity with a respectful enemy. But Lauterbach was no more submissive than Mücke. There are many accounts of what followed, including some by the central figure himself. Lauterbach was a chronic teller of tall tales and could not resist embroidering on stories which would astonish even if stripped of all adjectives and exaggerations. The various versions conflict in detail but the main thrust of the story is strongly corroborated; Lauterbach, clearly a man with an inflationary memory, told one of his versions to the American author Lowell Thomas, who recounted it under his own name, but written in the first person as if straight from the pen of Lauterbach without so much as an 'as told to' on the title-page. This odd literary form must itself have added to the confusion over detail but no matter: there are enough documents in both the German and the British records to show that, while he frequently exaggerated – unnecessarily – for effect, Lauterbach was not lying.

The British ship clearly caught the Germans aboard *Exford* by surprise – they had no time to scuttle her, but did fiddle the compass to show false readings, causing her to run aground briefly on the way to Singapore. Baillie-Hamilton allowed Lauterbach to retain his sword, in keeping with Churchill's order that the men of the *Emden* should be afforded all the honours of war (it is remarkable that an officer temporarily detached from his ship to look after a prize should bother to take his sword, even if he was a German and even if the times were more formal). On arrival at Singapore on 15 December, the Germans were marched to Tanglin barracks, where they were cheered by their compatriots interned since the beginning of the war as enemy aliens. Lauterbach, the only officer among the new captives, was lodged in a three-room bungalow of more than adequate comfort. He was offered the alternative of living in a hotel but only on condition that he gave his parole that he would not try to escape, which he refused to do. On the 16th, a British general came to inspect the barracks and the prisoners from the *Emden*, who paraded smartly. On the 17th Lauterbach was taken to the headquarters of Admiral Jerram himself and explained to the British C-in-C, China, how the *Exford* had come to run aground; once again he refused to give his word that he would not try to escape.

Tanglin barracks were occupied by the Fifth Light Infantry, Indian Army, a regiment recruited from among the warlike Punjabis, but the soldiers were Moslems, not Sikhs. Lauterbach dealt with a Major Catton, whom he describes as the commanding officer. There were about 850 troops in the battalion, which was far from home and suffering from something of a decline in morale, partly no doubt from having to serve as prison guards. While conditions for Lauterbach and the middle-class German civilians were more than satisfactory, the same could not be said for those imposed on the lower ranks, such as Lauterbach's sailors. He and others complained repeatedly but little enough was done. The Germans noted that the British officers were hard on their Indian troops and liberal with punishments. But the thirty-seven-year-old seadog was allowed to order tropical suits from a local tailor and to buy delicacies from a shop-owning friend. He even acquired a few yellowing and dog-eared German newspapers.

Soon the big buccaneer's thoughts turned to escaping. Among the Germans already in the camp was Second Officer Johann Merckl from the good old *Markomannia*. He, two German civilians and a loyal local servant of one of them joined Lauterbach in starting work on a tunnel on 27 January 1915, the birthday of the German Emperor. Lauterbach persuaded a lady who mysteriously came all the way from Shanghai to look him up, a woman of half Chinese, half French extraction, to smuggle some maps to him and organise a local boatman to meet the escapers on or about 23 February with a view to crossing the Strait of Singapore, to the islands on the other side which were part of the Dutch East Indies. The rumbustious mariner was crafty enough to befriend several of his Punjabi guards. He learned they were due to leave for France on 16 February, a fact which did nothing for their morale, and he did his best to fan their smouldering anti-British sentiment into the flames of open revolt, assisted by his acolytes among the Germans in the camp. His efforts were rewarded on a scale even he had not envisaged on 15 February, when the troops ran riot. They shot and bayoneted as many of their British officers and NCOs as they could find. Lauterbach consistently claimed to have fomented the mutiny, which was a thoroughly nasty affair that was no less hastily put down by other units. The British did not disagree. After his escape that night, they eventually put a price of £1,000 on Lauterbach's head, twice as much as they put on Mücke's.

Abandoning the fifty-foot-long tunnel out of the barracks dug by his escape team with some relief (its diameter had been dictated by his bulk), Lauterbach declined the invitation of the mutineers to lead them – he says they chaired him round the camp on their shoulders – and led a total of sixteen Germans out into the darkness at 8 p.m., through a hole in the fence of corrugated iron and barbed wire. Six of them became separated in the night and were eventually rounded up by the British. Uproar surrounded the Germans as they stole away. As Jerram telegraphed the Admiralty on the 16th: 'Right wing of the Fifth Light Infantry mutinied . . . murdered some officers and European civilians . . . fighting going on intermittently . . . situation serious but hope it is now in hand.' Sailors and marines helped in the suppression. Two days later he wired: 'Rather more than half of Fifth Light Infantry surrendered, captured or killed . . . sixteen German prisoners escaped, six of whom reported to be with rebels . . .' By the 27th he could report that the six Germans had been recaptured while the remainder had escaped to the Dutch islands.

They did so by heading westward to the coast, where they bought two dugout canoes from local people and took to the sea in the Malacca Strait after midnight. They lay flat as searchlights reached out towards them, and after a fourteen-hour journey south-westwards reached the island of Karimon off the coast of Sumatra. There they hired a sampan and sailed on to Sumatra itself, up the estuary of the Kampar River looking for a Dutch official to whom to report. A customs officer put them up for two days. They continued their journey by dugout, two men to a canoe, across the largest island in the Dutch East Indies, along beautiful streams and through the enchanting territory of a local sultan for whose benefit they sang, *Deutschland, Deutschland über Alles*. They had to seek shade during the appallingly humid heat of the day between breakfast-time and evening, when movement was impossible. Even though their journey, on foot as well as on water, took them through this cloying climate and over mountains and other rough terrain, Lauterbach

144

shed only five and a half pounds in weight. Meeting alternately with hostility and helpfulness from the Dutch officials they came across, they pursued their march ever north-westwards until they reached Payakombo. From there they completed their journey to Padang overland by rail on 5 March 1915.

At Padang, Lauterbach learned that the reward for his capture now stood at £600 (it had been lower and was to increase later). He reported to the Dutch authorities, and eventually a district court ruled that he should be allowed his freedom locally, pending a ruling from the Netherlands, which had been officially requested by the British to hand over any men from the *Emden*. Later he was allowed to pass on by boat to Batavia, the colonial capital on the island of Java, where on 16 April 1914 a higher court ruled that he should go free unconditionally. Regardless of the enormous distance involved, Lauterbach was absolutely determined to get back to Germany. Because of the large price on his head (multiply by twenty-five for today's value) he decided that the best way was to keep going east, even though that meant a journey twice as long as the other way, and also crossing the Pacific, the Americas and the Atlantic. Going east, unlike going west, he could avoid the entire British Empire. The German consul-general at Batavia gave him money and despatches to take to China, and Lauterbach, having parted from all but one of his companions, who were content to stay on Dutch soil, made his way by train, boat, pony and on foot along the chain of islands of the East Indies until he reached Cebu, at which he found within twelve hours a steamer to take him to Manila in the American-controlled Philippines, where he spent eight days. It had taken him more than six weeks in all to get there, and as a precaution he disguised himself in several ways, including a period done up in the finery of a rich Arab merchant.

Lauterbach sent several nose-thumbing postcards to people he knew in British colonies in the Far East, including one to Major Catton at Tanglin barracks, who had emerged unscathed from the mutiny and was decent enough to forward the adventurer's mail. To an uncle resident in Sweden he wrote a long letter from China, which he reached on 13 June. This, the first lengthy account of his exploits thus far, was written in the middle of that month and is less likely than subsequent versions to suffer from recollective inflation. Boasting of his resourcefulness he wrote: 'Sometimes I am a Swede, sometimes a Belgian, sometimes a Dutchman, and I have passports for all . . . The English are vexed that I have escaped. What a stupid race they are!' He adds, with typical modesty: 'This account reads nicely enough in a letter, but I have had some very dangerous and trying experiences, demanding courage and energy to see them through.' Curiously enough the letter fell into the hands of British naval intelligence in August 1915, before Lauterbach had finished his travels. It was passed to London by the British naval attaché in Petrograd (the former St. Petersburg), Commander Grenfell, who reported that it had been 'intercepted by the military censor'. A remarkably alert Russian official must have spotted it as it made its way across his country on its way to neutral Sweden (or else the Russians were opening everything, which is more likely). The letter revealed Lauterbach's plan to get home via Japan, America and Norway. Naval intelligence duly alerted everyone it could to be on the lookout. The physical description is accompanied in the Admiralty records by the remark: 'heavy drinker and smoker, a good type of blustering Prussian.'

Lauterbach shed his last companion, a German company manager called Schoenberg, in Manila after many wanderings in the Philippines to add to those in the Dutch East Indies. Schoenberg wanted to go to San Francisco whereas Lauterbach had to go to China. He got to a small northern port on a Japanese collier and then travelled down the coast disguised once again as a Dutchman, via Tientsin, where he looked up a German marine pilot who owed him $500, Nanking, where he looked up *Kapitänleutnant* Brunner of the *S90* of Tsingtao fame who was interned there, and Shanghai, where he met his old friend, Captain Dewar, the British harbourmaster, for a drink, and gave a talk on the voyage of the *Emden* at the local German club. He handed over his despatches from Batavia to the German consulate in Shanghai and then went into hiding in the home of a woman-friend of long standing and English origin, who warned him of a plot by British agents to kidnap him and take him back to Singapore. Four men, he recalled, tried to seize him as he left the German club but he escaped by jumping into a river. A shot was fired after him. He then hid on an interned German ship in the port, whose captain was a former subordinate.

Now Lauterbach, as resourceful and irrepressible as ever after all these scrapes, proceeded to acquire a real American passport in the name of W. Johnson, petty officer in the US Navy, via American friends in Shanghai who must have arranged to steal the document, and had two appropriate uniforms made. He then sailed on an American passenger ship to Nagasaki. Despite having planted the story of his own capture aboard ship off British Columbia via a reporter friend in the *North China Herald*, Lauterbach had a nasty turn in Nagasaki when Japanese officials boarded his ship and demanded that 'Mr. Johnson' step forward. The Japanese had obviously been alerted somehow that Lauterbach was aboard. Amazingly, another man stepped forward, announcing that he was indeed *Colonel* Johnson of the American army, and would they mind telling him what the fuss was about? In Yokohama harbour, Lauterbach found a man searching his cabin – a Japanese detective who said he was 'looking for German officers'. The policeman showed Lauterbach around the city, where posters offering 250,000 yen for the German's capture were on view in several places. The sleuth licked his lips at the idea of winning such a reward. Back on the other side of the world Lauterbach could not resist sending the detective a sarcastic postcard.

Still on the same ship, Lauterbach went on to Honolulu, where he found his old command, the *Staatssekretär Kraetke*, in internment. Guessing that the Americans might enter the war against Germany one day, Lauterbach gathered all his gear and coolly deposited it with the local US customs post, from which he was able to collect it after the war. The rumour that he was aboard the ship from Japan had surfaced in the American press, despite the fact that the Japanese had failed to find him. When local reporters boarded the ship, he got a slightly-built German to stand in for him so that a completely misleading description was circulated. He reached San Francisco without further incident and then crossed the United States to New York by train, this time disguised as a Dane. His arrival on the East Coast leaked out after he had called at the German consulate-general. Eventually he continued his journey home by bribing his way aboard a neutral Danish freighter, whose captain 'employed' him as a stoker for a consideration of $200 paid in advance by Lauterbach, at Hoboken. When the ship was near the Orkney islands, off the north of Scotland, she was held up by a British armed merchant cruiser as a suspected blockade runner, escorted into Kirkwall harbour and detained there for five days. The British searched the ship extremely thoroughly and even made sudden shouts in German in the hope of tricking a German runaway into betraying himself (it was well known that Germans were getting home in disguise on neutral ships). The Danish ship was at last allowed to sail on to Oslo, and from there to Copenhagen, where the German naval attaché provided Lauterbach with papers. On 10 October 1915 Julius Lauterbach made the seven-hour train and boat journey to Warnemünde, the family home near Rostock, where he was given a hero's welcome by the band of the local regiment his father had once commanded, the burgomaster and a large crowd. The band played *Zu Lauterbach hab' ich mein' Strumpf verloren*, to the tune of, 'Where, oh where has my little dog gone.' The overgrown puppy was back and would soon be presented to Admiral Tirpitz and the Kaiser himself. The scarcely less remarkable continuation of his war is described in Part III.

13

IN THE HANDS OF THE
TURKISH ALLY

Captain Minkwitz took the *Emden* detachment round the Horn of Africa, sailing the *Choising* along its northern coast until he was in striking distance of the Perim Strait at the entrance to the Red Sea. He approached its western shore after dark on 7 January. Mücke planned a landing on the eastern shore of the Red Sea in the vicinity of Hodeida, some 150 miles north of the Strait. The *Choising* hugged the western shore so as to approach the chosen spot from due west before dawn on the 9th. The collier anchored a few miles off Hodeida (now Al Hudaydah) and lowered her largest boats, numbers three, four, five and six, with a total of fifty-three men aboard. The incorrigible troublemaker in the party, Stoker Jakob Kreutz, was to stay aboard the *Choising*. Mücke ordered Minkwitz to return to the same point off Hodeida for the next two nights, to await a signal telling him either to head for Massawa in (then Italian and therefore neutral) Eritrea or to pick the detachment up again. To the disembarked forty-nine of the original landing party were now added the two from the *Rheinland* who had joined the *Ayesha* as she left Padang and two officers from the *Choising*, Reserve Sub-lieutenant R. Geerdts and Ship's Doctor Heinrich Lang. They rowed towards some lights which they assumed were those of Hodeida, only to discover when they were up close that they belonged to a ship at anchor (Captain Minkwitz had seen them too – they were those of the French cruiser *Desaix*). The four boats sheered off to the south and eventually made land without further incident some six or seven miles south of Hodeida. After the near-miss with the enemy warship, Mücke, lacking news of the war, wanted first to establish in whose hands the territory on which he had landed now lay. It ought to be under Turkish rule but might have been seized by the French or the British from their respective territories on either side of the Red Sea. He hoped to gain the necessary intelligence quickly so as to be able to decide whether to withdraw back to the *Choising* or try his luck with the local Turks and their Arab clients. He had with him a flare pistol with rounds of various colours for signalling his choice. The boats were very heavily laden and took on a lot of water, even though they had been carefully prepared, their timbers soaked in water aboard the *Choising* to close cracks and then painted several times. Provisions for a few weeks, all the small arms, personal possessions, even most of the lifebelts from the *Choising* (a most wise precaution and a tribute to German thoroughness, as we shall see) – and of course the war ensign from the *Emden* – were taken ashore.

The resourceful and determined sailors of the *Emden*'s landing party now found themselves out of their element. Up to now their evasion had been by water, even if the first stage had been passed aboard a neglected and puny schooner and the second on a fire-damaged rustbucket of prodigious slowness. Now they had landed in the Yemen on the shore of Arabia where the beach merges with the desert inland. And to the mirages commonplace in the Arabian desert were soon to be added the illusions, deceptions and illogicalities of the people, both Arab and Turkish, who lived their precarious lives there in a far-flung province of the Ottoman Empire, itself fossilised by centuries of decay but still of major importance both as Germany's ally and as the main source of such authority as there was in all of Araby. Such information as Mücke had about the effect of the war in Europe on the Near and Middle East was nearly three months old, although of course he knew that Turkey had entered the war on Germany's side at the end of October 1914, his reason for the present landing. But he also guessed that the British and the French would be doing everything in their power to undermine the Turkish position in the entire region because Turkey's intervention in the war had effectively cut off their ally, Russia. The unwelcome sight of the French armoured cruiser suggested that Hodeida might be in French hands. Extreme circumspection was therefore required. Mücke's plan was to land in the dark, hide in the sand dunes during the day, send an officer on a scouting expedition to Hodeida after dark and decide on whether or not to go back to the *Choising* when he returned, on the basis of the information he brought back.

The Germans dragged their equipment through soft, muddy sand for hundreds of yards before reaching dry land. During this exhausting process, completed in daylight, two Beduin were sighted, separately. Both made off. Then a man in a blue and red uniform of suspiciously French aspect rode up on a camel. He and the bedraggled intruders could find no common language: the officers tried German, English, French, even in desperation Malay, all in vain. The man rode off in the direction of Hodeida, to the north. Mücke now expected French troops to appear shortly and prepared to disperse his men to hiding places in the desert. It was already very hot and they were all desperately tired. But before they could disperse, a mass of Beduin armed with rifles ancient and modern appeared and spread out at a distance of about a quarter of a mile from the detachment. The two groups improvised defences against each other and waited, Mücke determined not to fire first in the hope that he might be able to negotiate. His four Maxim guns and the fact that the Beduin were obviously not regular troops gave him some confidence. Soon about a dozen of them approached, unarmed and waving at the Germans. Mücke rose to his feet and dropped his sword-belt to the ground. But once again the language barrier seemed insurmountable. Words and gestures failed; so did the production of both the naval ensign and the black, white and red tricolour of the Reich. Eventually one of the officers had the wit to produce a gold, twenty-mark coin about the size of a sovereign. Gold spoke where all else failed: the Kaiser's head was recognised and understanding dawned. 'Aleman, Aleman,' the tribesmen exclaimed. Eventually one of their number who had some halting English explained that Hodeida remained in Turkish hands. The Beduin seemed genuinely delighted that the Germans had landed and appeared to nurture healthy anti-British and anti-French sentiments. The sailors learned that they had at first been taken for British or French invaders. The tribesmen were all for the Kaiser and had even heard of the *Emden*, but they lacked enthusiasm for their Turkish masters. There was much jubilation and firing of elderly *jezails* into the air.

Meanwhile, a small column of Turkish troops had been sighted, approaching the position in about company strength. The detachment found German and French-speakers among the officers and introduced themselves. The Germans were politely escorted into Hodeida, where the sailors were led off to a Turkish barracks and the officers taken to the house of a wealthy Arab for refreshment and a change of clothes. In the late afternoon, Mücke and his officers were introduced to the Turkish authorities. They met the local administrator, one Raghib Bey, the garrison commander (confusingly, another Raghib Bey with the rank of colonel), his French-speaking subordinate Major Gallib, and a German-speaking army doctor, Nedim Bey. The Turks strongly advised their guests against proceeding any further by sea. The British and French had set up a naval blockade off Kamaran Island, some fifty miles up the coast, they said, and they were searching every boat, no matter how small. Spies in French or British pay would in any event warn the enemy. When Mücke raised the only alternative possibility, of continuing the homeward march by land, the two Raghibs blandly assured him this was entirely possible, while their inferiors vehemently disagreed. Mücke repeatedly pointed out that he was in no position to judge for himself whether a continuation by land was feasible: 'I would rather seek to go further by sea by any means at all than run the risk of getting stuck on land,' he told them (according to his own report).

He was told that it would take two months to get the detachment overland to the nearest relevant railhead, then at Al Ula on the famous Hijaz railway, a daunting 850 miles as the crow flies, to the north-west, but probably closer to 1,000 miles as the desert traveller marches. From there they could take a train to Damascus and then across Asia Minor to the Bosporus. Against his better judgement, Mücke committed himself by going back to the coast with his flare pistol and firing the prearranged signal to the *Choising*, in the early hours of 10 January. She was to make a run for the neutral port of Massawa on the other shore of the Red Sea, and from there to try to sneak southwards with provisions for the *Emden*'s sister-ship, the *Königsberg*, which had been cruising off East Africa.

(Captain Minkwitz saw the signal, even though he had been obliged by the unhealthy interest shown in his ship by the French cruiser *Desaix* to steam in an irregular circle. Boldly trusting to his neutral, Italian disguise, he affected unconcern until the Frenchman sailed away and then moved to a position where he could watch the sky over Hodeida. On seeing the signal, he set off for Massawa, which he reached without further incident on the 12th. Learning there that the *Königsberg* had apparently ceased operations – she was bottled up in the Rufiji River – he decided to stay put in the hot and dreary port and mailed a report of his mission to North German Lloyd on the 15th. When the Italians came into the war later that year, they expropriated the *Choising* and interned her crew. The ship was coarsely repaired and put to work in the Mediterranean as a supply vessel. Renamed the *Carroccio*, she was one of three ships in a small Italian convoy which came under fire on 15 May 1917 from Austrian warships commanded by Admiral von Horthy when he raided the Otranto barrage across the mouth of the Adriatic. She went to the bottom under the guns of two destroyers.)

Mücke began all too soon to regret his decision to send the *Choising* away. 'I cannot accept that it was unknown to the authorities that continuation of the journey by land was out of the question,' he wrote in his report. 'Every child in Hodeida knew that even strong Turkish units could not get through the country, which was in revolt all around.' He began to speculate as to why the Turks had deceived him. Were they saving face by concealing the chaos inland or did they believe that the local Imam, the true repository of Arab loyalties in the area, could be persuaded to arrange safe conduct for the westerners? He already guessed that the Turks, to whom deviousness seemed to be second nature, assumed as a matter of course that the detachment was not what it claimed to be but was some kind of British or French force. If they were either they could be slaughtered and their equipment seized; if they really were Germans they could come in useful against local Arab rebels. Either way, the Turks did everything they could to keep them in the Yemen. Later he learned from Turkish sources how right he had been: 'The authorities did not accept us as Germans but believed for a long time that we were Britons who were playing a comedy,' he wrote afterwards. 'Several weeks after our arrival Turkish officers said to our doctor that we were playing a very good comedy. Other Turkish officers told us later, there had been a plan to let the disembarked column camp at night near Hodeida and then to attack and kill.' The Germans found out only later that there had been a plan to massacre them on the way to Hodeida the very day they landed. The Hodeida garrison consisted of 300 Turkish infantry plus cavalry and artillery, and there were some 800 armed Beduin in Turkish pay. All these 1,100 fighting men were to fall on the exhausted sailors at the first water hole. Fortunately the German-speaking Turkish officers made their way round the detachment and satisfied themselves that all the strangers actually spoke German, which fact caused the plan to be shelved.

After cooling their heels as far as the climate permitted for ten days, the Germans learned that the Turks had begun to build a special barrack block for them. Mücke could get no sense out of the authorities. He demanded to know when the detachment could move on, only to be told that negotiations with the local Imam were still continuing and nobody could say. The man attached to the party to 'protect' its officers from 'nuisance' turned out really to be there to prevent them having contact with local Greek and Armenian traders and the like. Turkish officers who warned the Germans to be on their guard against spies among the Greek and Armenian minorities were seen drunk with them. The Turks tried to establish direct authority over the Germans by such means as offering to pay them, giving them Turkish uniforms and (very foolishly) trying to treat Mücke as a subordinate. The German commander reacted by spelling out his position unmistakably: he led an independent formation of the German Imperial forces and would act on his own responsibility until such time as he received orders from his German superiors. It is not difficult to imagine the chill precision and suppressed rage with which

152

the resolute and always correct Saxon officer, of noble ancestry and a naturally xenophobic turn of mind, would have clarified the situation to what he regarded as a bunch of smarmy, two-faced, undisciplined orientals! Yet the Turks stayed polite – and the Germans stayed put. But Mücke at least got an official loan on account of the German Empire from the Turks of 150 Turkish pounds in gold, and also persuaded them to let the sailors prepare their own food, the appalling quality of which he was able to improve with the money. Once this domestic breakthrough was achieved, the numbers down with stomach trouble declined dramatically.

After a frosty dispute with the local deputy military commander, Lieutenant-Colonel Kadri, in which the Turk told Mücke to his face that the detachment was now under Turkish command and demanded a report of events aboard the *Emden* and after, the German had had enough. He could not go forward to the Hijaz railway, nor could he go back to the sea; but it was open to him to go sideways, north-east to Sanaa, the regional administrative capital and base of the Turkish army's VII Corps (part of the Turkish 4th Army based on Damascus). With dreadful duplicity, some of the locals in Hodeida had blandly asserted that the climate at Sanaa, some 100 miles away across the desert, was much superior to the malarial Hodeida. So he determined to try his luck and chose 27 January, the Kaiser's birthday, as an auspicious day to start the march. But first the great day had to be marked with a parade, and inevitably, wearisomely, there had to be a row with the Turks about the protocol for the occasion, which the hosts were bent on using as a means of establishing their authority over the German detachment. An ornate dispute developed about who would salute whom and who would take the salute and how, and when, and where . . . Eventually the occasion was so organised that nobody lost face and the Germans kept their independence (for what it was worth). The Kaiser's flag flew over the sand, but not so high that it could have been seen from enemy ships offshore. After a lavish banquet, the Germans set off, leaving Dr. Lang and three sick men behind and marching into the relatively tolerable temperature of evening on a scratch collection of horses, mules and donkeys. Their equipment was carried by a separate camel-train. The sailors' mistrust of the animals, especially the frisky mules, was heartily reciprocated and it took Mücke more than an hour to enforce some kind of order. Almost needless to say, the preparations promised by the Turks for their route, including food dumps, water supplies and the like, did not exist. On departure, the officers were given food and there was nothing at all for the ratings. The Turkish guides were amazed when the officers shared their supplies with the men. In fact, some food for the column had been sent by a different route, and Mücke sent messengers from among the guides to have it brought up to join them. As a precaution he gave each man eight days' supplies to carry and set aside some for the sick men left behind, who were to follow on when fit.

On the second night's march a band of robbers on camels came up but sheered off when they saw the machine-guns and the Turkish gendarmes who provided the corps of guides. The Maxims of the Germans were the most awesome infantry weapon in the whole of southern Arabia, which did not run to much beyond the ubiquitous rifle and the occasional elderly cannon. Turks and Arabs alike cast envious eyes at the water-cooled machine-guns whose mere presence, unfired, may have saved the Germans on more than one occasion. They were also to prove themselves handsomely in action. On the third day the Germans' caravan completed the crossing of the narrow strip of coastal desert and reached the foot of a high escarpment with peaks up to 12,000 feet high which barred the way to Sanaa. There was nothing for it but to undertake the long climb. The promised caches of supplies still did not materialise; only at Manakhah, just over halfway along their route, did they find assistance, and then in full measure, from the friendly, efficient and hospitable local garrison. The major in command was a Mesopotamian of commendable professionalism, and the grateful Germans took two days off under his protection. Mücke visited local dignitaries for reasons of protocol and believed he had found encouraging quantities of pro-German sentiment among them.

The rest of the march to Sanaa was hard but free of incident, and the Germans arrived there on 6 February, earlier than locally expected, to be greeted by an entire batallion turned out as guard of honour and a military band, which made a brave but inaccurate attempt at *Deutschland, Deutschland über Alles*. A huge crowd and an impressive collection of worthies were present to welcome the men from the legendary *Emden*, whose reputation had reached even here. The men were led to a barracks; Mücke and the officers, to the amazement and even irritation of their hosts, having learned from recent experience, insisted on staying with them instead of in the town. The power in Sanaa was the commander of the military in Yemen, Ahmed Tewfik Pasha, with whom Mücke conducted complex and frustrating, but always polite, negotiations culminating in a long series of telegrams in which Mücke tried to pin the general down and the general smartly sidestepped all responsibility. The German officer learned from local contacts that Sanaa boasted what was probably the worst climate in the region and the Europeans would have been much better off in Hodeida. At one stage four-fifths of his men were sick. Mücke came to the conclusion after two weeks of fruitless argument that there was no way out overland from Sanaa either; there was no choice but to go back to Hodeida. But for this he needed money, and apart from one British silver shilling he still had from the German consul in Padang, Mücke now had none. His T£150 had long since been spent on food and mounts, bribes and water. But he persuaded a retired Turkish general in Sanaa to lend him money against a receipt, on the grounds that he was bound to lose his capital when local rebels overwhelmed Sanaa! The erstwhile First Officer of SMS *Emden* remained in full possession of his wits. Using the contacts of a friendly and interested Austrian windmill engineer who just happened to be in town, Mücke was also able quietly to hire the necessary mounts. Tewfik did everything he could to delay the Germans' return to the coast, insisting that there should be farewell festivities which could well have gone on for ten days. The Germans now dug their heels in. Well supplied this time with provisions, they set off for Hodeida, a journey no less arduous but rather less uncertain than the outward one, a journey which Mücke hoped might also profitably be diverted from the stated destination.

During his stay in Sanaa he had come across a Turkish marine engineer who told him that he had been in charge of a small steamer intended to carry supplies for an Italian–Turkish railway project in the Yemen, abandoned because of the war. The Turk implied that the ship had been 'mothballed' but remained seaworthy and that 200 tons of coal intended for it were heaped on a nearby beach, only a few miles away from Hodeida. Mücke and a handful of his men therefore rode on ahead of the rest to examine the vessel with a view to continuing their journey in her. The plan was that if the advance party found the ship in good order, the rest of the detachment would turn off the route to Hodeida and proceed to the coast to join her. Once at sea, a way might be found of seizing something larger. But, of course, all was not as advertised. On reaching the promised ship, the disappointed Germans saw only her funnel. The rest was under water, silted up with sand and covered in marine vegetation. The wreck looked to have been submerged for half a dozen years. For purposes of dissimulation against both spies and the Turkish authorities, Mücke had put it about that he hoped to continue his journey by sailing boats from Isa Bay opposite Kamaran Island. He had asked for some *sambuqs* (small dhows with lateen sails) to be made ready. The hapless engineer who had told the tall stories about the ship for which he was responsible shrugged when taxed with his lies by Mücke, who had brought him along with the advance party. It was not healthy, he explained, to give bad news to the authorities. It was now 8 March, two months to the day since the *Choising* hove to off the coast south of Hodeida. It really was time to get a move on after all the frustration caused by the incompetence or indifference of the Turkish authorities.

Mücke managed to find two *sambuqs* for hire and had them brought to Yabana, a small harbour on the same stretch of coast between Isa Bay and Hodeida, that very morning. In the afternoon, the advance party sailed down the coast in them to Hodeida. The Germans learned the next morning that for the first time since the war began a British gunboat had appeared along the coast opposite Kamaran Island and had probed the beach of Isa Bay with its searchlight for hours. Was this the result of mere espionage? Or was it more complicated, with the Turks playing a role in ensuring that the enemy got wind of Mücke's plan, to convince him to stay for the rest of the war and help to pacify the Yemen? Mücke did not care very much at this stage, being determined now to continue the journey home by sea. The two boats were sent back to Yabana with orders to wait while Mücke went off to investigate the appearance of a large Imperial German flag in the middle of Hodeida during his absence. The proud banner marked the return of the German vice-consul from a period of lodging aboard a ship, chosen by the official as a refuge after a quarrel with the local Turkish authorities. The vice-consul turned out to be an Italian national who also represented his native country in Hodeida (it must have seemed logical at the time it was done to make such an arrangement, because Italy was even at this stage technically a member of the Triple Alliance with Austria and Germany, though everyone knew that she was now on the brink of entering the war on the side of the Triple Entente). Nonetheless this worthy saw no conflict of interest in proposing to the internationally renowned German heroes that the detachment should be feted once again, this time by a banquet organised by himself. Invited to choose a date, Mücke suggested Sunday 14 March. He knew now that word of the great beano would be in the ears of the Turks and the enemy within hours and therefore that the 14th would be an excellent day for the Germans to slip away. He sent a message to the officers leading the detachment back from Sanaa to ride hell for leather towards Yabana without sparing the mounts, so as to be there on the Sunday afternoon. Mücke himself and his small advance party, as well as Dr. Lang and the three sick men who did not go to Sanaa but were now recovered, stole away that morning. The ruse worked like a charm: the two boats were ready, the caravan from Sanaa arrived at 4 p.m. as ordered, all the equipment was piled aboard, the flag run up, and with three heartfelt cheers for the Kaiser, the German sailors entrusted themselves to their element once more. Back in Hodeida the apoplectic vice-consul's banquet went cold and there was no sign of his guests of honour.

14

THROUGH THE BRITISH BLOCKADE

There had been much speculation around the world about what fate the *Emden*'s vanished landing-party could have met. The discovery of the *Exford* and the capture of Lauterbach and his companions had of course revived the already legendary story of the cruiser at the end of 1914, and with it renewed guesses about the missing fifty. Although Mücke took his men ashore and reached Hodeida on 9 January, it was only when he reached Sanaa nearly a month later that the survival and whereabouts of the detachment were revealed to an astonished world. Unlike the plotters and cynics at Hodeida, Tewfik Pasha took the Germans at their word and reported their arrival to Constantinople. The message reached the Turkish Grand Headquarters on 8 February by telegraph and was passed on to the German naval authorities by the German General von Bronsart, on liaison duty at GHQ. Lieutenant-Commander Hans Humann, in charge of the 'Germania' *Etappe* at Constantinople, was assigned the responsibility for the detachment's approach to the capital. Admiral Wilhelm Souchon, head of the German Navy's Mediterranean Division and simultaneously of the Turkish Navy, moved swiftly but diplomatically to assert his overall authority over the *Emden* detachment, whose immense propaganda value he was not slow to see. (Souchon had made his name by a dashing escapade of his own which had the most far-reaching effect on the course of the war. In August 1914 he raced the length of the Mediterranean from west to east after shelling the Algerian coast, eluding the French and British navies, in the battle-cruiser *Goeben*, escorted by the light cruiser *Breslau*. Persuading the dithering Turks to let him through the Dardanelles, Souchon later personally brought Turkey into the war on Germany's side by leading his ships under her flag in a bombardment of the Russian Black Sea coast. Turkey's involvement enormously extended and prolonged the war by virtually cutting Russia off from her allies and drawing significant British and French naval and military forces into a largely disastrous series of ventures against the surprisingly robust 'sick man of Europe'.)

The news from Sanaa prompted a flow of telegrams between Constantinople and Berlin and much jubilation in both places. The Reich Navy Office wired its acceptance of all expenses relating to getting the detachment back to civilisation. From the start, the Germans firmly rejected hints from the Turks that they would like to retain the detachment's services in the Yemen. Humann went to see Enver Pasha, the pro-German and German-speaking Minister of War and persuaded him to overrule the army's plan to keep the Germans where they were, or at any rate in the service of the 4th Army of Jemal Pasha. Souchon directly ordered Humann on 11 February: 'Detachment *Emden* should be brought to Mediterranean Division . . . tell Mücke he can leave part of his detachment in southern theatre if individuals wish and if they can be attached to German Military Mission members down there . . .' It was to be assumed that it was highly unlikely a group of men who had been through so much together would voluntarily split up. The Admiral was determined to make the most of the opportunity the detachment presented, and Humann spent much of the ensuing fifteen weeks sending messages into the chaotic deserts of Arabia and hoping for replies. The link with the Yemen was distinctly precarious: one method was via the Italian cable to Massawa, and then by steamer across to Hodeida, which took four days; later, as the sailors moved slowly northwards to the railhead, messages were sent to the nearest telegraph station and forwarded by camel-rider or horseman. Nonetheless, once contact was established, a lively if erratic traffic developed.

The Kaiser was naturally delighted to hear the news of the re-appearance of the detachment and on 11 February he conferred the Iron Cross, First Class, on Mücke and the Second Class on all the others in the party. Two days later a package containing the medals and a covering letter was despatched to Souchon's headquarters. The Germans in Constantinople started preparing an immense reception for the returning heroes. Meanwhile, news of the detachment's survival reached the outside world through the Associated Press. The American news agency's correspondent in Aden picked up the story and wired it to the AP office in Berlin via the Turkish, Austrian and German cable networks for forwarding to head office in New York (the direct route would have been across British Imperial territory and was subject to British military censorship). The story broke on 17 February.

Although Mücke was in fragile contact with German authority

from Sanaa onwards, he and his men were far from being home and dry. Their most dangerous adventures still lay ahead, did they but know it, and the return to the sea on 14 March was not without risk, given that the enemy also knew roughly where they were. Extrapolating over-optimistically from the AP report, the German press had the *Emden* men already in Damascus and expected momentarily in Constantinople that same week.

The Kaiser's naval ensign flew over the smaller of the two *sambuqs* hired by Hellmuth von Mücke; Sub-Lieutenant Geerdts was in command of the other, aboard which were also the sick of the party – several men were suffering from malaria, dysentery and even typhus after the trials and dreadful climate of Hodeida. One boat was about forty feet long, the other about forty-six. Before leaving, Mücke had learned that the British now had at least three ships patrolling a blockade line touching Kamaran Island: the armed merchant cruiser *Empress of Russia* (transferred from Jerram's command) and two gunboats. They were there to cut Turkish communications, which had to go by *sambuq* because of the turmoil among the Arabs inland. Armed *sambuqs* supplemented the blockade. The Germans therefore split up after arranging a rendezvous north of the line, in the hope that one boat would get through if the other did not. As daylight found them becalmed on Monday, 15 March, the Germans in each boat could see *sambuqs*, which they assumed were part of the blockade line, similarly immobile on either side. When the wind picked up a little, both boats got through unnoticed, to the amazed relief of their crews. On the 16th the two *sambuqs* sighted each other again and thenceforward sailed on together, now that the main danger appeared to be past. They passed slowly northward through the dangerous but at the same time protective coral reefs of the Farzan Bank which runs for hundreds of miles along the eastern coastline of the Red Sea, trusting to the shallow drought of their flat-bottomed boats, each of which carried about thirty-five men (Germans and Arab crew).

On Wednesday, the 17th, however, the second boat under Geerdts struck a reef and sank up to her masthead. The light was already failing as the men took to the water, wearing the lifejackets so prudently brought from the *Choising* and preserved in the desert. Not a man was lost, despite the fact that each *sambuq* had as its sole lifeboat one two-man dugout canoe, and Mücke's boat had to do its rescue-work in the dark with only a bonfire on deck to guide the shipwrecked men. But the fire served to dry out the torchlights among the gear they had brought all the way from Direction Island from the

Emden's stores and these were eventually ignited; Mücke risked firing off a few flares from his signal-pistol to help the swimmers. The sick men were of course most at risk and were given pride of place on the surviving boat. Once fifty men were aboard her, it became clear that she could take no more – her gunwales were all but awash. Everything that could be thrown overboard, including fresh water, was now abandoned: Mücke retained food and water for three days, and such guns and ammunition as had been stored on his boat. Eventually every man was accounted for on board the surviving *sambuq*, the officers from the lost one being the last to be rescued. The survivors revealed that their boat had freakishly come to rest on a ledge on an otherwise vertical reef: it could easily have gone straight to the bottom, in which case the sick at least, if not many others, would have drowned.

Throughout the pandemonium of the rescue operation, which was probably the last thing the German sailors needed after their adventures thus far, a *sambuq* manned by rebellious Idrissi tribesmen had watched from a few hundred yards away. At first they had sent their own dugout to help, but when they saw mere Europeans struggling in the water, they left them to their fate. Mücke sent an Arab messenger in a dugout to offer the men of Sheik Idris £10,000 in gold for help; the captain sent a message back saying that £100,000 would not move him to assist infidels. Mücke considered seizing the unfriendly vessel but rejected the idea – despite the fact that his own overloaded boat could barely float – for fear of adverse political consequences: he would be using force against Turkish subjects, even if they were in murderous revolt and in cahoots with the British (infidels too, but favoured on the grounds that my enemy's enemy is my friend). In daylight on the 18th, Mücke had his best and fittest swimmers dive on the wreck to salvage what they could – the two Maxims and some of the small arms as well as some ammunition were recovered. The detachment's medical supplies were not.

After the disaster of the sinking, the weather took pity on the Germans and produced a splendid southerly wind of just the right strength to carry them a distance it could easily have taken them a week to cover in the changeable conditions normal in the area. They went ashore at Al Qunfidhah, well over 300 miles up the coast from Hodeida, a splendid achievement in only four days even without the loss of one *sambuq*. The Germans were lavishly received and fell upon the lamb and rice the local Turkish dignitaries provided at a banquet. Mücke negotiated the hire of another, much larger *sambuq* and set off again on 19 March. In five days they completed their planned voyage by arriving without incident at Al Lith, which lay

161

inside the northern extremity of the Farzan Bank. The coral reefs had cost the Germans a boat and a scare but had protected them against British interference; to continue by sea without such protection would have been foolhardy. They were now about halfway to the railhead at Al Ula. There was nothing for it but to go on by land. Mücke took two days to assemble the necessary supplies, spurred on by local reports of intense British vigilance at sea in an area hitherto untroubled by their attentions. In the early hours of 27 March Seaman Keil became the first fatal casualty of the detachment, from typhus. He was taken out to sea in a rowing boat at daybreak and buried in the water; on the shore a firing party saluted him with three volleys from their rifles.

Mücke became the first Christian to enter the home of the Sheik of Al Lith, who nonetheless proved helpful in the crucial task of assembling some ninety camels. On the evening of Sunday, 28 March, after the heat of the day had passed, the Germans resumed their agonisingly slow march to the north. Their destination this time was Jiddah.

15

THE BATTLE OF THE DUNES

If not exactly blasé about the uncertain art of camel-riding, the Germans by now gave little thought to spending fourteen to sixteen hours a day mounted on the Ship of the Desert, exhausting though it was. The riding day began about 4 p.m. and lasted until about 9 or 10 a.m., when the heat made it essential to rest in whatever shade could be improvised. Progress was agonisingly slow but the trek passed without noteworthy incident for three days, on a monotonous diet of mutton and rice washed down with dubious water from holes in the sand. The fourth day's trek began on the afternoon of 31 March from a waterhole said to be only a day's march from Jiddah. The Germans, warned of the particularly wild rebels in the area, were escorted by a Turkish officer and seven gendarmes and rode with a round 'up the spout' of each weapon and the safety catch on. At the waterhole they were met by seventeen more gendarmes, under an officer who brought greetings from the Turkish civil and military officials in the city. The area through which they now rode was notorious for its lawlessness even in those turbulent parts and bore the name, literally translated, 'Father of the Wolf'. They were riding through dunes which allowed them a maximum visibility of a quarter of a mile in any direction, despite the clear moonlight. Suddenly to their right, a dozen or so Beduin on camels appeared briefly and disappeared again. They were assumed to be part of a band of forty robbers known by the Jiddah authorities to be marauding in the area. As a precaution, Mücke rearranged the column from a single file into a double one, the camels in each tied nose to tail and the men warned to stay alert. When the sun rose and the likelihood of attack seemed to have faded, Mücke took a slow ride of inspection down the column. When he was about halfway along a whistle shrilled loudly.

The startling sound was followed by a volley of rifle fire, and then by a hail of bullets from all directions. Mücke leapt off his camel and led a few men at a stumbling run through the sand to the head of the column, where a fierce exchange of shots was in progress. The hostile

163

fire was coming from a position ninety yards ahead; only the muzzle flashes could be seen. Most of the Germans and their Turkish escorts were up front, while a small group covered the rear of the column. Each end of the train of camels was carrying two of the four Maxims, which now as never before came into their own. Mücke ordered their immediate deployment and soon the reassuring stutter of their sweeping fire gave the attackers pause. Their salvoes died away.

Mücke took advantage of the lull to reorganise his defences, showing in the process a natural aptitude as an infantry officer. Such camels as were still standing were made to squat on their haunches for cover and to present a smaller target. Ammunition was distributed, the best of it (that part which had not gone down with the sunken *sambuq* and been recovered by the divers) hurriedly loaded into the machine-gun belts. Apart from the Maxims, the sailors now had thirteen German rifles from the *Emden*, ten old and three new rifles subsequently acquired from the Turks as replacements for those lost in the sinking, and twenty-four pistols, of little value except at close quarters. Those with rifles had already fixed bayonets without being ordered to do so.

There seemed to be about seventy attackers facing the head of the column as it dug into the sand; but when full daylight had come, a total of about 300 could be seen encircling the position. Mücke boldly decided to risk cold steel and ordered a series of bayonet charges, accompanied by bloodcurdling German yells, forward and then to either side to drive the attackers back. Desultory fire gave way to flight: the manoeuvre had created a no man's land of well over 1,000 yards between the Germans and the Beduin at a cost of just one sailor wounded. Only seven of the Turkish gendarmes were still with the column; the rest had ridden off at the first sign of trouble and were later found to be in Jiddah. A few of the handful of Arabs accompanying the column as guides and servants had been wounded; the Germans counted at least fifteen dead in the positions their bayonet charges overran. Many camels had been killed.

Mücke instinctively decided to head back towards the sea: with that at his back he could at least be neither surrounded nor easily outflanked. He organised his small force into a scattered square with screens of riflemen ahead, behind and to either side and the camels in half a dozen short rows in the middle, carrying the wounded, the sick and the supplies, now reduced to a minimum, and of course the machine-guns, two each at front and rear. The Kaiser's ensign flew at the centre. Barely had this formation been set in motion when the Beduin once again peppered it with gunfire from all sides. The dunes shielded the attackers and gave the Germans no targets; fortunately the Beduin were terrible shots. One German sailor was killed, and Sub-Lieutenant Schmidt, commanding the rearguard, was badly wounded. Once again the machine-guns were able to bring relief, even though the camel carrying one of the rear Maxims was shot dead and the weapon was almost lost. The firing died down as suddenly as it had begun.

A couple of the remaining gendarmes now ran towards the Beduin positions waving white cloths and one of their colleagues told Mücke they had gone to seek terms. Clearly this was no mere attack by robbers; several hundred men were involved, and the Germans' position seemed hopeless. They could defend a stationary position with the machine-guns, but these could not be fired on the move; yet they could hardly stay in the desert forever, waiting for their strength to be reduced piecemeal, something even the poor shooting of the attackers was bound to achieve eventually. But in the meantime the sailors dug themselves in as much as possible, burying their water-containers and building a low defensive wall round their position. In the centre a higher protective wall covered the wounded and sick. The dead Seaman Rademacher was buried on the spot. At each corner stood a machine-gun protected by heaps of sand.

The gendarmes came back with the 'terms': the foreigners could go free on payment of £11,000 in gold, surrender of all arms, all camels, all food and all water! Mücke replied: 'Firstly, we have no money, and secondly we are guests in this country. Get the money in Jiddah. Thirdly, it is not a German custom to surrender weapons.' After delivering this defiant message to the Beduin, the Turkish gendar-merie officer who had carried it made off for Jiddah. Nearly all the gendarmes and most of the camel-drivers, all Arabs, had also vanished. Another exchange of fire took place in which the well dug-in Germans took no casualties. After dark, Sub-Lieutenant Schmidt died of his wounds and was also buried on the spot. Mücke sent an Arab to steal through the enemy line during the darkest period between sunset and moonrise and report their plight to Jiddah.

At sunrise the Beduin poured more of their seemingly infinite supply of ammunition into the German position, now thoroughly dug in and strengthened during the night. To conserve ammunition, the fire was returned only in short bursts, enough to stop the enemy risking an advance. The Germans stewed in the sun all day, sand in their weapons, their eyes and ears and mouths, their food and water, constantly having to shore up their crumbling defences of sand. The temperature in the sun touched 65° C (150° F). Night fell again, during which Stoker Lanig died of his wounds. Two of the last remaining gendarmes were sent, disguised as Beduin, to make another attempt to get the news to Jiddah. The third night under siege came and went until the sun came up on 3 April. There was one day's water left, enough for one mug per man morning and evening. Mücke saw no choice but to try to make a break for Jiddah that night. The situation was desperate; after being marooned on Direction Island, the voyages on the *Ayesha* and the *Choising*, the journey up the eastern shore of the Red Sea, exposure to typhus, malaria, dysentery and stifling heat, the sinking of the *sambuq* and treachery on all sides, after five months' hard slog against all the odds, the one group of survivors of the *Emden* that had not been captured by the British seemed doomed to die in the desert sand. It was high time the cavalry appeared.

And so it did. The Germans heard in mid-morning a new outbreak of shooting at a distance from their position and not directed at them, on the seaward side of their camp. Meanwhile, a man waving a white cloth came from the Beduin line towards them with a message that the besiegers were now prepared to forgo their demand for the surrender of guns, ammunition, camels, food and water if only the besieged were prepared to pay £22,000 in gold. 'My answer is not worthy of mention,' Mücke modestly recorded afterwards. But he took his time about giving it; he had guessed that the distant exchange of fire might indicate relief in the offing, and it might become possible to catch the attackers between two fires. A few more harmless volleys were fired at the German position; then silence fell. With the utmost caution, the Germans raised their heads and searched the surrounding dunes with their field-glasses. The Beduin had vanished into thin air. An hour later, two men on camels appeared waving a white flag. They identified themselves as messengers from the Emir of Mecca, whose second son, Abdullah, was on his way to the rescue at the head of a column of camel-riders.

In due course, a troop of magnificently accoutred warriors appeared, riding in double column and numbering about seventy. They rode up to the German position as if on a sightseeing expedition, taking no precautions at all, under a red banner with gold Arabic lettering and preceded by a couple of drummers. The Germans rubbed their eyes in disbelief. Abdullah told Mücke that he had been sent by his father as soon as news of the attack had reached Jiddah; he apologised profoundly for what had happened and claimed to have driven off the raiders. He would now lead them into Jiddah; meanwhile, he had brought fresh water for them. Mücke found all this extremely suspicious but saw no choice: he had to fall in with the princeling, and at least his troops seemed to offer insurance against renewed attack, especially if the sailors stuck as closely as possible to them, their weapons discreetly at the ready. Mücke determined that at the first sign of another onslaught he would personally put a pistol to Abdullah's head. As the Germans rode away from their position they looked back; to their amazement the Beduin had reappeared and were swarming over the abandoned supplies looking for loot and ignoring Abdullah's men and the Germans only a few hundred yards distant. There could now be no doubt at all that there was a connection between the attackers and Abdullah, and Mücke ostentatiously fiddled with the flap of his pistol-holster. Abdullah insisted that there was no danger any more.

After dark, Mücke asked for a break for his exhausted men and engaged Abdullah in lively conversation in French. On the pretext of admiring the magnificent rifles of the Emir's troops, he was able to establish that none of them had been fired recently while he dispensed flowery compliments to their owners as if to the manner born. This proved that the rescue operation had been completely contrived and that the 'exchange of fire' which preceded Abdullah's appearance on the scene had been a fiction. But there was as yet no explanation or theory to account for the elaborate deceit. They spent this fourth night by a well and for the first time since leaving Al Lith the Germans were free to wash and cook; but to the amazement or amusement of their elite escort, they took up a defensive position with sentries posted and machine-guns in place. In the darkness they could see the searchlights of the British sea-patrol playing along the coast off Jiddah.

The next morning the fifty surviving Germans and their splendidly caparisoned escort came under the walls of Jiddah. The sailors rode along crowded streets full of cheering people to the barrack square, where a guard of honour of a battalion of Turkish troops as well as Arab auxiliaries awaited them. A Turkish colonel offered greetings and expressed his regret that the Germans had been attacked only a day's march from his garrison. Looking around the faces of the assembled men in uniform, Mücke was interested, if hardly surprised after all that had happened, to see among them most of the gendarmes of his previous 'escort' who had fled during the fighting. The whole affair took on a surrealistic aspect in recollection as the Germans were feted, their wounded cared for, the sick treated and the rest magnificently entertained in a ceaseless round of feasting.

16

THE LAST EVASION

Convinced beyond argument now that honesty was the worst policy in dealing with the Turks and the Arabs alike, Mücke adopted a policy of self-reliance and dissimulation from the moment of his arrival in Jiddah. As he went the rounds of one banquet after another, he listened and learned and at the same time let no one doubt that it was his intention to go on by land. Presumably his listeners believed this because they wanted to; they must have had a very low opinion of the Germans to think that they would, after all their dreadful experiences, want to spend a moment more in the desert than they had to. Mücke was soon totally certain that the attack on the detachment at Ras al Aswad had been organised by the Emir of Mecca, the Grand Sherif Hussein, and carried out by his second son, Sherif Abdullah, who had 'come to the rescue' only because the Germans resisted so effectively with their feared machine-guns. The attackers, he learned, had lost forty dead and thirty-six wounded, a fact which no doubt gave the sailors grim satisfaction. Arabia was a thieves' kitchen at this stage in its history, and it was not long before Hussein was to throw in his lot with the British, as represented by Lawrence of Arabia, to advance the cause of independence from the Turks. What is more, less than two months after the *Emden* detachment passed this way, a group of six German servicemen who had made a comparable march from the south coast of the Arabian peninsula via Sanaa and Hodeida and thence by the same route as Mücke's men (after escaping internment in the Dutch East Indies) was wiped out by Beduin, who mutilated their bodies, on the very outskirts of Jiddah. Hindsight at least shows that Mücke was right to suspect that another attempt to make progress by land would only invite a better organised and more determined onslaught on the column.

Always on the lookout for an opportunity, Mücke met an Egyptian who spoke fluent English but was thoroughly anti-British and ran boats from Egypt across to Jiddah with British aquiescence (they did not want the anti-Turkish Arabs to starve as a result of their blockade). The German commander, after due thought, decided to trust this man to hire him a large *sambuq* and to keep quiet about the deal. Meanwhile, ostentatious preparations for continuing the march northwards overland continued; messengers were sent in all directions, animals were reserved, food stockpiled and advice taken about the best route amid constant assurances that the venture would be safe. Mücke now borrowed a motor-boat for a surreptitious scouting trip which revealed that the British gunboats of the blockade were nowhere to be seen; he assumed that the spies had assured them that the Germans had decided to go on by land. Finally, on the evening of the 8th, after barely four days in teeming Jiddah, Mücke detected a sturdy and apparently steady southerly wind, gathered his men, led them as unobtrusively as possible with their equipment and supplies down to the harbour and loaded the *sambuq*. The idea was to leave the spies no time to warn the British. Even so, before they could sail away, the Turkish colonel in command of the garrison came down and pleaded with them not to risk the sea passage but to go on by land, which he swore on his honour was safe.

The Germans took their own counsel and sailed away, this time guided by an excellent pilot, even though the sheiks who were supposed to accompany them as hostages did not show up. Mücke was worried about this; he had already at various stages of the long journey adopted this Turkish custom of taking hostages and paying them off when the next one was taken. But the pilot said that the four machine-guns were worth more than twenty such hostages. They sailed through the blockade line without seeing anything that night and reached the comparative safety of a coral reef parallel with the coast some thirty miles north of Jiddah. During the second night, that of the 9th to 10th, a ship's searchlight played over the reef by which they were anchored at the time, without picking them out. From now on the Germans proceeded up the coast, using the reefs as cover, in short hops from one small port or fishing village to the next. They were able to obtain fresh fish by barter as they went, and in general were received with courtesy and friendliness by local sheiks during the three weeks of the last stage at sea, a voyage of nearly 400 miles. Their destination was the coastal town of Al Wajh; Al Ula, the railhead, lay about 100 miles east of it and inland. In fact the protection of the reef ran out some ten miles south of Al Wajh, so they disembarked for the last time at that point on the coast on 28 April, taking their weapons and food and water for one day. The *sambuq* was sent on with the rest of their supplies and arrived safely. The detachment was met by a handful of gendarmes who sent for camels, and they reached Al Wajh in the evening of the 29th.

There they were received with honour by the local sheik, Suleiman Pasha. After two days' rest, the *Emden* detachment set off on the last stage of the long journey to the railhead, escorted by Sheik Suleiman and his men. The way inland started in the all-too-familiar desert but soon became rather less stifling as the caravan began to climb into a mountain range offering pleasant landscapes and plenty of fresh water. It was now cool enough to march by day and sleep at night. To the astonishment of their plentiful escort, the Germans dug in every night, setting up the famous machine-guns and posting sentries: this was no time to be careless, so close to the major goal of the station at Al Ula. The nights were chilly now, extremely so in comparison with what had gone before; but the terrain offered excellent visibility by moonlight and gradually the sailors began to feel more secure. Sheik Suleiman's territorial boundary was reached a few hours' march short of Al Ula. At that point the Beduin proved just as ready to dig themselves in as the Germans because the neighbouring sheik was hostile to them and likely to attack if he saw profit in it. Suleiman decided to take the risk of accompanying his guests a day's ride into his neighbour's territory to ensure they reached the station safely. Here at least, the Germans thought, was an honourable man. Although the last stretch offered several places ideally suited to an ambush, the column came through safely. A few miles out of Al Ula they learned from men met on the track that the local sheik was engaged in a conflict in another part of his lands. Mücke therefore decided to ride on ahead into town with Suleiman, the sheik's two sons and an escort of a few Beduin camel-riders. He wanted to enquire about hiring a special train and finding lodging for his men, as any good officer would. As he topped the ridge overlooking the town, he surveyed it with his field-glasses and saw the double line of the railway glinting in the sun, paralleled by a row of telegraph poles. It was an extraordinary moment after an exceptional ordeal, not long before noon on 7 May 1915. By midday, *Kapitänleutnant* Hellmuth von Mücke and his escort were down in the town, where a no less extraordinary reception awaited.

17

'FOR GERMANY'

What followed Mücke's descent from the mountains at Al Ula may well be the nearest equivalent German history has to offer to that famous British moment in 1871, when Henry Morton Stanley, the journalist, met Dr. David Livingstone, the missionary explorer who had been 'missing' for an unconscionably long time, near Lake Tanganyika and made his immortal presumption. A renowned journalist was on hand at Al Ula too, to greet the returning *Kapitänleutnant* Hellmuth von Mücke and his men, and his despatches record the first direct contact between the undefeated warrior and a compatriot, namely himself. The reporter was Emil Ludwig of the *Berliner Tageblatt*. Herr Ludwig had been anticipating this historic moment for nearly three months, from hearing of the detachment's reappearance in Arabia through the long journey eastwards to the long wait at the railhead, and it shows in his copy, which at the same time succumbs to the overpowering emotion of the event and becomes a kaleidoscopic, disjointed jumble of impressions full of adjectives, adulation and the historic present. Yet it still manages to ring true, despite its abandonment of that excellent if elusive principle, clear thoughts clearly expressed.

The dialogue when Stanley met Livingstone is remembered in fact as a monologue: everybody knows the question, 'Dr. Livingstone, I presume?' but nobody seems to know the reply, if any – possibly because it was a question presuming the answer Yes. Herr Ludwig's shining hour, as he recorded it, was marked by a snippet of true dialogue in what can only be described as the finest journalistic tradition:

'A bath, or Rhine wine?'

'Rhine wine!'

The circumstances being as they were, the account of the great escape of the *Emden* landing party and its long journey home has to be drawn in the main from the official reports Mücke made at or near the time and from his subsequent writings. Ludwig's breathless double despatch to his paper, following his initial, short and sharp message recording the sailors' safe arrival at Al Ula, is the first account by an outsider of any part of the adventure since Captain Minkwitz's reports to his owners, which were passed on to the German Navy Office, and it incorporates a verbal snapshot of their condition when they emerged from the wilderness. He sent two long cables, both what we would call 'colour pieces' today, one datelined 7 May at Al Ula, the other the next day at Tabuk, the first important stop on the Hijaz railway from the point where the detachment ended its long march and took to a train.

For all these reasons it seems appropriate to quote the reports of Emil Ludwig *in extenso* below. They were news millions of Germans wanted to hear (and millions of non-Germans found absorbing and cheering when relayed) and they are translated by the author from the cuttings in the German archives. (*Berliner Tageblatt*, 11 May 1915.)

Al Ula, 7 May

The *Emden* caravan reached here this evening, Captain Mücke in advance as reported earlier. We were still sitting waiting when suddenly Arabs stormed in: 'They are here!' From the rugged mountains a small caravan descended. I ran up to it. The tall, blond man had already dismounted and smiled at my welcome. He stood there in a completely ruined tropical uniform with his involuntary beard and the bluest seaman's eyes, next to his white camel. 'A bath or Rhine Wine?' was my first question, "Rhine wine!" the decisive answer. Then we sat in the stationmaster's room, and without any fuss Mücke began to tell his story.

Truly an odyssey, on water and on land. In between times, he opened letters ('Have I got the Cross?') and he found newspapers which one after another reported his First Class [Iron] Cross, a Bavarian and a Saxon decoration. He smiled, blushed and was as happy as a child with a present. 'It really is too much,' he cried, 'but the Saxon Order of St John pleases me most – my father wore that.' In between times, questions about Müller's fate, about the Carpathians and the Dardanelles [campaigns began while he was cut off from war news] and fragments of reports about the *Emden–Ayesha*. Another caravan was reported unexpectedly quickly. 'I must go and meet my men,' and we approached a large caravan. Thirty Beduin, with the Turkish flag at their head, then, all intermingled, Germans, fine blond sailors dressed in fez or turban on camels, and in between melancholy-looking Arabs. 'Boys,' the captain called to them, 'you have all got the Cross, and you,

Gyssling [Sub-lieutenant] a Bavarian on top.' – 'Hurrah!'
echoed across the red and flat desert. The German flag was raised.
A handshake for the new arrivals. 'Boys, this is paradise; come on,
Sekt is flowing here. And there is a genuine railway line!' – 'When
do you want to leave?' asked the Turkish major. 'In three hours,
as fast as possible, through the night and the morning.' Even
before he reports his arrival to his parents, he wires his request for a
new command against the enemy. I have never seen such simplicity
[combined] with such fame as with all fifty *Emden* men. 'Have you
got newspapers here?' – 'Piles of them.' – 'How goes it for
Germany?' a young voice asks from the blond circle. 'For Germany.' I said, as I listened to the names of the three dead, 'for
Germany' said the expression of the tired men, sitting in rows,
silent. Four lambs are slaughtered and roasted on the fire. The men
bathe, larking around like children, and look happily from the
desert at the coaches of the special train, but on all faces [there] lies
the hundredfold adventure, 'for Germany.'

All this is relatively controlled, except for the closing passage which
is a little on the toothsome or purple side. The headline reads: 'The
meeting with the *Emden* caravan on the Hijaz railway,' and the
sub-heading reads (of course), 'For Germany!' The second despatch
is placed under the first, and is somewhat less inhibited.

Tabuk, 8 May
They are asleep. It is not yet sunrise. The joy lasted a long time
yesterday evening. But I could not sufficiently admire the self-
discipline which, even on this well-earned day of celebration, never
betrayed itself. The seriousness, the fundamental attitude of the
serviceman underlay all the cheeriness. When the locomotive was
reported ready for departure, Mücke called: "Departure! Boys, I'll
command a train just once in my life." Then he sat with the officers
among the men. There was fun at every station, only because they
were real railway stations which came up automatically without the
risk of adventure. All everyone wanted was full speed for Germany. Mücke wants to cut short all the feasts prepared for him.
There is nothing he wants more than a command in the North Sea. I
went along the corridors of the train just now and saw them
sleeping. They lie crosswise or lengthwise, wherever there is room,
comrades bound [together] by nine months through seas and
deserts, and I realise how young they all are. None over thirty, and
their commander thirty-three. Of the officers only Sub-lieutenant
von Gyssling was on the *Emden*. Willman, from Oldenburg, joined

173

in Padang. Dr Lang and Sub-lieutenant Geerdts are taken over from the *Choising*. This ship of North German Lloyd, the third and last ship that bore the expeditionary force of the *Emden*, took the crew and the supplies on 16 December at sea off the coast of Sumatra. The *Ayesha* was sunk the same evening. On 9 January they left this ship in turn before Hodeida, in the hope of being able to take the land route through Arabia. The march went wrong. Having lost two months, they had no choice but to take a small sailing boat of fourteen metres in length, and broke their way through the Red Sea in new adventures. All are well and in good spirits; but they laugh in amazement to see themselves described as 'heroes' in the newspapers.

At least Herr Ludwig got most of his facts right amid the florid prose. One of the few quibbles a pedant could raise against the foregoing is the award to Sub-Lieutenant Gyssling of the ennoblement prefix 'von' to which he was not in fact entitled. And in the first despatch he gives the round-figure total of fifty for the strength of the detachment when it reached Al Ula. There were in fact forty-nine. It was a good story all the same.

18

TRIUMPH IN CONSTANTINOPLE

The destination of the *Emden* detachment was now Constantinople, as it was still called in those days. The entire journey from Al Ula to the eastern shore of the Bosporus dividing Asia from Europe could be done at that time by train, except for two stretches towards the southern end of the line which were not complete and had to be traversed on foot or mounted. The line ran roughly parallel to the northern end of the Red Sea in what is now Saudi Arabia, and then through Jordan, Syria and Anatolia to the railway terminus at Haydar Pasha, between Scutari and Chalcedon and across the water from Stambul, on the European side. From there they would go back to Germany by train via Austrian territory, to individual celebrations in their home towns. But it was in Constantinople that they formally returned to duty with the Imperial Navy, and it is there that the story of the landing party's wanderings reaches its natural end.

The train journey to the capital of the Ottoman Empire became a leisurely and triumphal progress that lasted more than two weeks, with several stops for celebrations on the way, a series of feasts which verged on becoming a new challenge to the stamina and endurance of the detachment. Meanwhile, there was a great deal of detail and correspondence to deal with. Mücke had taken every opportunity to report to his superiors – a letter from Padang by post to his father with a covering note asking him to forward it to the Admiralty in Berlin was his first effort. This was the report written on paper from the SS *Kleist*, which took a good ten weeks to reach his father, on 11 February 1915. Mücke Senior sent it on by registered post the same day (and complained eleven days later in another letter to the Navy that he had received no acknowledgment). Of course by that time, the report from Padang had been overtaken by the telegram from Sanaa via Constantinople; and only a few days later, Captain Mink-witz's report was forwarded by North German Lloyd. Mücke sent another letter to his father as he left Jiddah on 27 January, which arrived on 15 March for forwarding; it contained a warning not to expect anything further for six to eight weeks. But on 23 February the leader of the detachment wrote again from Sanaa, and this report reached his father on 1 April. Curiously enough, this letter has three lines heavily scored out, a fact the German Admiralty attributed to *British* censorship! This is not as fantastic as it sounds, because an important means of communication from the Arabian peninsula in its permanent state of upheaval was via the then still neutral Italian steamer connection from Jiddah to British-ruled Egypt (the British allowed it to continue, as we have seen, so that their desired ally, the Grand Sherif of Mecca, would not be affected by the blockade of Jiddah against the Turks). But if it was a British military censor who made the deletion, he was clearly an ignorant one who did not appreciate the significance or perhaps the identity of the writer. The route the letter took is not known; but it must be assumed that the German Admiralty had a reason for its explanation of the deletion.

Both Mücke's subordinate officers from the regular navy, Sub-Lieutenants Schmidt and Gyssling, had friends in high places in the form of their respective fathers. Rear-Admiral Schmidt was at that time serving with the Baltic Fleet at Kiel; Lieutenant-General Gyssling was in command of the 6th Bavarian Division with III Corps based at that time at Vigneulles, near Verdun, in northern France. Both senior officers wrote to the Admiralty after the news of the detachment's reappearance in Arabia became public knowledge, asking for news and for letters to their sons to be forwarded. On 8 April, Mücke got off a telegram to the Admiralty reporting the battle with the Beduin, which arrived only on the 20th; the Foreign Office in Berlin received a report from the Embassy in Constantinople four days earlier; Humann was told two days earlier still of the arrival at Turkish GHQ of a report of the battle from 4th Turkish Army headquarters in Damascus. The news was released to the German Press on 22 April, and on the 24th, General Gyssling sent a telegram saying, 'Request news of son' to the Admiralty, which replied: 'Your son not wounded. Letter follows.' The Admiralty was obliged to write to Admiral Schmidt to tell him that his son had been killed. He was sent a copy of Mücke's message: 'We have fought three days with Arabs sent by British south of Jiddah. Sub-Lieutenant Roderich Schmidt, Seaman Rademacher, Stoker Lanig killed. Seamen Mauritz and Koschinsky seriously, Witte slightly, wounded. Seaman Keil died of typhus at Al Lith.' This was the final casualty list of the *Emden* detachment.

Relatives of the other members of the detachment were naturally no less anxious for news and the opportunity to have letters forwarded, and eventually two sackloads of mail were assembled in

Commander Humann's office for forwarding as soon as this became practicable. Among the stack of mail for Mücke was a letter from a publisher in Mannheim asking him if he was interested in writing a book about the long march home, an admirable display of business acumen.

As Ludwig reported, Mücke sent a message to his naval superiors reporting his return and asking for a combat posting against the British in the North Sea, followed immediately by another to his family to say he was safe and sound, from Al Ula before the train left. But it was in Damascus a few days later that he really got busy with telegrams, mainly to Humann in Constantinople. He wanted to know whether the Kaiser's all-round Iron Cross award also covered the men who had attached themselves to the *Emden* detachment at Padang and Hodeida, and whether the medals would reach them in time for their arrival in Constantinople. He also sent off a very detailed 'shopping list' of items of uniform, with sizes and quantities carefully given. A selection of workaday uniform had been sent down the Hijaz railway to meet them; but Mücke wanted parade uniforms, and asked for everything from officers' swords (four) to epaulettes, caps, boots, buttons and 'housewife' sewing kits. These were provided from the stores kept for the thousands of German sailors of the Mediterranean Division in Constantinople, who manned the *Goeben*, the *Breslau* and other craft of the Turkish Navy in the Black Sea.

The biggest reception for the returning heroes while they were on their way to Constantinople was given by the sizeable German community in Damascus (military advisers, businessmen and diplomats). At Aleppo there was another celebration, and it was there that the mail from home was waiting, together with the medals and the uniforms. As the train progressed in its stately way north-westwards, there were scenes of enthusiasm at every scheduled halt, and goods wagons attached to it steadily filled with gifts of all kinds. The fan mail from all manner of people in Germany and elsewhere in the world outweighed by far the personal letters from home, and the most outlandish people wanted the opportunity to bask in the *Emden* heroes' reflected glory. A Mr. Har Dayal of the Bureau of the Hindu National Party in Stambul wrote to Admiral Souchon: 'The Indian Nationalists resident in Constantinople wish to meet the heroes of the *Emden* when they arrive here in order to express their sympathy and admiration. I hope you will kindly comply with our request.' This appeal was written in English and dated 13 May; it was repeated by the same hand in French a week later, whereupon Souchon agreed.

Entirely in keeping with the German delight in organised festivity, especially on the grand scale, a truly vast *Fest* was being prepared for the men from the *Emden* by the enormous German community in the Turkish capital, which (of course) formed a *Fest*-committee to arrange the welcome to end all welcomes. The German brewery in the city and the concessionaire of a pleasure garden were willingly recruited to help organise a monumental *Bierabend* (beer-evening). The celebration was to take place on the evening of Whit Monday, 24 May 1915. The Navy was also naturally deeply involved; a batch of rifles for the march through the city was collected from the *Breslau*, and the German steamer *General* was to accommodate them during their stay. Meanwhile, sailors who were to hand out the food and drink in the beer-garden were issued with books of tokens which collectively entitled each man to six half-litre bottles of beer, five bread rolls with filling, one pair of sausages and a packet of twenty cigarettes! Admission was to be by ticket only, to keep out the 'demi-monde', as the impressive surviving collection of organisational paperwork in the German archives prudishly explains. The jollifications were to terminate at 10 p.m. or at such earlier or later time as Admiral Souchon himself might order. And so it was.

On the afternoon of Whit Sunday, 23 May 1915, the special train pulled into Haydar Pasha station in a cloud of smoke and steam. Forty-nine men in brand-new German naval uniforms detrained, formed up and marched to the head of the platform where Admiral Wilhelm Souchon stood waiting to receive them, flanked by staff officers standing stiffly to attention. The *Emden* detachment, the only German military formation in the First World War that returned from overseas to rejoin the fray, the only survivors of Graf Spee's Cruiser Squadron not in captivity, formed up in a double line, the four officers and Dr. Lang in front. At right flew the tattered naval ensign from the *Emden*, attached to the pole of a boathook by rusty nails. *Kapitän-leutnant* Hellmuth von Mücke, First Officer of the lost SMS *Emden* and leader of its landing-party, raised the hilt of his sword to his lips and lowered its point in salute. Looking the Admiral in the eye, he said: 'Beg to report, landing-party from SMS *Emden* numbering five officers, seven petty officers and thirty-seven men, present and correct.'

PART III

GLORY AND AFTER

The stately ship is seen no more,
The fragile skiff attains the shore;
And while the great and wise decay,
And all their trophies pass away,
Some sudden thought, some careless rhyme,
Still floats above the wrecks of Time.

William Lecky, *On an Old Song*

19

THE LATER CAREERS OF
THE PRINCIPAL FIGURES

Commander Karl von Müller of the *Emden* entered the officers'
section of the British prisoner-of-war camp in Valetta, Malta, on 7
December 1914. His captivity was uneventful for the most part and
the conditions of confinement tolerable – at least for the officers;
Müller had several disputes with the British about the less blissful
circumstances of his men, no doubt motivated by his customary desire
to do his best for his subordinates. But at least the climate was very
pleasant most of the time, which helped Müller to overcome the
occasional bout of malaria all the more quickly, and he had regular
access to his fellow-officers.

On 8 October 1916 there was a brusque and fundamental change in
these conditions of tolerable tedium. As he was having breakfast,
Major Jellicoe, of the camp staff, arrived suddenly to tell him that he
was to report to the Governor of Malta at 9 a.m. No reason was given.
Müller had been taken to this official once before for an exchange of
courtesies, and he was not concerned, merely curious to know what
was going on. Smartly dressed in civilian clothes appropriate to the
climate – solar topi, lightweight navy-blue blazer and white
flannels – Müller was met at the gate by Jellicoe and the camp
commandant and driven, to his surprise, to the harbour. Jellicoe
escorted Müller in a steam pinnace to the old British battleship, HMS
London (15,000 tons), which was at anchor but with steam up ready
to sail. Asking no questions, Müller boarded the ship and doffed his
sun-helmet in the direction of the quarterdeck and then towards the
waiting captain and his officers. The courtesy was not returned. The
captain wordlessly pointed to a companionway that led below deck
and four sailors and marines, at least two of them armed with rifle and
bayonet, crowded Müller below. He was taken to a compartment

with bars over the porthole and a sentry took up his post outside the door. A few minutes later the ship began to move. Müller had nothing with him apart from the clothes he stood up in.

The captain of the *London* soon came to see him and stiffly apologised for the fact that his personal belongings had been left behind. They would follow 'on the next steamer'. Meanwhile, he would be allowed an hour on deck mornings and afternoons. On going to the lavatory, Müller found he was closely, almost offensively, escorted front and rear by armed sentries. When the captain came back in the afternoon, Müller complained that he was being subjected to treatment unworthy of an officer-prisoner. The captain said he had the strictest orders to watch him closely on the voyage to England: no other officer, for example, was allowed to speak to Müller. But only one sentry followed him to the lavatory from now on. The next day, the captain relented enough to provide a few toiletries and some fresh laundry as well as reading matter. On 16 October the warship docked at Plymouth, and about noon two British Army officers and an NCO fetched him and took him in a closed van to a military prison. There he was placed in a bleak and bare cell on his own. Müller demanded to see the prison commandant and told that officer that the treatment to which he was being subjected constituted a clear breach of the Hague Convention; he objected strongly to being treated like a common criminal. This kind of thing would never happen to a British officer in Germany. The commandant said nothing could be done unless Müller gave his word of honour not to try to escape; the German Commander said coldly that under these conditions he would refuse on principle to give his parole, and he would complain to the American Embassy in Britain (the neutral Protecting Power at that time) about his treatment. Later he was transferred to a room in the administrative block, where he was locked in after being required to surrender one boot, to discourage thoughts of escape. The room was closely guarded, and inspected regularly throughout the night. Two days after his arrival, at midnight on the night of 18 October, Müller was put on a train, under armed guard, and sent via Bristol, London, Nottingham and Derby to the prisoner-of-war camp at Sutton Bonington, near Kegworth, Derbyshire.

No explanation for this sudden change in circumstances was ever made to Müller, from whose account the foregoing is chiefly drawn. No explanation seems to exist in the British or the German records either. Müller, apart from the occasional representation to the authorities on behalf of his men and the periodic bout of illness, had not been a troublesome prisoner in Malta by any means: on the contrary, he behaved with correctness throughout. The abrupt transfer to Britain was apparently reserved for him alone: the rest of the *Emden* officers and men, apart from the wounded who had gone to Australia in November 1914, stayed on at Fort Verdala in Valletta until the end of the war. Apart from a brief security clampdown, they were not moved even after Sub-Lieutenant Erich Fikentscher escaped with a civilian internee in a rowing-boat to Sicily in April 1916 (as Italy had joined the war on the Allied side, he was imprisoned there, but was repatriated in an exchange in autumn 1917). Only Müller was ever moved.

But he was by a large margin the most distinguished German naval officer in captivity; and the German Navy had enraged the British just two days before he was bundled out of Malta. The Germans had pursued unrestricted submarine warfare between February and September 1915 against merchant shipping. Just as this campaign was beginning to produce results of great value to Germany (because so damaging to the British), the Kaiser succumbed to political pressure, prompted by fear of American intervention in the war, and called a halt to the North Sea underwater campaign. After the inconclusive Battle of Jutland (in which four of Mücke's men went down with the light cruiser *Wiesbaden*) in 1916, the admirals pressed for a resumption of the U-boat campaign. They felt the High Seas Fleet could not affect British surface superiority or offset the distant naval blockade which they rightly saw as the main threat to Germany. On 6 October Admiral von Holtzendorff, Chief of the Admiralty Staff, won a qualified victory by persuading the Kaiser to agree to a new submarine offensive in the North Sea – on condition it was done in accordance with prize rules (the same as those followed by the *Emden* and other undisguised surface raiders, which had been expected to challenge and investigate before sinking). Even though such conditions put submarines at an almost crippling disadvantage, negating their very purpose as a weapon of stealth and surprise, the British were alarmed by the orders they heard going out to the German Navy (having been given a captured German naval codebook by the Russians at the beginning of the war, a coup comparable with the 'Ultra' operation in the Second World War, the Royal Navy was usually extremely well informed on its enemy's movements) on the same day. In the absence of any other explanation it seems reasonable to put down the sudden transfer of Müller in unprecedented conditions of maximum security to bureaucratic vengefulness at the Admiralty in London, which was still a long way from finding any more practical answer to the submarine threat.

On 26 September 1917, Commander von Müller managed to break

out of the camp at Sutton Bonington, but was recaptured within hours. In November he was sentenced to 56 days' close arrest in solitary confinement as a punishment. His malaria was playing up severely at this time, and in January 1918 he was sent into internment in the Netherlands for treatment, as part of a humanitarian exchange of prisoners. In October 1918 he was finally repatriated just as the war was coming to an end. He was promoted full captain (*Kapitän zur See*) and given an administrative post in the Navy Office, from which he retired in January 1919.

During his internment in the Netherlands, which proved distinctly more beneficial than imprisonment in a damp camp in Derbyshire, Müller was allowed at his own request one period of home leave on parole by the Dutch authorities, in March 1918, when he went to stay with his parents in Blankenburg in the Harz Mountains. He made use of this period to deliver the fullest possible account of his stewardship as captain of the *Emden*, which he was asked to do as a result of a row which had broken out between the Admiralty and the Kaiser's Naval Cabinet, or more precisely between Admiral von Holtzendorff, the Chief of Admiralty Staff, and Admiral Georg von Müller (no relation), Chief of the Kaiser's Naval Cabinet and his principal ADC. Since the retirement of Grand Admiral Alfred von Tirpitz, 'father' of the Imperial Navy, in honoured disgrace in 1916 from the post of State Secretary in the Navy Office, the centres of power in the Navy had been reduced from three to two. Holtzendorff, not unreasonably, wanted the captain of the *Emden* to be given Germany's highest decoration for gallantry, the still prized if inevitably somewhat devalued Order *pour le Mérite* (cheapened, for example, by the fact that pilots automatically earned one on achieving a certain number of 'kills'). But it was not as if the blue and white enamelled Maltese cross worn at the collar was commonplace. Holtzendorff's request to the Kaiser was passed to Admiral von Müller for attention, and the Chief of the Naval Cabinet sent a frosty note to his colleague which read as follows:

Before I place Your Excellency's recommendation for the award of the Order *pour le Mérite* before His Majesty the Emperor for decision, I request [your] kind clarification of the following points:

1) Was it not a mistake to make an approach to the Cocos Islands with their wireless station?

2) Can the running aground of SMS *Emden* on the reef after her last battle be defended from every military and seamanlike point of view?

3) Did the captain render honour to the flag in the fullest

184

measure when he had the white flag hoisted, apparently to save the lives of the rest of the crew?

4) Did no possibility exist for the captain to destroy the ship and her weapons in such a way that nothing could fall into enemy hands?

I should also be grateful to Your Excellency for a brief description of the last action of SMS *Emden*, which can serve me as a further exhibit for my presentation to His Majesty.

The Admiralty was furious and pressed harder, whereupon Admiral von Müller responded with a broad hint that his namesake, for all his popularity, ought to answer to a naval court-martial for the loss of his cruiser and might well have been made to do so but for the grace of the Emperor. He wrote to say that the Kaiser now required the fullest possible explanation of the circumstances surrounding the loss of the *Emden*.

It was in response to this that, on 15 March 1918, the Admiralty sent Admiral von Müller the report of Commander von Müller on the fight with the *Sydney*, which later became Part VI of the captain's account of the entire cruise of his ship. Admiral von Holtzendorff himself penned a summary of points contained in the report as a detailed answer to his unfriendly colleague's four questions (which certainly went to the heart of the matter). It ended with the courteously expressed *envoi*: 'The circumstances under which the showing of the white flag took place will, I trust, allay the doubt of Your Excellency as to whether the captain of the *Emden* rendered honour to the flag . . . . I permit myself the hope that His Majesty will award the decoration requested by me at once.' The Kaiser agreed, and wrote in his own hand on the top copy of Commander von Müller's report, 'He is fully justified.'

On 21 March 1918, the following telegram arrived for the erstwhile captain of the *Emden* at Blankenburg:

Commander von Müller. On the basis of your report, laid before me by the Admiralty Staff, on the last days of My cruiser *Emden* and her final battle, I hereby award you the Order *pour le Mérite*, in warmest recognition of the expedient and gallant conduct of yourself and your crew. You have conferred high honour on the name of your ship for all time, giving the entire world a brilliant example of the most decisive and chivalrous conduct of cruiser warfare. I gladly accept the proposals mentioned at the end of your report for decorations for the officers and crew. Wilhelm I. R.

At this distance, the exchange between the two admirals looks unseemly. Admiral von Müller had just turned 64 and was, as ever, not in the best of health; this handicap helps to explain his comparative lack of seagoing experience. Before the war, British diplomats in Berlin had reported him to be 'notoriously pro-English', while the professional assessment of the Royal Navy was that he was 'one of the ablest men in the German Navy'. He was also a teetotaller opposed to drinking by others, and a supporter of Tirpitz's 'big navy' policy. Having become a highly influential professional courtier at the end of his career, the Admiral no doubt felt it part of his duty to save the Kaiser from his subjects, especially the ones with real influence. He was himself awarded the Order *pour le Mérite* just before the end of the war. Holtzendorff's position as naval Chief of Staff, effectively the administrative head of the navy as a fighting force (although it came under the overall command of the General Staff) was simpler – he wanted to see one of his officers get what he saw as the man's just deserts for outstanding conduct. It is entirely reasonable to conclude that both men were doing their duty as they saw it, however petty the argument now seems. Commander von Müller was duly grateful for the distinction.

After retiring from the navy early in 1919 on health grounds, Müller withdrew to Blankenburg, modestly declining the endless invitations to appear in public and talk about his role as the last corsair. He politely rejected also the importunities of publishing houses. 'I performed no special deed but only did my duty,' he would say privately. 'Were I to write, I would regard myself as arrogant, and I should not be able to escape the feeling that I was coining money from the blood of my comrades. I cannot do that, and I shall never write about myself.' In the light of this attitude, we are fortunate indeed that the row over his award led to his being ordered to write a lengthy report of the *Emden*'s cruise which was preserved intact in the archives for posterity. He kept his word and his silence – there is nothing else from him except for a few private letters. Those to his parents (he was unmarried) were written in the knowledge that an enemy censor would read them, as we have seen.

But he was not so retiring as to have no strong opinions. He rejected out of hand an invitation to join the 'German Nobility Association' (of which the 'von' in his name indicated him to be a minor member). This organisation acted as a 'trade union' of the aristocracy in the precarious republic which the Reich became after the Kaiser's abdication in November 1918. He reacted by saying that Germany was riven by class divisions when she needed unity. He was elected as a 'German National' (traditional German liberal) deputy

186

to the Brunswick provincial parliament, and it was in that city that he died suddenly on 11 March 1923, before his fiftieth birthday, burned out by malarial fevers and no doubt cleaned out by the great inflation which was then at its height. His overriding interest in the last few years of his life had been the welfare of the survivors of the *Emden*, and he managed to attend one reunion. To the end he was a man nobody knew.

CAPTAIN GLOSSOP

The man who destroyed the *Emden*, Captain John Glossop of HMAS *Sydney*, diligently pursued an otherwise unremarkable career, even though he attained his final rank of Vice-Admiral in 1926. He was not awarded the knighthood that normally automatically accompanies this rank under the Buggins-turn rules of that most peculiar of institutions, the British honours system; but he was made CB (Commander of the Order of the Bath) and was also appointed to the French Legion of Honour and the Japanese Order of the Rising Sun (third class). This fifth son of a former Vicar of Twickenham on the western fringe of London retired in 1931 and died at Weymouth, Dorset, on 23 December 1934 at the age of 63, leaving an Australian widow, a son and a daughter and earning obituary notices in *The Times* of both London and New York.

HELLMUTH VON MÜCKE NOISILY FADES AWAY

The becoming modesty of his former captain was a weakness not shared by Hellmuth von Mücke, especially after his remarkable feat in getting his men home through territory all but unknown to Europeans at the time. He was soon involved in a row with the diplomatic service over the allegations of treachery he made against his 'hosts' in Arabia in the report he wrote on his return. The Resident Minister in Constantinople, Baron von Oppenheim, in a critique of Mücke's report addressed to his ambassador, Baron von Wangenheim, rejected the claim that the attack on the detachment in the desert had been initiated by the Emir of Mecca or his son, Sherif Abdullah. Secure in the superior knowledge of the Arabs gathered in his well-appointed office in the Turkish capital, Oppenheim dismissed the hundreds of Beduin attackers as no more than a band of robbers seeking money or a ransom, quite a normal local custom. They might have friends or contacts at court in Jiddah but these would hardly include the Emir or his sons, who would be too clever to do down the heroes of the *Emden* in any case. The suspicious circumstances outlined by Mücke (see Chapter 15) were airily dismissed as par for the course. The Turks had permitted only one version of the attack to appear in their censored newspapers, attributing it to robbers who might have been incited by the British and describing Abdullah as the saviour of the Germans. Oppenheim asked that Mücke adhere to this version in all public pronouncements, for the sake of Germany's political interests, and indeed that his superiors should order him to do so, as he was about to give talks on his experiences.

Faced in August 1915 with this document by the Admiralty, Mücke responded:

It did not need the intervention of Herr von Oppenheim to make me present the events in Arabia to the outside world in the manner current relations and political tact require. I refer in this connection to my telegram from Jiddah, which provided the basis for the official Turkish account. The account which the reporter, Herr Ludwig, gave to the German papers also came solely from me and passed the German and Turkish censorship without objection. These accounts were made long before I got to Constantinople . . . I cannot forbear from giving expression to my astonishment that Herr von Oppenheim has used the reports I made to him personally on his express wish about the true circumstances of the case to prepare an official report, and that he wants, on the basis of this report, to have my superiors order me to adopt a course of conduct which I have observed since long before the appearance of Herr von Oppenheim.

Mücke's reply is dated 6 August 1915 (Oppenheim's note was dated 6 June) and was written at Wilhelmshaven, where, after promotion to lieutenant-commander, he was leading the 15th Half-Flotilla of torpedoboat-destroyers with VIII Flotilla – he had got his wish for a North Sea command.

The tone of this blistering apologia helps to explain why the rest of Mücke's naval career did not live up to the apparent promise of his work on the *Emden* and his leadership qualities there and in the desert. It also points towards the reasons why this remarkable man was doomed to lifelong frustration and eventual oblivion. Refusal or sheer inability to compromise is one thing under military conditions when one's life and that of one's men are at stake; but they do not win friends or followers in civilian life, where people prefer to be persuaded as to what is good for them, even in the still deferent Germany of the postwar darkness and confusion. Weighed down by medals after his return, Mücke never lost an opportunity to give lectures on the *Emden* and the detachment; he wrote enormously popular and successful books which were already on sale before the end of 1915. Eventually he produced half a dozen volumes on his war experiences and also helped in the production of a silent film on the *Emden* made in Munich in 1926. His lectures up and down the country remained a big draw for years after the war, but he failed to translate this personal drawing power into the political movement he made many different attempts to create. In the psychological sense he never recovered from his finest hour.

In January 1916, Mücke briefly took command of the German river boats on the Euphrates in Mesopotamia, working with the Turks; before the end of the year he was back in Germany as a staff officer at the Admiralty. After only four months he was given command of the Danube Half-Flotilla; after only five months in that post he was assigned, in August 1917, to the battlecruiser *Derfflinger*, based at Wilhelmshaven with the High Seas Fleet, as navigation officer. In May 1918, he moved again, to the command of the first section of the Second Torpedoboat Division. He was demobilised without further promotion after the war. This jerky, restless and notably undistinguished close to his naval career speaks for itself. Obviously his superiors did not know what to do with a man like Mücke in a service that became increasingly frustrated and impotent, apart from the submarine arm, as the war wore on and ultimately exploded in mutiny, which he witnessed in the north German ports. Equally obviously, he was not about to be accommodating. He had become completely impossible to work with.

After the war he went to live in Potsdam and devoted himself to writing books, which made him financially independent for the rest of his life, thanks to the 'trench editions' of his *Emden* and *Ayesha* titles. He began to look for a political home but, as was only to be expected, he quarrelled with one group after another. His ideological appetite leaned towards the romantic, nationalistic, authoritarian Right. It is no exaggeration to conclude that he was close to being one of nature's fascists. He had a brief flirtation with the German National People's Party, and then the National Socialist German Workers' Party (the Nazis), which he left in disgust when Adolf Hitler took it over in 1921 – Mücke did not like the new style of personality cult! There was probably no room in any of the bewildering array of political parties of the day for any two personalities if one of them belonged to Mücke, an interpretation borne out by his subsequent career, such as it was. But the lectures went on successfully, doing much for interest in the navy at home and for sympathy for Germany when he made a popular tour of the American lecture circuit. When he came back, he sat down to write his *magnum opus*, a political trilogy under the generic title 'Line', the quality he had decided was lacking in all contemporary political groupings of any note. Only the first volume appeared in 1931, and it was a flop. In the end, nobody would listen to him and he became in effect a political party of one member. When Hitler came to power constitutionally at the beginning of 1933 and founded the 'Third Reich', Mücke applied for permission to emigrate and was refused: it was officially assumed that he would make propaganda against the Nazis abroad, which was probably a shrewd guess.

He lived quietly now in the shadow of official disfavour, an unperson left alone for the sake of his past heroism (and because a few friends and former comrades quietly saw to it that he was left alone), despite his well-known hostility towards the Führer and the state he had created. Most of his officer-colleagues of the *Emden* served in the Second World War as admirals or senior officers – two vice-admirals, Schall and Witthoeft, one captain, Fikentscher, two lieutenant-commanders, Geerdts and Prince Franz Joseph von Hohenzollern – while he was obliged to sit on the sidelines, producing handbooks for coastwise navigation. The silence continued after the war, when Mücke, now into his sixties, became all but a recluse. He had lost a son on the eastern front. He retired to Schleswig-Holstein in the far north of West Germany and died of a heart attack at Ahrensburg on 30 July 1957 at the age of 73, a pathetic victim of his own character and that of his country, protagonist in a personal tragedy of unfulfilled promise and disappointed aspiration.

THE OTHER WAR OF JULIUS LAUTERBACH

Julius Lauterbach, the last man from the *Emden* to escape back to Germany and the only one to do so alone, did not remain idle for long after his celebrated return home eleven months and a day from the destruction of the cruiser. First he reported to his employer, the Hamburg–America Line in Hamburg, and then he was called to Berlin by the Navy Office and temporarily attached to Tirpitz's staff to write a report on the *Emden*'s voyage. He was granted an audience by the Emperor and Empress, dined out in high places on the story of his experiences and even had a brief meeting with Sir Roger Casement, the Irish nationalist. At the end of 1915 he was promoted to *Kapitänleutnant* of the Reserve and posted to Kiel, the Baltic station commanded by Prince Heinrich, first on the submarine crew training ship *Mars*, then as captain of the auxiliary vessel *K*, then as administrative officer of the First Commerce Protection Half-Flotilla. This little formation was made up of small converted vessels which were intended to lure and attack submarines in the Baltic. He took a prominent part in the sinking on the same day in May 1916 of two submarines, one Russian, the other British, by ramming, depth-charges and gunfire. In August his little force sank another British submarine off the Danish North Sea coast. In October, they were caught and fired on by some British destroyers off the south-western Swedish coast. Lauterbach's vessel, the *Marie*, was badly damaged and he and a few comrades were rescued by a Danish steamer which took them to Elsinore. After a week's treatment for light wounds, Lauterbach was released from hospital and repatriated.

As if all that were not enough, on 1 January 1918, after Russia had been knocked out of the war and the Baltic was a German lake, Lauterbach was appointed captain of the *Möwe* (the name means gull), the most famous German surface-raider of the war after the *Emden* herself, though of a very different and in no way comparable stamp. The difference was that the *Möwe* was a disguised merchant ship used for blockade-running, minelaying and attacks on unsuspecting enemy ships. She was the forerunner of the kind of surface-raider Germany deployed quite successfully in the Second World War. Her original captain, Commander Graf Dohna-Schlodien, established himself as a naval hero. Converted into an armed auxiliary cruiser from the prewar Africa-run fruit-boat *Pungo*, 4,778 tons, she had four 150 mm. (5.9 inch) and one 105 mm. (4.1 inch) guns, all concealed, and space for 500 mines. On her first cruise of twelve weeks to early March 1916, she accounted for one British cruiser and fifteen merchant ships, returning home with some 500 prisoners. On her second cruise of four months, rather later that year, she sank no less than twenty-seven merchantmen totalling 121,000 tons, operating in the Atlantic and penetrating deep into the southern hemisphere.

By the time Lauterbach took her over the *Möwe* was in use as a short-range minelayer until sent to Finnish waters in April, where she stayed for four months in support of German troops who had intervened in the Finnish civil war between pro- and anti-Bolshevik forces. He captured a Russian gunboat and eight steamers she was escorting by firing a shot across her bows and ordering them all to surrender as if he were the advance guard of an entire fleet, which of course he was not. The Russians were furious. He led them all into captivity.

Back in Kiel in early autumn 1918, he was apparently able to maintain discipline aboard his ship, even though the great naval mutiny was going on all around. At the very end of the war he went to Latvia in the *Möwe* to bring home some German naval officers, stores and a handful of troops – they had been trapped there by the turmoil inside post-revolutionary Russia. It was his last voyage on the *Möwe* and the Armistice was already in force when he got back. Lauterbach then went down with a bad case of the influenza which reached epidemic proportions and killed untold millions across Europe after the privations of the war. There was no merchant ship for him to command in the shambles of Germany after the defeat, but it was not long before Lauterbach became involved in the unrest of the German revolution which had grown out of the naval mutiny and spread to many parts of the prostrate Reich. He joined one of the *Freikorps*, the volunteer militia recruited from among veterans which became a way of getting round the 100,000 limit put on the German Army by the Treaty of Versailles, and was soon involved in ugly street battles with Spartacists (marxist revolutionaries), including a siege of the City Hall, where he was trapped with 300 others by Spartacus League supporters. In the end General von Lettow-Vorbeck, hero of the amazing defence of German East Africa, had to march into Hamburg to restore order. All this happened in the early months of 1919.

Eventually, with a loan from his mother, Lauterbach started a shipping business based in Berlin, operating a single, elderly schooner in the Baltic trade. He was soon doing well enough to acquire three more schooners; but the appalling economic and social troubles of Germany in the 1920s, largely attributable to the crushing burden of the reparations imposed by the Treaty of Versailles, led Julius Lauterbach to emigrate to San Francisco, where he became very successful in the shipping business. He died in America after the Second World War. Fran Maria Lauterbach-Emden, the wife he married when he was forty (for a bet which required him to wed within three months!) was still living in Cologne in 1982.

20

ECHOES

On Saturday, 14 November 1914, the City Council of Emden fore-gathered for a ceremonial memorial session in honour of the lost ship that had been thrust upon it as a 'godchild' and had made the city's name a byword for chivalry throughout the world. It resolved to send a telegram of condolence to the Kaiser: 'Deeply saddened by the destruction of Your Majesty's glorious ship, the light cruiser *Emden*, and the great loss of life lamentably accompanying its destruction, Your Majesty's most loyally obedient City Council of Emden begs permission to express its most humble condolence to the said All-Highest.' The almost untranslatable, grovelling phraseology conforms with the stifling etiquette the subjects of the Hohenzollerns were required to exhibit to the rulers of their *arriviste* Empire. The said All-Highest condescended to reply as follows: 'Grateful thanks for your telegram of sympathy on the occasion of the saddening yet so heroic end of My cruiser *Emden*. The gallant ship won further laurels for the German war-flag even in its final battle against the superior enemy. A new, stronger *Emden* shall arise, on whose bow the Iron Cross will be affixed in memory of the glory of the old *Emden*.'

On 1 February 1916 the Imperial promise was kept. A light cruiser with the provisional name 'Replacement for *Nymphe*' was launched at Bremen and named *Emden* (II). A giant Iron Cross was attached on either side of the bow, a unique distinction. It was one of seventy-four German warships that went into internment in Scapa Flow after the Armistice as hostages for German good behaviour while the Treaty of Versailles was being negotiated, and eventually became the flagship of the Flag Officer in charge of them, Admiral Ludwig von Reuter. It was from her deck that Reuter issued the unprecedented order to scuttle the entire fleet on 21 June 1919, to prevent it falling into enemy hands. *Emden II* herself did not sink and was later handed over to the French Navy, which used her for experiments with explosives and scrapped her in 1926. Before internment, *Emden II* served as a flagship with the destroyer flotillas and also took part in one of the first 'combined operations', against islands in the eastern Baltic in 1917. In the same year the German submarine *U50* was lost in the North Sea, with all hands. Among them was Lieutenant Eugen Gyssling, one of the three officers landed on Direction Island by the *Emden* and a major support for her First Officer during the long march home.

While the scarred wreck of *Emden II* was still being maltreated by the French Navy, the shrunken German Navy resolved not to let the *Emden* tradition die: its first postwar cruiser was launched on 7 January 1925 at Wilhelmshaven and, inevitably, christened *Emden* (III). From the beginning it was a special honour to command this ship, which also bore the Iron Cross at the bows, and which came to specialise in the training of officers for a new *Reichsmarine*, limited in numbers and tonnages by the Treaty of Versailles but, ship for ship and man for man, no less excellent than the Kaiser's. Four of her captains became admirals (including Karl Dönitz, Hitler's naval supremo and briefly his successor as Führer). One of her commanders was Captain Robert Witthoeft, once the torpedo officer of *Emden I*, in 1930 and 1931. On one of a series of world cruises for training purposes, *Emden III* anchored off North Keeling Island on 16 March 1927, from where she sent a commemorative signal to the city of Emden. On the same voyage the ship discovered a spot-depth of 10,497 metres in the Philippine Trench on the floor of the Pacific. In accordance with international usage, the point was named the Emden Deep, and was known as such until 1945, when the USS *Cape Johnson* got a slightly deeper reading close to the same spot, which was renamed in her honour. After a busy war in the North Sea and the Baltic, *Emden III* was caught off Kiel by British bombers and sank in flames in the last days of the Second World War. She was blown up on 3 May 1945 and her remains recovered for scrap in 1949. One year later a Japanese salvage company was allowed to remove the remains of *Emden I* from the reef at North Keeling Island for scrap. During the war, there occurred a curious and ironic coincidence which was also a tragedy for the Royal Australian Navy. A German auxiliary cruiser disguised as an ordinary merchantman and named *Kormoran* in honour of *Emden I*'s first prize, caught out HMAS *Sydney* (II) off the western coast of Australia, not all that far from the Cocos Islands, and destroyed her with the loss of all 645 lives aboard on 19 November 1941. Herself crippled, *Kormoran III* was obliged to scuttle.

It was Hamburg's turn to build the next *Emden*, number IV, and she was launched on 21 March 1959, entering the service of the West German *Bundesmarine* (Federal Navy) on 24 October 1961. This third reincarnation of the *Emden* and her legend is a frigate built for anti-submarine warfare and full of modern electronics, which have been updated from time to time. As this is written, she is reaching the end of her useful life and is due for retirement from active service in October 1983. But, as we shall see, the *Emden* tradition has already been salvaged in advance of her paying-off.

The British and the Australians did not forget their honoured marine enemy either. In January 1915 Admiral Jerram reported on a visit to North Keeling Island by the *Pioneer*, an old P-Class cruiser, to inspect the wreck of the *Emden*. He telegraphed: '*Pioneer* after visiting Keeling Islands reports that there are two intact safes on board *Emden*. As they may contain important papers or money I am sending *Cadmus* there again to endeavour to obtain them or contents. She will leave Singapore 23 January and will also take explosive to destroy guns of *Emden*.' The Admiralty replied from London: 'If it can be done without risk, salve one or more of *Emden*'s guns.' On 9 February Jerram was able to report: 'Mexican dollars value £500, two guns, gun mountings, one torpedo, one searchlight taken off *Emden* by *Cadmus*.' It will be recalled that HMS *Cadmus* had been given the unpleasant duty of burying the dead of the *Emden* after the battle. Some of her gleanings from the wreck can also be seen in Sydney, New South Wales, today.

In 1932, the Australian High Commissioner in London, Mr. Bruce, presented one of the *Emden*'s nameplates to President Hindenburg in Berlin. In 1977 Australian television made a film of 'The Cocos Incident'.

The news of the survival and homeward march of the *Emden* landing-party broke just as representatives of north German local authorities were meeting to discuss common problems. The city of Emden was also represented. It was from this meeting that a unique idea first arose for honouring the men who had sailed and fought the *Emden* so gallantly and then provided the world with such a superb 'follow-up' in the form of the detachment's return. It was resolved at the meeting to approach the Reich Minister of the Interior with a proposal that former crew members should be permitted to add the suffix 'Emden' to their family names. There was no legal provision or precedent for such a privilege and the idea promptly became entangled in red tape and arguments among lawyers, of whom Germany has seldom experienced a shortage. But after the First World War the proposal went through, and more than 100 *Emden* veterans availed themselves of the right to change their names in this way. They included Captain (and *Kapitänleutnant* of the naval Reserve, retired) Julius Lauter-

195

bach-Emden, Erich Fikentscher-Emden and even Prince Franz Joseph von Hohenzollern-Emden.

The city of Emden jealously guards to this day the tradition, the reputation and such mementoes as it has been able to accumulate of its floating godchild and her successors. A memorial was set up after she was lost and a fund opened for relatives of the dead. Her captain was later presented by the city not only with a certificate of honorary citizenship (comparable with being made a freeman of an English city) but also with a handsome model of the ship. All this was voted at the special meeting on 14 November 1914.

The old naval barracks near the harbour in the city of Emden are still in use, but no longer for sailors. The West German Army took them over long since. At the 'Karl von Müller Barracks' there is a bronze tablet with the ship's coat of arms and a picture of her in bas-relief. The inscription reads:

SMS *Emden*, captain Commander Karl von Müller, sank large numbers of merchant ships in the Indian Ocean, destroyed the oiltank-installation of Madras, annihilated the Russian cruiser *Zhemchug* and the French destroyer *Mousquet* in the harbour of Penang. Was run aground on the Keeling Islands on 9 November 1914, pursued by the superior force of the enemy and after a fierce battle with the Australian cruiser *Sydney*; almost half the crew fell for the Fatherland. Glorious ship – may the city whose name you carried round the world never forget you.

SMS *Emden*, launched on 26 May 1908 and destroyed in war six years later, was the last undisguised commerce-raiding cruiser to practise classic cruiser-warfare. The radio which trapped her made her so and her role passed to the 'Q-ship' and, much more importantly, to the submarine. Stealth and deceit supplanted chivalry and 'prize rules'. Karl von Müller goes down in history as the Last Corsair.

EPILOGUE

On 2 March 1915 an Order in Council was promulgated in the *London Gazette* which decreed that officers and crews of British warships present at the capture or destruction of any armed, hostile ship should share in the distribution of prize money, calculated at £5 for each man aboard the enemy vessel at the start of the engagement. The Order was retroactive.

On 22 August 1916, Captain Samuel Evans presided at a Prize Court in London which had been convened to hear and judge claims from the crews of Royal Navy ships that had taken part in the Battle of the Falkland Islands where Graf Spee's Cruiser Squadron was destroyed. At the end of the court's day, a separate hearing took place in which the officers and crew of HMAS *Sydney* claimed Prize Bounty for their defeat of SMS *Emden* at the Cocos/Keeling Islands on 9 November 1914. Commander Maxwell Anderson, RN, appeared for the claimants and Mr. M. Shearman for the Crown.

Commander Anderson opened the proceedings by claiming the sum of £1,645 on behalf of the crew of *Sydney*, stating that there had been 329 men aboard the enemy ship at the start of the engagement which destroyed her. He then gave a summary of the events of 9 November 1914. 'This case is of interest as providing the first instance in naval warfare where a white flag was shown,' the Commander said.

He based his claim on the calculation that the *Emden* had had a full complement of 397. Of these, as he was advised (slightly inaccurately), fifty-two had been put ashore on Direction Island before the start of the action as a raiding party and sixteen had been sent away in the captured collier *Exford*. Of the remainder, 131 had been killed in the battle and 214 captured after it. The Commander made so bold as to suggest that as the landing party had gone ashore immediately before the action and the prize crew was placed aboard the *Exford* on its eve, these sixty-eight men could legitimately be seen as part of the *Emden*'s crew at the start of the action. 'If the Crown has no objection to paying for these people, the claimants have no objection to receiving it,' the Commander said disingenuously, hoping to add an

197

extra £340 to the bounty. It all depended on one's interpretation of the relevant passage in the Act of Parliament under which the Order had been made – on what precisely was meant by the phrase 'start of the engagement'. Mr. Shearman faithfully took HM Treasury's traditional, narrow view and objected.

The President was in expansive mood. 'In my view, not taking too narrow a construction on the words of the Act of Parliament, the words "on board", if they are in fact part of the crew, and in attendance in some form or other, not having left the vessel entirely, and doing work as part of the crew, I am entitled to treat them as persons on board within the meaning of the Act of Parliament. I therefore have great pleasure in allotting £5 per head, calculated on the 397, the bigger figure, and the Prize Bounty will be £1,985.'

But before delivering this generous judgement, the President pressed Commander Anderson on the fact that the *Sydney* had returned to the wreck of the *Emden* and raked it with broadsides after the German ship had patently run aground. Captain Evans clearly thought this unsporting or at least excessively cautious or zealous, a graceless *coup de grâce* for a gallant foe. Commander Anderson did not demur; the *Emden* had indeed been palpably *hors de combat*: 'A beached and burning ship, my Lord – a dead bird really.' So much for the erstwhile 'Swan of the East'.

The Times of 6 October 1920 carried the following item:

THE COCOS ISLANDS

In the course of an article on the Cocos Islands which appeared in the Empire Number of *The Times* on May 25 last, the following words occurred:

"Last year the German Government punctiliously presented the present [*sic*] Mr Ross with a very neat craft in place of the one which was taken."

Subsequent investigation has proved that Mr Ross has not yet been compensated for the seizure of his schooner.

So much for the non-existent *Ayesha II*.

On 17 December 1980 the frigate *F210* was launched at Emden, Lower Saxony, West Germany, due to enter service in October 1983. Like other Type 122 (*Bremen* Class) frigates, she should bear the name of a West German state such as Bremen. But at the special request of the Emden City Council the Federal Navy changed her name.

So much for *Emden V* . . .

A NOTE ON SOURCES

Two short accounts of the *Emden*'s war-cruise serve as a very good *hors d'oeuvre* for serious study of the subject. J. G. Lockhart's 'Of the Company of the Privateers' can be found in *Great Sea Stories of All Nations* (Harrap, London, 1932); and 'The Cruise of the Emden' by Lionel Fanthorpe is in *Warships and Sea-Battles of World War I*, extracted from Purnell's *History of the First World War* – an excellent 'part-work' (Phoebus, London, 1973).

The most recent full-length account in English is *The Last Cruise of the Emden* by Edwin P. Hoyt (André Deutsch, London, 1967). This is a racy and readable book which on occasion sacrifices accuracy for its spanking pace – more thorough research and expert assistance with the German language would have helped. As Mr. Hoyt is a former foreign correspondent who has turned his attention to contemporary history, including German naval matters, I should not throw stones. The main thing is that I enjoyed his book.

The latest book in German is both very recent and exhaustive: *Die Kaperfahrten des Kleinen Kreuzers EMDEN* by R. K. Lochner (Heyne Verlag, Munich, 1979). This work is so thorough that it tends to subordinate readability to rigid adherence to chronological order, being organised more like a diary (including the occasional entry on the lines of, 'Not much to report today') than a book. It is thus a work for naval history buffs like me rather than the general reader – I found the immense detail fascinating. That said, the trail so painstakingly marked out by Herr Lochner was of immense value to me. As an account it is surely definitive, and it also includes a splendid collection of photographs and maps as well as an invaluable bibliography. The overriding virtue of this book is its thoroughness.

Apart from the primary material in the German and British national records, which were the principal sources of this book, there is a long list of works of all kinds by participants and witnesses, from lengthy books to short articles. The most prolific is Hellmuth von Mücke, the *Emden*'s First Officer, whose first two books, *Emden* and *Ayesha*, were published by Scherl, Berlin, in rapid succession in 1915, within months of his return home. The former was translated into English and published as *The Emden* by Ritter and Co. of Boston,

Mass., in 1917. Scherl also published in 1917 *1000Pf Sterling Kopf-preis – tot oder lebendig, Fluchtabenteuer des ehemaligen Prisenoffiziers SMS Emden* ('£1,000 on his head, dead or alive, the Escape Adventures of the former Prize Officer of the *Emden*') a title of an order of magnitude reminiscent of its author, Julius Lauterbach. I also read *Lauterbach of the China Sea* by Lowell Thomas (Hutchinson, London, 1939), which was entertaining and quite informative after a discount of fifty percent for exaggeration!

For general background I relied upon *History of the First World War* by the incomparable B. H. Liddell Hart (Cassell, London, 1970; and *The World Crisis* by Winston Churchill (Thornton Butterworth, London, 1923–7). Of special worth (and exceptional quality) on the opening moves of the war, which determined its magnitude as a world catastrophe and foreshadowed its outcome, is *August 1914*, by Barbara W. Tuchman (Macmillan paperback, London 1980, reprinted 1981). Brilliant is the right word for it.

The official German history of the war at sea was written by Erich Raeder, who eventually rose to the supreme rank of Grand Admiral and commanded the German Navy for the first part of the Second World War. There are several versions; I consulted volume 2 of *Der Kreuzerkrieg in den ausländischen Gewässern* ('The Cruiser War in Foreign Waters'), which deals with *Emden, Königsberg* and *Karlsruhe,* the three 'loners'. Raeder relies heavily on Commander Müller's official report on the *Emden* but adds some very valuable background material (Berlin, 1923 and 1927).

I also found *Coronel and the Falklands* by Geoffrey Bennett (Batsford, London, 1962) extremely helpful on the doings of the rest of Graf Spee's Cruiser Squadron; and *German Raiders of World War II* by August Karl Muggenthaler (Robert Hale, London, 1978) contains a great deal of comparative material showing how surface raiders changed their tactics from one war to the other. The chaos in Arabia at the relevant time is impressively chronicled in that strange work, *Seven Pillars of Wisdom* by T. E. Lawrence ('of Arabia') which reappeared as a Penguin in 1962.

The majestic sixth edition of *The Times Atlas of the World* (London, 1980), whose spellings I have used when in doubt, and *Jane's Fighting Ships* (various editions) were essential props throughout.

INDEX